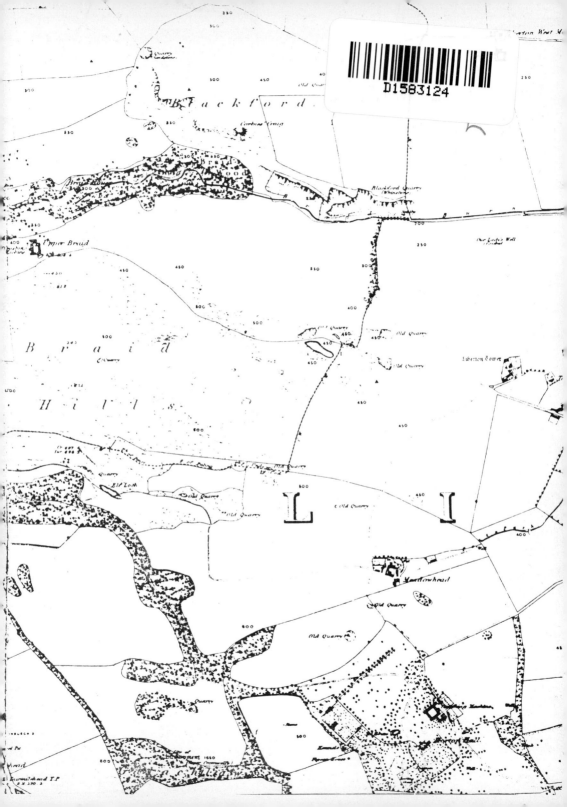

Historic South Edinburgh

VOLUME TWO

From John Adair's Map of Midlothian, 1735

Panoramic view of Morningside from Churchhill

Photograph by Mr W. R. Smith; by courtesy of Miss Sheila Fletcher

Historic
South Edinburgh

BY CHARLES J. SMITH

VOLUME TWO

CHARLES SKILTON LTD
Edinburgh & London

© Charles J. Smith 1979
Made and printed in Great Britain
by C. I. Thomas & Sons (Haverfordwest) Ltd
Haverfordwest, Pembrokeshire
and published by
CHARLES SKILTON LTD
2 & 3 Abbeymount, Edinburgh 8

Reprinted 1982

VOLUME II

CONTENTS

LIST OF ILLUSTRATIONS

Courtesy of the National Library of Scotland

Endpapers

INTRODUCTION

In the preparation of this second volume on *Historic South Edinburgh* I have been particularly indebted to the many people who have expedited its appearance. Mrs Jean Desebrock, B. Litt. (Oxon), has been especially helpful in skilfully and effectively editing a lengthy manuscript, and the bibliography. In a book ranging over such a wide area and encompassing much detail, the compilation of the index has been a meticulous and laborious task. In the preparation of this, I have been entirely dependent upon the professional skill and much valued patience of Mrs N. E. S. Armstrong, M.A., F.L.A., Head of Reference and Information Services of Edinburgh's City Libraries, and the continuing assistance of Miss Sheena McDougall, A.L.A., and the staff of the Edinburgh Central Library's Edinburgh Room. Mrs Irene Combe has given invaluable help in the typing of the manuscript and especially the bibliography and index. Much assistance from Mr Robin Hill, Assistant Curator of the City of Edinburgh District Council Museums, has also been greatly appreciated.

Special attention has been given in this volume to obtaining appropriate illustrations and my brother, Mr W. R. Smith, B.Sc., M.B.K.S., L.R.P.S., has spared no effort in this field. Mr Bill Weir of the Edinburgh University Library's photographic department has again provided invaluable assistance and advice.

I also wish to express my indebtedness to Mr Ian Hobbs, authoritative lecturer and popular guide on South Edinburgh, for providing valuable information on Swanston and to Mr Gerald Shepherd for first awakening my interest in the stay of the War Poets, Siegfried Sassoon and Wilfred Owen, at Craiglockhart Military Hospital and for kindly allowing me to draw upon his notes. In further study, the assistance of Sister Valerio of the Convent of the Sacred Heart has been invaluable, and the permission of Messrs Faber & Faber Ltd for the reproduction of Siegfried Sassoon's poetry is also much appreciated. In addition I am happy to acknowledge Mr Duncan McAra's book, *Sir James Gowans: Romantic Rationalist* (Edinburgh, Paul Harris, 1975), as the source of the material of that architect's fascinating buildings, from which I drew in Volume I of my book.

Finally, in this concluding volume I express my sincere appreciation to the vast number of residents in South Edinburgh who have assisted in so many ways and given of their time. I should like to think that what has been committed to print is very much a work of collaboration. Without such kind and willing assistance this contribution to the history of South Edinburgh would not have been possible.

Edinburgh from Braid Hills

From the painting by H. G. Duguid, engraved by C. Rosenberg, 1851

By courtesy of Edinburgh City Libraries

CHAPTER 1

The Jordan Burn

Still murmuring on through Morningside, the Jordan Burn, now largely
hidden, is an ancient witness to the development on its banks of a hamlet,
later a village, which was to become a populous, bustling suburb. For
centuries, and until 1856, the Jordan was Edinburgh's official southern
boundary. Many famous men of history have crossed its banks from the
south; and there is even evidence that the Romans built a bridge across
the Jordan.

Early records refer to the "river", which also features in romantic
poetry, while in an important book on Scottish rivers Morningside's own
stream enjoys pride of place in the opening chapter. The mushroom
growth of Morningside in the late nineteenth century was heralded by
"the builders careering like wild colts" across the Jordan to apply their
"tinkling chisels" to the construction of a modern suburban Promised
Land. In more recent times Morningside residents have been alarmed to
hear the sound of water murmuring under their floorboards; the frontages of buildings, revealing signs of subsidence, have had to be
demolished; building programmes have been delayed — all on account of
Morningside's relentlessly flowing stream.

Over many a Morningside dinner table a long controversy, sometimes
resulting in the setting up of exploration groups, has raged: where does
the Jordan rise? Where may it be seen? What is the course through
Morningside on its way to the sea? No chronicle of the district would be
adequate without an attempt to answer these questions — hopefully once
and for all. These answers are the fruits of a long, careful systematic
search through records and in the field.

The first documented reference to the Jordan Burn occurs in the
"Protocol Book of James Young" under the date March 23rd, 1497.
Young was an Edinburgh Notary Public who recorded the principal events
in the city, including the transfer of property between its citizens. His
entry for the above date describes the disposition of land at Nithirbrad
(Netherbraid), within the ancient Barony of Braid. In defining the
boundaries of the land in the transaction he refers to "the Buckstane,
Plewlandsike and the Powburne on the north". The Pow Burn was the
name by which the Jordan Burn was known until about 1760, "pow" being
derived from the Scandinavian word for pool or sluggish stream. The
name Jordan was later given to the section of the burn between its source
(described below) and, approximately, what is now Mayfield Road. This is
the part which flowed through Morningside's Biblical area. After that the
original name Pow Burn was retained.

253

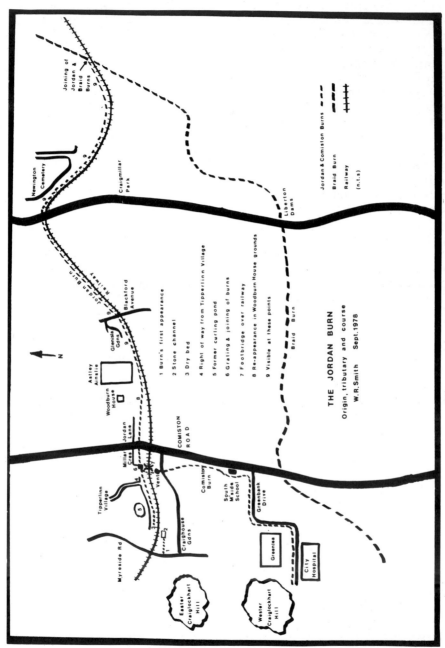

The course of the Jordan Burn

By courtesy of Mr W. R. Smith

254

While the other documented references to the Jordan Burn do not occur until the late eighteenth and early nineteenth centuries, in *Marmion* Sir Walter Scott describes the Scottish army encamped, in 1513, on the area of the Burgh Muir which today is occupied by the Astley Ainslie Hospital, describing it as "between the *streamlet* and the town". Young's reference of 1497 was just sixteen years earlier than the scene Scott describes. In charters of the many feus within the land of Canaan boundaries are frequently defined in terms of "the straad", "the streamlet" or "the burn of Braid". (This last reference was not to the more southerly Braid Burn; it is simply another title for the Jordan which flowed along and formed the northern boundary of the estate of Braid.) In 1692 there was some damage to property when the then substantial stream overflowed its banks. Edinburgh Town Council, apparently responsible for the burn, paid compensation to James Russell "tennent in Canaan for the damage caused to his crops". Russell farmed a substantial area of Canaan for nearly fifty years.

Sir Thomas Dick-Lauder, in his entertaining book *Scottish Rivers,* written in 1846 and dealing in general with Scotland's mightier rivers, amusingly devotes his first chapter to the Jordan, which skirted his own extensive lands south of Grange House. He describes people and places of interest on the Jordan's then largely unbuilt-upon banks. Certain of his anecdotes are interspersed in my description of the stream which follows.

Apparently even in Sir Thomas's day "the precise place of the Jordan's origin was productive of much contradictory speculation". On one occasion, he recounts, he collected together "about a round dozen . . . sages of Modern Athens" to impress one of his distinguished friends with their conversational brilliance. The after-dinner talk, however, fell flat; the evening seemed a failure. Then, with a concealed gleam in his eye, their host introduced a subject which, at last, made the dining-room echo with animated conversation. Said Sir Thomas: "It is a strange thing that, though the little stream of the Jordan runs through our grounds here and within less than half a mile of this house, no-one can tell us where its source is." The result was sensational: excitement, commotion and a noisy debate ensued as the erudite guests proffered their theories of the Jordan's birth. In the Pentland Hills, insisted one; at Hunters' Tryst, smugly replied another. Innumerable sources were dogmatically proposed. Sir Thomas Dick-Lauder listened with patience and tolerance, finally suggesting the source described hereafter.

In more recent times, Wilfred Taylor of *A Scotsman's Log* has fanned the embers of debate, which continued to smoulder since Sir Thomas Dick-Lauder's day, by raising yet again the same questions. With the object of finally answering them, he entertainingly describes the researches which he and a journalist colleague pursued. They were the two exclusive members of the Morningside Night Exploration Society, the activities of which were frequently conducted by moonlight.

The systematic study of the Jordan Burn now presented, which takes into account the theories of certain other writers, began at Craiglockhart Hill, above the pond in what was for long known as The Happy Valley. A burn, it had been suggested, flowed from the pond's northern end. This was found to be correct. A burn does leave the pond here, flowing parallel to Lockharton Crescent. That this burn proceeded to flow through Morningside was, however, soon proved to be inconsistent with the law of gravity as the level of this stream at Meggetland Terrace is below that of Myreside. The former was identified as the Stank Burn which flows under the Union Canal to Slateford, past Westfield Avenue and into the Water of Leith at Roseburn.

The next area of investigation was Craighouse Hill above Myreside as it is near here that the Jordan Burn can first be seen. No watercourse could, however, be traced on Craighouse Hill. Myreside, with its ancient village, took its name from the area of "myre" or marshland in the vicinity referred to in the records as "the common myre" and shown on old maps as at the western extremity of the Burgh Muir. Cadell, in his study of Edinburgh's ancient lochs, notes that a large sheet of water existed in the region of Myreside in prehistoric times and relates that, when the suburban railway line was being cut through solid rock between Myreside and Craiglockhart Station, geological evidence was discovered of the existence there of an ancient loch. This may well be related to the origins of the Jordan Burn at this point. Abercrombie and Plumstead, in their *Civic Survey and Plan for Edinburgh* (1949), include a map which shows Jordanville Loch in the vicinity of Morningside. Reference to the Edinburgh City Engineer's plans revealed that an old water-pump house had for long existed on the west side of Craighouse Road, just within the wall of the Edinburgh University recreation ground. It now seemed clear that it was within this immediate vicinity that the Jordan Burn arose. On the east side of Craighouse Road at this point entry was made to the allotments beside Craighouse Cabinet Works. Slightly to the north of the latter, a few yards east of the railway bridge, in an area overgrown with bushes, the first unimpressive and virtually stagnant source of the Jordan Burn may be seen. Alongside the north wall of the Cabinet Works, the burn, polluted and unattractive, makes its sluggish way. This is the first identifiable source of the Jordan. It may be noted that Sir Thomas Dick-Lauder cited this as the Jordan's source, traced no doubt during his own explorations. Certain early maps also indicate this as the source. The investigations now recorded were, however, uninfluenced by earlier conclusions.

For some ten or twenty feet here, high up on the southern embankment of the railway line, the burn moves slowly on to a point behind the wall of the Balfour Kilpatrick works in Balcarres Street. It is interesting that, in this short length of its course, it is contained in an unusual channel with stone slabs on its base and sides. Half-way up the side-slabs are overflow holes — seldom necessary it may be thought, in recent times. This man-made channel then comes to a dead end and from this point the meagre flow of water makes its way down the railway embankment to the permanent way, where a phenomenon occurs which no-one seems able to explain. The water which has trickled down from the tiled channel now begins to follow the western slope of the permanent way, going back in the opposite direction from which it has come, towards the old Craiglockhart Station. Even more enigmatic — and frustrating for its tracker — it suddenly disappears down a hole and is lost! When consulted, the Engineer's Department of British Rail pondered this mysterious happening but could offer no explanation or indication of the course the Jordan had now taken.

Morningside's river is not to be written off so easily. Crossing to the north bank of the permanent way, investigation of a very obvious and much reported natural channel at the foot of the northern embankment seemed strongly to indicate that water had flowed there at some time. Excavation at certain points revealed dampness but no significant flow of water. At this point the channel ran parallel to the southern boundary wall of the Royal Edinburgh Hospital. Old plans and descriptions of the hospital grounds indicated that pond-like areas formed there at times. Indeed, curling ponds had once existed within the hospital precincts in this area and these had been the scene of many animated contests.

There is little doubt that the Jordan at one time flowed past the boundary wall of the Royal Edinburgh Hospital. Indeed, Sir Thomas Dick-Lauder's account of the burn's course confirms this. When describing this stretch of the Jordan, he noted certain features of the hospital in 1846, thirty-three years after the foundation of the original East House by Dr Andrew Duncan. The hospital report for that year listed what were then considered to be the principal causes of insanity among those admitted for treatment: "Anxiety on account of friends going abroad. Bad treatment by step-mothers. Domestic misfortunes. Desertion by husbands and wives. Disappointed affections. Enlistment of sons. Fright. False accusations. Grief at the loss of relatives. Pecuniary losses and misfortunes. Political agitation. Poverty. Religious enthusiasm. Vanity..." Sir Thomas remarks upon the vast changes which had even by then taken place in the attitude towards and treatment of the insane. He notes especially new developments under Dr Mackinnon.

Where the Jordan once flowed and now trickles past the southern wall of the Royal Edinburgh Hospital, at the point where it is joined by the east wall running downhill from Morningside Terrace, it is still possible to trace the route of the old right-of-way coming down from the ancient village of Tipperlinn, in line with what became Morningside Terrace but now terminating abruptly at the telephone exchange at the end of Maxwell Street. The original reason for the preservation of the ancient right-of-way from Tipperlinn was to give the women of the village access to the Jordan Burn to do their washing, either at the nearest point for them, where today the southern and eastern boundary walls of the Royal Edinburgh Hospital meet, or perhaps, by proceeding further along the right-of-way, where the Jordan was joined by the tributary about to be described. In earlier times there would appear to have been plenty of water in the vicinity of the telephone exchange.

For long the precise course of the Jordan at the foot of the steep pathway which is a continuation of what is now Morningside Terrace, and of the burn which flowed into the Jordan a little east of this point, were difficult to discover. By a stroke of good fortune, at the time that our field studies were being carried out, the preparation of the foundations for the new Maxwell Street telephone exchange revealed invaluable evidence of the waters in this vicinity. To the consternation of the builders and delight of Jordan Burn researchers, the bulldozers brought much of interest to light. The engineers on the site reported that in their excavations, just yards southwards of the old Tipperlinn right-of-way, a very old pipe, approximately nine inches in diameter, was unearthed, in which there was a damp muddy deposit, although certainly no evidence of the steady flow of a burn. This pipe followed what was traditionally believed to be the course of the Jordan coming from Craighouse Hill in the west, as indicated in old maps of the area and in Sir Thomas Dick-Lauder's description. The pipe had obviously been installed to channel the Jordan underground, possibly when the railway goods yard was first laid out on this site.

If no more could now be seen of the Jordan than a damp deposit in an old cracked pipe (duly removed by the site engineers), was it to be concluded that Morningside's ancient river had dried up for ever? Were this so, what was the source of the burn still flowing, albeit largely underground, past the back gardens of Nile Grove and Jordan Lane, and surfacing most pleasantly as it passed Woodburn House in Canaan Lane, Blackford, Mayfield and Cameron Toll? The telephone exchange excavations were to confirm the traditional explanation reflected in certain old maps and Sir Thomas Dick-Lauder's book.

The bulldozers literally uncovered a mystery which had long fascinated Morningside residents, especially those who as children had lived near Maxwell Street and played in the lane climbing from the north side of this street steeply up to Millar Place. Many had placed an ear over an iron grating at the point where the lane was joined by the ancient right-of-way from Tipperlinn: beneath could be heard, sometimes strongly, sometimes faintly, the sound of running water. This, they believed, was the Jordan Burn. The subsequent excavations revealed, however, that it was not the Jordan — now a mere muddy trickle in an old pipe — but a vigorous little tributary, the waters of which meet those of the Jordan under the grating.

Again, over the years, many observers with sharpness of ear had heard the rush of water under another grating which was on the left as one entered from Balcarres Street the pathway leading over the railway footbridge at Morningside Station. The water sounded deep underground, and beyond the grating its course could not be traced. Excavations at the old railway goods yard were to solve the mystery, however, bringing to light a strongly flowing stream.

What, then, was the source and the course of this substantial tributary which had for so long been transfusing life into the almost moribund Jordan Burn? Residents on the south side of Comiston Drive have long been proud of the pleasant stream flowing just beyond their garden walls. Many built picturesque little footbridges across it to what was originally the Poorhouse Road. Closed many years ago, it ran closely parallel, on the north, to Greenbank Drive, which leads to the City Infectious Diseases Hospital. This burn, which tradition and old maps suggested was a tributary of the Jordan, without naming it, was, for the purpose of our research, called the Comiston Burn.

Since the Comiston Burn is first to be seen in the garden of a villa just west of the junction between Morningside Grove and Greenbank Drive, investigation began at this point. Just beyond the western boundary wall of this villa is the Merchants of Edinburgh Golf Club, on the southern slopes of Craighouse Hill. As golf club members are well aware, after heavy rain the valley at the foot of these slopes is often waterlogged. No trace of a burn could be found in this area on the south side of Craighouse Hill but note was taken of the City Engineer's Department's advice that, when the golf club car park was laid out at the foot of this hill, provision had to be made for the drainage of hill water. This area, therefore, seemed likely to be the source of the Comiston Burn, though this was not conclusive. Just as the Jordan had its life-giving tributary, so too, it seemed, did the Comiston Burn, which, partly or principally originating in the catchment area of the valley of the golf course, was also apparently joined by a little stream emanating from another source.

On the south side of Glenlockhart Road, almost opposite the golf club car park, the bed of a small stream may be seen, which occasionally bears water and disappears under the road. This southern source of the Comiston Burn demanded further investigation. Running alongside a footpath parallel to the boundary wall of Greenlea, the course of the little stream may be followed southwards. At one point a narrow pipe carrying surface water from the nearby Greenbank estate delivers a modest contribution to the stream. Where the path ends, as Greenbank Drive turns at right angles past the frontage of the City Hospital, the stream also disappears. There is no trace of it on the other side of the road, within the hospital railings. Proceeding along Greenbank Drive on its Greenlea side, there is occasional evidence of the course of a small stream. Just west of the main gates to the City Hospital and the little lane which continues on to Firrhill School, in ground at the foot of Craiglockhart Hill, a water-

259

course was quite distinctly seen, filled with decaying leaves and muddy soil. This seemed to be the source of the stream which flowed along the north side of the last stretch of Greenbank Drive, then turned northwards, running under Glenlockhart Road into the main course of the Comiston Burn.

The Comiston Burn flowing past the back gardens on the south side of Comiston Drive may be seen from the railings on the left (where Comiston Drive turns off from Comiston Road), in the back garden of what was once the lodge at the entrance to the former Poorhouse Road. It then passes under Comiston Drive and under the rear playgrounds of South Morningside School. At one time, before the adjacent houses in Craiglea Drive were built, the burn might have been visible from the little lane just beyond the row of shops on the south side of Craiglea Drive. It now proceeds downhill on the west side of Comiston Road and more than one report has attributed the cracked lintels of the flats in this stretch of Comiston Road to the ceaseless underground flow of the burn.

At Morningside Drive, the Comiston Burn passes under the Dunedin Masonic Hall and the shop opposite, then proceeds under Belhaven Terrace. Here it veers slightly westwards and, passing under Balcarres Street, suddenly reveals itself to the attentive ear, if not the eye, as it flows under the metal grille to the left of the entrance to the pathway which leads from Balcarres Street over the railway footbridge. That the sound of running water under the grille comes from a considerable depth is evidenced by the fact that the ground level of the lane is much higher than that of the railway line, under which the Comiston Burn passes. The stream then enters the former railway goods yard, now something of a wasteland at this southern point, and makes its way, running parallel to the lane, beyond the footbridge, passing the end of Maxwell Street and the entrance to the grounds of the telephone exchange. At the point already described it flows at right-angles into the now feeble waters of the Jordan Burn and surrenders its identity.

The excavations on the site of the telephone exchange revealed that the Comiston Burn, which enters the former goods yard from under the railway line, had not always flowed in its present direction. An old course was found running in a north-westerly direction towards the Jordan Burn pipeline, near the south-western corner of the Royal Edinburgh Hospital grounds. The first revelation of the Comiston Burn's present course came when a large flagstone was uncovered near the old weigh-bridge hut just inside the entrance of the former goods yards, at the end of Maxwell Street. Below lay a channel, the base and sides of which were formed from similar large flagstones some two feet six inches square. Through this the Comiston Burn, once a mere trickle at Greenbank Drive, now flowed strongly. The flagstone channel was replaced by large concrete pipes and the old course to the north-west was filled in. Morningside residents who witnessed the prolonged preparation of the telephone exchange site will

Jordan Bank Cottages on the Jordan Burn

Photograph by Mr W. R. Smith

remember the veritable underground loch produced by the liberated confluent Jordan and Comiston burns, and the slow but relentless action of the pumps which eventually withdrew their invading waters, until, at last subdued, they were channelled anew, still to assure the Jordan's ancient onward journey.

Now flowing underground between the very high wall which was originally the southern boundary wall of East House and the low wall and railings of the back greens of the north side of Maxwell Street, the Jordan flows between the shops at 356-8 Morningside Road, above which the original tenements were demolished on account of the burn's erosion of their foundations. There is a narrow concrete channel, revealed some time ago during road repairs at this point, in which the burn passes under Morningside Road and continues beneath the lane at the south wall of a modern supermarket. This very old lane, once a pathway, and the old toll-house which stood beside it, have been discussed in an earlier chapter. During the building of the supermarket at the entrance to the lane, considerable delay occurred while the burn was safely confined to a concrete pipe.

Until the end of the last century, when it was covered over for most of its course through Morningside in order to facilitate the great building programme, there were many pleasant open stretches of the Jordan, notably at the point where it now flows under Morningside Road. Here the burn was quite wide, but not too wide to be leapt across by village boys, who preferred this adventurous method of crossing to using the little wooden bridge known as the "Briggs o' Braid", or simply "the Briggs". The Briggs o' Braid is frequently given as a location in old property titles. Some confusion has arisen over the name. It sounds as though it refers to a bridge over the Braid Burn, which is much further to the south, up Comiston Road. The name Braid was applied to the little bridge over the Jordan simply because the land immediately to the south at this point was the beginning of the Braid estate. On the north bank the estates of Morningside proper and Canaan ended. The bridge lay on the ancient Western Hiegait, which skirted the western fringes of the Burgh Muir and was one of the principal routes into Edinburgh from the south. Thus it was across the Briggs o' Braid in its most primitive forms that invaders from the south — the Roman legions, Edward I of England and subsequent English armies — entered Edinburgh. In later times, during the '45 Rebellion, Bonnie Prince Charlie and his Jacobite army, coming by Slateford, Colinton Mains and the path along the Braid Burn, crossed the Briggs o' Braid on his way to Holyrood.

The Jordan Burn, having crossed under Morningside Road, passes the rear of Braid Church, and continues along the natural valley between the back gardens of the houses on the north side of Nile Grove and those on the south side of Jordan Lane. The houses at the far end of Jordan Lane have wooden doors in their back garden walls which once gave entrance from a pathway along the north bank of the Jordan, hence the street's original name, Jordan Bank. These doors, now mostly boarded up or unable to be opened because of the gradual alteration in ground level, today lead into a narrow walled lane directly above the burn. Certain of these Jordan Lane houses have little stone-built sheds at the foot of their gardens once used as wash-houses, with hand pumps for drawing water from the Jordan. At the foot of the garden of Braid Hill Cottage at 20 Jordan Lane, the Jordan surfaces for a few feet. Stone steps lead down to the water, alongside which is an old iron hand-pump. It was here that the first attempts were made to verify, before the telephone exchange excavations provided conclusive evidence, that the Comiston Burn was a tributary of the Jordan. At the point where the Comiston Burn disappears underground below the railings on the left at the entrance to Comiston Drive from Comiston Road, a small amount of innocuous flourescent dye was added to the stream. An hour later the waters of the Jordan in the garden of Braid Hill Cottage showed the first traces of discolouration.

The Jordan now passes under Woodburn Terrace, where the houses at the gable-end of the flats on the east side seem to have escaped the damage inflicted on other buildings in Morningside built over the Jordan or its tributary. Perhaps the builders of Woodburn Terrace wisely stopped short for this reason. The Jordan emerges from under Woodburn Terrace into the pleasant grounds of Woodburn House, entered from Canaan Lane, and here contributes to a delightfully idyllic rural scene. Two little waterfalls enhance the burn's charm as it murmurs onwards through a glade of tall, venerable trees, the setting signifying the origin of the name Woodburn. It is here that the Jordan may be seen at its best, recalling its charm of earlier days.

The southern slopes of the Astley Ainslie Hospital grounds now accommodate the Jordan as it continues eastwards, close to its early travelling companion, the old suburban railway line. In earlier times the burn formed a natural hazard on the ladies' nine-hole golf course which existed here before the hospital was built. Visible from the road-bridge over the railway line at Oswald Road, the Jordan next flows on through what was formerly the old farm of Blackford, on the site of which the once bustling suburban railway station of this name came to be built. While only a few scattered stones of Blackford House now remain, fortunately the sturdy two-storey farmhouse itself still stands. Long after the farm's disappearance it remained the pleasant home of a family whose lives were spent as farmworkers here. The house is still occupied today, a relic of past days amidst the picturesque and quaint surroundings of Glenisla Gardens. In the garden of the farmhouse, the old stone bridge over the Jordan, once a popular subject for photographers, has been carefully and imaginatively preserved and laid out with pleasant flower-beds.

The early days of Blackford House and its pleasant surroundings have been picturesquely described by Sir Thomas Dick-Lauder. He gives a delightful portrait of his friend Miss Memie Trotter, then in her nineties, last of a branch of the notable family of Mortonhall estate. Perhaps a secret of Miss Trotter's longevity was her daily bathing in the waters of the Jordan, even in advanced years!

There is something of Jekyll and Hyde about the Jordan: its course alternates between calm, pleasant settings and scenes of aggressive destruction, the latter occurring at Blackford as well as Morningside. Immediately beyond its attractive manifestations at Blackford farm, the burn emerges into view just beyond the bridge at the foot of Blackford Avenue and flows onwards in a very narrow channel which is nothing more than a ditch. Yet in this innocent-looking and apparently subdued stretch the Jordan has been secretly taking its toll. A few years ago, as passers-by noted with some curiosity, teams of workmen were engaged for months on a major and expensive operation. Running parallel to the burn from the old Briggs o' Braid at the foot of Morningside Road is the Powburn sewer, a large concrete pipe nearly five feet in diameter. Just beyond the bridge at Blackford Avenue the Jordan had gradually eroded the soil under a considerable stretch of the unsupported sewer pipe so that it had, at certain points, cracked and collapsed. After months of work the offending Jordan was diverted from the sewer into a new concrete channel.

Once more in safe captivity, "the little streamlet" which Lord Marmion viewed from Blackford Hill continues along what were the southern fringes of the Grange House estate and onwards to Mayfield

Road. On the west side of Mayfield Road, just before it flows underneath, the burn, which for some distance has gone underground, may again be seen emerging from a small tunnel on the north side of the railway embankment. On the banks of the burn, at the point where it reappears from under Mayfield Road, was the ancient village of Powburn. In 1663 Sir James Keith was baronet of Powburn, but this title became extinct. A large villa, Powburn House, in its latter days a favourite summer resort of wealthy Edinburgh citizens, was advertised as vacant in 1773 in the *Edinburgh Advertiser* which described it as, "A desirable mansion, pleasantly situated from the Grange Toll Bar, with coach-house and four-stalled stable." This house and the village were eventually swept away as Edinburgh grew southwards.

Just beyond the one-time village of Powburn, the Jordan flows under the now derelict Newington Station, under Mayfield Gardens at the foot of Minto Street, and then washes the southern boundary wall of Newington Cemetery. At the foot of Lady Road at Cameron Toll there is a little parapet from which the Jordan may be seen as it leaves the cemetery's precincts.

Now the long persevering flow of Morningside's own river, far from its source, is nearly at an end. Re-appearing from under Lady Road, it compensates for its ignominious and uncomfortable confinement during so much of its travels by enjoying the last luxury of expanding into a new open concrete channel. At times, after heavy rainfall, it has even had the pleasure of welcoming ducks here to its open waters. Its early polluted and sluggish origins at Myreside are long forgotten.

Finally, its end in sight and as if reluctant to accept it, the Jordan once again becomes sluggish and enjoys a last rendezvous with its travelling companion, the suburban railway line. Just south of the University recreation grounds at Peffermill, within the district of Greenend — an area which in ancient days was also a great myre or marshland — the Jordan is at last received by its more southerly Morningside neighbour, the Braid Burn, and carried along by the latter's more powerful waters. If the Jordan's surrender of its proud name to that of Braid is painful, it does not last for long, for soon both streams lose their identity to become the Figgate Burn. Passing through the hinterland of Portobello, the last days of the Jordan and Braid are quickly spent, and skirting the walls of the man-made waters of Edinburgh's open-air swimming pool, a stone channel under Portobello promenade hastens the death agonies of Morningside's two rivers.

CHAPTER 2

Beyond the Jordan :
Plewlands . Craighouse

The first signs of the transition of the village of Morningside into what, in a relatively short time, was to become a rapidly expanding suburb were heralded by Robert Louis Stevenson in *Edinburgh: Picturesque Notes,* published in 1878. Describing the steep descent of Morningside Road from Boroughmuirhead and Churchhill, he notes that at the foot of the hill, just as the road is about to climb again, it passed the toll-bar and then "issued at once into the open country". "Even as I write these words," Stevenson continued, "they are being antiquated in the progress of events, and the chisels are tinkling on a new row of houses. The builders have at length adventured beyond the toll which held them in respect so long and proceed to career in these fresh pastures like a herd of colts turned loose."

This expansion of Morningside beyond the city's ancient southern boundary, the Jordan, roused Stevenson's wrath. He had come to know the old village well in his younger days when walking through it on his way from the city to Swanston Cottage. Recalling how Lord Beaconsfield had once proposed to hang an architect by way of stimulation, he advocated similar measures to save "these doomed meads from the ravages of the builders. . .It seems as if it must come to an open fight," he wrote, "to preserve a corner of green country unbedevilled."

But, despite Robert Louis Stevenson's words of regret and protest, the march of progress was not to be halted. On the open country beyond the toll a vast residential building programme was soon to begin. The owners of the estate of Braid, the Gordons of Cluny, had feued out extensive lands over an area between what are now Nile Grove in the north and the Hermitage of Braid in the south, Comiston Road in the west and Blackford in the east. Here was to arise the attractive residential district with streets bearing the names of the Gordons' Aberdeenshire estates, Cluny, Midmar and Corrennie, as well as that of their Edinburgh family seat, the Hermitage of Braid. Similarly, on the large Plewlands estate, extending from what is now Maxwell Street and the old village of Myreside southwards to Greenbank Crescent, and from Comiston Road eastwards to Craighouse and the fringes of Meggetland, another vast residential area was to be built. Together, the development of the Braid and Plewlands estates, completed by 1900, resulted in the mushrooming of classical "villadom" on a scale which even Robert Louis Stevenson's fertile imagination had not conceived. Yet "the doomed meads" were not entirely obliterated: much pleasant open green space was preserved.

There were other factors which towards the end of the nineteenth century were leading rapidly to Morningside's growth and transformation. The Jordan Burn had ceased to be Edinburgh's southern boundary in 1856. The latter was then extended southwards to a line crossing Comiston Road at Comiston Drive, later to the old Braid Hills tramway terminus and finally, as today, to Hillend Park and along the ridge of Caerketton and the aligning range of the Pentland Hills. Road tolls in Scotland were abolished in 1883, and by that date the old toll-bar at the Briggs o' Braid had, in any case, been swept away and the Jordan Burn covered over by Morningside Road. There was no longer any financial deterrent to those choosing to reside south of the old city boundary. Further, with the gradual extension and improvement of transport facilities from the city, Morningside ceased to be the remote village of earlier days.

While Robert Louis Stevenson does not specify where "the chisels are tinkling on a new row of houses", Maxwell Street, just beyond the old toll-bar, was built just a year before the publication of *Picturesque Notes,* as the inscription high above the south-east corner of the street indicates, so that it may well have been its construction to which he refers. Writers to the Press at the turn of the century have described Maxwell Street as the

Braid Iron Church, built in 1883, from a water-colour by E. Michie
By courtesy of Rev. Roderick Smith, D.D.

266

Laying the Foundation Stone of Braid Church, October 1886

By courtesy of the late Miss E. Proudfoot

first scene of new building across the Jordan. It is probable that Maxwell Street takes its name from Herbert Maxwell, a member of Edinburgh Town Council in 1591 and the owner of land in this area. On the wall at the south-east corner of Maxwell Street is the inscription "Watt Terrace". This may have been the original name of the short stretch of Morningside Road from this point up to Morningside Station. As was often done, it might have been given the name of its builder.

Before Maxwell Street was built, the area was apparently grassy parkland which in winter was frequently flooded and frozen over, providing a popular resort of skaters. The street has earned a place in Edinburgh's early annals of telecommunications. Alexander Graham Bell, inventor of the telephone, was born at South Charlotte Street in 1847. The Scottish Telephonic Exchange Limited was established in the city in 1879. Morningside's first telephone exchange (comprising two fifty-line units) was installed in 1893 in the house of a family named Swanson at 8 Maxwell Street. It is interesting that not many yards from this first Morningside exchange a modern Post Office telephone exchange was established in the former railway goods yard in 1974.

Ten years after the completion of Maxwell Street, the chisels began tinkling on the construction of Braid Church, opened in 1887. It was built only a few yards from the toll-house which, a year later, was dismantled stone by stone and rebuilt as the entrance lodge to the Hermitage of Braid. The site of the toll-house became part of the church's surrounding lawn. The history of Braid Church forms an interesting part of the annals of Morningside and reveals a number of sidelights on the general growth and development of the district itself. Braid was the first church to be built in Morningside after the establishment of the Parish Church at Churchhill fifty years before. While St Matthew's Parish Church, opened a few months after Braid, was established and fostered by the original Parish Church, Braid has always been proud of its independent origins.

Braid Church had its beginnings in a little iron church built in January 1883 on the site of the present-day junction of Braid Road and Comiston Road. The generous benefactor who provided £500 for the purchase of the iron church for long remained anonymous. He was, in fact, Dr John Kerr. The original congregation of seventy "adherents" were of the United Presbyterian Church (similar to but independent of the original congregation of North Morningside Church at Holy Corner). As its site was within the estate of Braid, the church adopted that name.

Nine months after the opening of the little iron church the small body of worshippers were officially formed into a congregation in October 1883. Amongst the members of the original Kirk Session was a very wealthy Councillor (later Lord Provost and Sir) James Steel, a generous benefactor of Braid. It is related that, during an official inquiry, he was asked to state his income. He gave the figure of £80,000. The official apologetically replied that it was not Councillor Steel's capital which required to be stated but his annual income. Steel reiterated that this was £80,000. This very substantial income was derived from stone quarrying operations and many building interests. Steel built many Edinburgh streets including a large section of Dalry, the Murieston part of this district being named after his estate in West Lothian, a name also chosen as the title of his subsequent baronetcy. In 1877 he purchased land from the Heriot Trust and on this built Douglas, Glencairn and Eglinton Crescents, Belgrave Place and Buckingham Terrace. He also built much of Comely Bank.

Steel represented the George Square ward in Edinburgh Town Council for thirty-one years. He presided at the opening of the City Infectious Diseases Hospital in Greenbank Drive in May 1903 (when it was known as Colinton Hospital or the Fever Hospital). The ceremony was performed by Edward VII, who immediately afterwards made Steel a Baronet. Steel died soon after demitting the Lord Provostship in 1903.

The little iron church of Braid soon proved too small for the rapidly growing congregation built up by the first minister, the Rev. Walter Brown, called from Galashiels. Proposals were made and funds gathered to build a new church. The site at the north-west corner of Nile Grove was acquired and plans were drawn up by George Washington Browne, who later became the leading Scottish architect of his time, for a church which would accommodate seven hundred and fifty people. The estimated cost was £5,000. This was George Washington Browne's first public building in Edinburgh. His later achievements were to include Edinburgh's Central Public Library on George IV Bridge, the Royal Hospital for Sick Children on Sciennes Road and the Scottish National Memorial to King Edward VII at Holyrood.

When first approached by Braid's minister, the Rev. Walter Brown, the architect asked him what style of church he and his congregation desired: a traditional ecclesiastical building or an auditorium? The minister was puzzled, asking what was meant by an auditorium. The architect explained that an auditorium enabled a semi-circle of people to gather eagerly round a speaker. The minister immediately chose the auditorium, hence the unique octagonal design of Braid Church which enables the preacher to see his whole audience at once and all to hear him equally well.

The iron church had become completely inadequate, despite small extensions, so that the new building was commissioned without delay. The foundation stone was laid on October 9th, 1886 and, after only nine months, the church was opened on July 10th, 1887. The final cost was £500 above the original quotation.

Even though the original Braid congregation had been very confined in their tiny iron church, their activities had steadily expanded. These throw interesting light on the Morningside of that time. A Home Mission Station had been established at Swanston, meeting in the village schoolroom. It had the active support of the farmer, Mr Finnie, and later of his widow. For a time, services were conducted on the village green, worshippers being summoned by hand-bell. In Morningside, the Boys' Brigade has always been traditionally associated with Cluny (formerly St Matthew's) Parish Church, the still thriving 55th Company having been founded there in 1914. In fact, a Boys' Brigade company had earlier been sponsored by the congregation of Braid's iron church, although it did not exist for long.

The rapid increase in the population of Morningside towards the end of the nineteenth century is reflected in the steady growth of the Braid Church congregation from seventy in the first year of the iron church, 1883, to almost eight hundred in 1900. Likewise, the area's geographical expansion led to the Braid congregation being divided into twenty-five districts. As Morningside grew southwards, a United Presbyterian Mission was established at Greenbank. Initially pioneered from Braid, in 1900 it became Greenbank Church. During a period of severe financial crisis soon after the new Braid Church was opened, many members (and non-members) lent money to the church at a very low rate of interest.

By the early 1900s Morningside had begun to take on the features of a modern suburb offering attractive housing. The city itself was moving into a new era of development and progress. At this time the Braid records throw light on prevailing health problems. An entry for 1907, for example, reports regular services conducted in the crowded tuberculosis wards of the City Fever Hospital at Greenbank, opened four years before. Originally established as a United Presbyterian Church, Braid had in 1900 united with the Free Church to become the Braid United Free Church. In 1929 it was reunited with the Church of Scotland.

Morningside Station was opened for passenger traffic in 1884. The story of the construction of the Edinburgh Suburban and South Side Junction Railway, as it was originally named, is linked with one of the most tragic events in the history of Scottish railways, the Tay Bridge disaster of December 28th, 1879. The Tay Bridge had been designed by Thomas Bouch of Comely Bank, whose workmanship, along with other circumstances of the tragedy, was later the subject of a Board of Trade Court of Inquiry. Proceedings opened in Dundee in January 1880 and were concluded in May of that year.

While Bouch awaited the Court's findings, he did not, as some reports related, retire into obscurity, dreading the verdict. He firmly believed that his design was without defect and, retaining his confidence, he meanwhile undertook other assignments. One of these was the preparation of plans for submission to Parliament in order to seek permission to proceed with the construction of Edinburgh's suburban railway. The steering of his plans through Parliament was apparently not easy; it involved Bouch in frequent train journeys to London. His diary for July 31st, 1880 read: "Travelling to London. Suburban Railway." For August 6th the entry is: "Suburban Railway before committee. Preamble approved. Travelled to Edinbro." On his arrival at Waverley Station after this particular visit Bouch felt unwell. His doctor advised complete rest and he retired to Moffat, where he died in October 1880. The Bill incorporating his plans for the Edinburgh Suburban Railway was eventually approved; this project was his last achievement. The conclusions of the Tay Bridge Disaster Court of Inquiry had been equivocal, and not unanimous. Bouch regarded himself as having been exonerated but certain press reports took the opposite view: the Court's verdict resulted in controversy.

The Parliamentary Acts authorising the construction of the suburban railway were duly passed in August 1880 and July 1882. By 1884, from the special "through platform" opened at Waverley Station, a double-line system was put into operation. The new suburban stations were at Haymarket, Gorgie, Morningside Road, Blackford, Newington, Duddingston, Portobello and Abbeyhill, and trains travelled regularly in both directions. Craiglockhart station was opened three years after the others, in 1887. The line from Gorgie to Morningside followed a gradual uphill gradient until the summit was reached just west of Morningside Road Station. At a number of points cuttings had to be made for the track, most

Trace horses from horse-drawn cars being rested at Morningside Station, c. 1900

Torrance's shop and tea rooms

By courtesy of Miss Jean Campbell

notably through deep rock east of Craiglockhart, which meant that the station offices there had to be built on the street bridge level, as also at Morningside Road and Newington. As mentioned elsewhere, a footbridge had to be built at Morningside Station to ensure the old right-of-way from the village of Tipperlinn, although by 1884 the village had long since disappeared.

A year after the inauguration of the railway, the Edinburgh Suburban and South Side Junction Railway Company amalgamated with its parent company, the North British Railway Company. The establishment of the suburban railway encouraged increasing numbers of people to take up residence in Morningside, a trend particularly evident in the 1930s, when, perhaps, the railway was at its peak, having trains arriving at Waverley Station every ten minutes during peak hours.

The opening of the railway goods yard and coal depot at the end of Maxwell Street proved invaluable to the farmers of Comiston, Hunter's Tryst and Swanston, and many older Morningside residents will recall the bustle there as farm carts went to and fro' loaded with cows, sheep, potatoes and turnips. Sheep were regularly brought by train to the goods yard and, with disregard for the flow of traffic, were driven across Morningside Road to graze in the fields below the Blackford Hill at the east end of Hermitage Drive. In the days before electricity and gas were used for heating, the constant stream of carts and lorries from the important coal depot added to the bustle.

Soon after the opening of Morningside Station the spacious crossroads area comprising Morningside Road, Balcarres Street, Comiston Road, Braid Road and Cluny Gardens became the hub of Morningside. Morningside Station was the terminus of the horse-drawn cars. Here the horses were changed and rested before the steep pull to Churchhill. Here, too, was the stance of the horse-cabs, the cabbies' shelter being just round the corner in Balcarres Street. The cabs, which included brake and pair and four-in-hand coaches, operated from 8.45 a.m. until 10 p.m. The cab fare to Waverley Station in about 1900 was 1/6d. Near the station telegraph boys waited until hailed by the postmistress of Plewlands Post Office at the beginning of Comiston Road, then set out on foot or bicycle with their urgent messages for the important people in the "big houses" then rapidly being built.

To complete the services which centred on Morningside Station, a group of enterprising Morningside businessmen, of whom Colonel Trotter of Mortonhall was chairman, decided to build a hotel. Thus at the corner of Braid and Comiston Roads a substantial five-storey building arose in 1884, the year the station was opened. It was designed to provide ample accommodation for short-term visitors to Morningside. Colonel Trotter proposed that this new creation be named the Pentland Hotel, while some partners preferred the Belhaven Hotel (nearby Belhaven Terrace had then just recently been built). The need for a decision did not arise. When the building was completed, financial resources to continue the enterprise were not forthcoming and the scheme was abandoned. The prospective hotel was sub-divided into the comfortable flats of today. The two small sculpted animal figures which still surmount the stone balustrade above the corner premises at 1 Comiston Road were placed there during the occupancy of the British Linen Bank, whose insignia they represented.

What has become a cherished landmark, the station clock, was installed in 1910. It was the gift of three Morningside Town Councillors, R. K. Inches, William Inman and William Torrance. During the construction of a new traffic control system in the Morningside Station area in 1968, the clock was removed and, when some considerable time passed with no sign of its replacement, many residents made inquiries in official quarters. All was well. The clock was duly re-sited, a new electrical mechanism having been installed. The station area regained its traditional appearance.

Another pleasant feature of the area were the tea-rooms above Torrance's bakery at the corner of Belhaven Terrace and Comiston Road. Owned by Councillor William Torrance, one of the donors of the clock, the premises were a popular rendezvous and no doubt many important discussions took place over Torrance's tea-cups. One, recalled by an elderly Morningside resident, occurred on October 7th, 1894 when the pioneers of Morningside's Baptist Church at Churchhill held their informal initial meeting here.

PLEWLANDS

The lands of Plewlands or Ploughlands are referred to as "Plewlandsike" in the Protocol Book of James Young under the date March 23rd, 1497. For long they were part of the extensive adjacent lands of Braid which comprised four hundred and twelve acres. Plewlands as such extended from what is now Maxwell Street and the southern boundary wall of the Royal Edinburgh Hospital (following the line of the western stretch of the Jordan Burn) southwards to what I have called the Comiston Burn, flowing behind the south side of Comiston Drive. What is now Comiston Road formed the eastern boundary, while on the west the frontiers were the ancient village of Myreside and the nearer fringes of Meggetland.

Amongst the earliest recorded owners of the Plewlands estate was Patrick Elois, an Edinburgh merchant and bailie who acquired the lands from his father soon after the death of James IV at Flodden in 1513. The Elois family were also owners for some time of Mortonhall. Shortly after Sir William Dick settled in the estate of Braid in 1631, he acquired and gifted to his son Alexander the lands of Plewlands. In 1719 Archibald Brown of Greenbank obtained partial possession. By 1760 Plewlands had been disponed to Henry Trotter of Mortonhall. *A Plan of the Barony of*

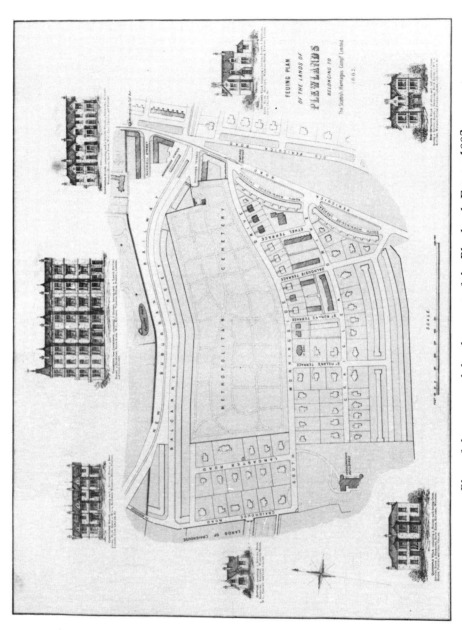

Plan of the proposed development of the Plewlands Estate, 1882

Braid dated 1772, shows the extensive area of Plewlands as "Mr Sievewright's Lands".

A large dairy farm with a tannery was established in Plewlands in the early 1800s. The farmhouse and extensive byres and steadings were situated close to the site of the present-day Morningside Recreational Park, entered from Morningside Drive and Balcarres Street. The farm is indicated and named in Edinburgh Post Office Directory maps until 1908. The following year its ruins are indicated but no longer named. Soon after this date these were swept away as the present-day residential district of Plewlands was gradually extended.

In the 1820s, immediately beyond and westward of the Briggs o' Braid, a farm-cart track led to Plewlands Farm, crossing the Comiston Burn near the point where today this little stream flows underground beside the railway footbridge at Balcarres Street. The farmhouse was a much-sought-after retreat for many notable Edinburgh citizens. One such who came to reside here in 1823 was the Rev. Robert Morehead, D.D., at one time Episcopalian Dean of Edinburgh. Dr. Morehead wrote of his Plewlands stay with some enthusiasm, describing the farmhouse as, "A most beautiful summer residence near Braid where I am alone with my daughter, Isabella. In the mornings, I study Hebrew," he wrote. "I sometimes think of writing my journal here in blank verse. There is a great deal of poetry scattered about me if I could catch it, and it is a pity to lose the power of versification. The poetry of life is the only poetry worth preserving. But I shall not strike it out from prose this morning."

In 1882 a feuing plan for the lands of Plewlands was published by the Scottish Heritages Company which had acquired superiority. Illustrated in colour, this showed that a fair degree of building of detached and semi-detached villas had already taken place on the south side of what was then, and for years remained, South Morningside Drive, later coming to be named simply Morningside Drive. Ethel Terrace, Dalhousie Terrace, the east side of St Ronan's Terrace and a short length of Craiglea Drive (on the north between Dalhousie Terrace and St Ronan's Terrace) had, by 1882, already been built. The considerable building programme proposed for the remainder of the Plewlands estate is indicated and the plan shows the different architectural styles of the houses and what accommodation they would offer prospective purchasers. In addition to proposed new streets which have since been built and named as planned, others are indicated which were either never constructed or else given different names. North Morningside Crescent and South Morningside Crescent are illustrated as little semi-circular streets near the west side of Comiston Road (then Penicuik Road). North Morningside Crescent was to have extended from South Morningside Drive to Craiglea Drive and South Morningside Crescent from Craiglea Drive to what became Comiston Drive, which is shown but not named in the 1882 plan. What today is Plewlands Terrace was proposed, rather strangely, as Lancaster Road. St

Clair Terrace and Morningside Grove were not then envisaged. According to Charles Boog-Watson's *History and Derivation of Edinburgh Street Names,* Ethel Terrace was named after its builder's daughter, Ethel Clark, while Dalhousie Terrace and other streets bearing saints' names are ascribed to "baseless fancy".

The Plewlands feu plan of 1882 also indicates other points of interest. The tramway terminus (a single line with a car turning) is shown at the Comiston Road end of Morningside Drive. Morningside Station is indicated in anticipation of its opening two years later in 1884. The Morningside toll-bar also appears. A year after the plan's publication, tolls in Scotland were abolished and the toll-house was dismantled.

What became Braid Road is shown as the Old Penicuik Road. Belhaven Terrace is also indicated as already built at the entrance to what is described as the Metropolitan Cemetery. While the origin of its name is not on record, Belhaven Terrace may have had some association with the little place of that name near Dunbar.

The construction of Balcarres Street was begun by 1884 and completed in stages over a period of fifteen years. The first part to be built, originally named Balcarres Terrace, commenced at Morningside Station, opposite Belhaven Terrace. Its south side consisted of the short row of tenements extending from the small triangle of ground on the right of the entrance gates to the cemetery to what was, in more recent times, George Horne's mission hall above two shops, now 1 - 10 Balcarres Street. After this the cemetery wall began. On its north side, in Balcarres Terrace, from the time of the street's original construction, was an important blacksmith's workshop, owned for many years by the Moyes family. By 1900 the north side of Balcarres Street, from the blacksmith's premises to those of Messrs McKenzie and Moncur (now Messrs Balfour Kilpatrick) had been completed. At this time Balcarres Terrace ceased to appear on the Post Office Directory maps and the whole length from Morningside Station to the beginning of what is now Craighouse Gardens became Balcarres Street.

It is possible that Balcarres Street was given its name by Bailie McKenzie, a heating engineer who, with his partner Mr Moncur, owned much of this part of the old Plewlands estate. McKenzie had built Appin Terrace in Edinburgh, naming it after his birthplace in Fife. He may have named Balcarres Street after Balcarres House, a notable residence in Fife with which he also had connections.

For some time before building extended beyond what is now 36 Balcarres Street, the road was a *cul-de-sac,* sealed off by a wall of railway sleepers. Beyond were the pleasant lower slopes of Plewlands farm and the Craighouse estate. In this area a nine-hole golf course was laid out and here two young Morningside residents who were to earn a place amongst the world's most celebrated golfers first learned the royal and ancient game. These were Tommy Armour and Bobby Cruickshank.

Water-colour of the Plewlands district, showing Plewlands Farm and other early features of Morningside, c. 1900, by a patient in Craighouse

By courtesy of the Royal Edinburgh Hospital

Tommy Armour's family lived in a cottage within the Craighouse grounds, his father being on the maintenance staff of the asylum. Born in Edinburgh in 1896, Armour's early promise first became obvious when, at the age of fourteen, he played with his brother Sandy in the winning team of the Edinburgh Western Club's Dispatch Trophy contests. Serving during the First World War in the Tank Corps, he was blinded in one eye, but his golfing ability was not impaired. In 1920 he won the French Amateur Championship and was amongst the first eight in the United States Amateur Championship. His subsequent achievements are legendary. He was a member of the British Walker Cup team in 1922. After leaving for the United States in 1926 and becoming an American citizen, he was in the American Ryder Cup team that same year. He went on to win the United States Open Championship in 1927, the P.G.A. Tournament in 1930 and the British Open Championship in 1931 — three of the world's four supreme golfing accolades. Tommy Armour was also the author of several best-selling books on golf. When his playing days were over he turned to coaching in Florida, his pupils including Richard

M. Nixon and many millionaires. Armour was the first recipient of the Frank Moran Trophy awarded annually to a Scot who has gained golfing distinction. His son became a leading surgeon in the United States.

Bobby Cruickshank, born at Grantown-on-Spey, also played his early golf at the short Balcarres Street course. A prisoner of war during the First World War, he later became a professional golfer and also went to the United States, where he was regarded as one of that country's best professionals in the 1920s and '30s. On account of the brilliance of Bobby Jones, Cruickshank found himself runner-up in many a championship he might otherwise have won. While his achievements were not so numerous or spectacular as Tommy Armour's, Cruickshank nevertheless became one of the world's most celebrated golfers.

The open area beside what is now a bus terminus was once occupied by Buchan's stall-fed dairy. In the mews-like premises reached through a pend between 45 and 47 Balcarres Street, a number of artists and craftsmen have worked in recent years. Morningside Cemetery at the entrance to Balcarres Street was opened in 1878. It is the resting place of many distinguished Morningside residents and of others from outside the district whose relatives chose this place of burial. Amongst the most notable names in the cemetery's register are Alexander Carlyle, M.A., nephew of the Sage of Chelsea, and his wife Mary Carlyle Aitken (who resided at one time at 30 Newbattle Terrace with their three sons), James Logie Robertson ("Hugh Haliburton"), poet and essayist, William Cowan, for long President of the Old Edinburgh Club (who bequeathed to the Edinburgh Public Libraries a valuable collection of books and relics relating to old Edinburgh), John D. Comrie, M.D. of the Edinburgh University Medical School, author of *History of Scottish Medicine,* and Alexander John Travers Allan, Scottish Amateur Golf Champion of 1897. On one gravestone, simple but significant words recall "Cummy", Alison Cunningham, the "dear old nurse" of Robert Louis Stevenson's early childhood, of his sleepless, illness-plagued nights at Heriot Row, and his dear friend until his death far from Scotland. Miss Cunningham spent the evening of her life in Morningside, residing for some time in Balcarres Street, and finally with her maternal cousin Mrs Murdoch at 1 Comiston Place. Here she died in her ninety-second year. Only Cummy's relatives and members of the Stevenson family attended her funeral to Morningside Cemetery and the only floral tribute placed on her grave was a posy of wild flowers from Swanston. In more recent times a representative of a new world of space exploration was interred in Morningside Cemetery. He was Sir Edward Appleton, Principal and Vice-Chancellor of Edinburgh University and a distinguished scientist of world renown who died in April 1965.

Morningside Drive, immediately south of Belhaven Terrace and originally named South Morningside Drive, leads into a district with a variety of fine houses. At the beginning of the south side of Morningside

Drive is Dunedin Hall, now the well-appointed premises of the Masonic Lodge Dunedin. Built soon after the feuing of the Plewlands estate began in 1882, this ornate red sandstone building was originally known as Morningside Hall or simply "The Hall". In addition to being used for social events in winter, it was also the meeting place of at least two em-

Morningside Hydropathic, later Morningside College

By courtesy of Edinburgh City Libraries

Invitation to the Opening Ceremony of Morningside College

By courtesy of Edinburgh City Libraries

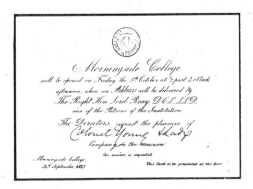

bryonic church congregations. The pioneers of South Morningside Free Church, later built in Braid Road, first met here in 1889, while in 1893 Episcopalians from south of the Suburban Railway, outwith the parish bounds of Christ Scottish Episcopalian Church at Holy Corner, held their first meeting here.

The hall later served the social needs of many Morningside organisations. For a period it was the property of the Morningside Unionist Club. In 1926 it was purchased by the Lodge Dunedin, which had originally met in a warehouse in Clyde Street and later in the hall of the Lodge Abbotsford at Churchhill. What had been known from its establishment as Morningside Hall then came to be known as Dunedin Hall.

A feature of Morningside Drive is its stately procession of venerable trees growing up through the narrow pavement on the north side. Morningside Recreational Park with its once popular bowling green and tennis court is still a happy playground for local children. The park was laid out on land once occupied by Plewlands farm and the farmhouse ruins remained here until the late 1920s.

A short distance uphill on the west side of Morningside Grove, on the site of the semi-detached villas between 28 and 38 Morningside Grove, once stood an impressive five-storey building, the Morningside Hydropathic. It is shown as already in existence in the Plewlands feuing plan of 1882 although the precise date of its establishment is not on record. Surrounded by thirteen acres of pleasant grounds, the Hydropathic was built at a cost of £20,000. It had over one hundred bedrooms and one of its corridors was a hundred and forty feet long by twelve feet wide. An attractive feature of the establishment was its heated indoor swimming pool.

By early 1882 the Morningside Hydropathic had closed, re-opening later that year, after alterations, as the well-appointed Morningside College (or Academy) for Boys. The windows in the long corridor had stained-glass panes depicting the College arms, those of the City of Edinburgh and various Scottish symbols. Cricket and football pitches, tennis courts and a cycling track were laid out in the extensive grounds. All resident masters were either Oxford or Cambridge Honours graduates. The course of studies was wide, ranging from the classics to carpentry and metal-work, and scholarships were available to both residential and day pupils. As already described, the College moved in 1889 to Rockville in Napier Road and later to Falcon Hall.

This removal proved fortuitous for the development of one of the city's great hospitals the Royal Edinburgh Hospital for Sick Children. In 1848 two Edinburgh doctors, Dr Charles Wilson and the famous Dr Henry Littlejohn (fourteen years later Edinburgh's first Medical Officer of Health) visited Paris, where they were most impressed by *L'Hôpital des Enfants Malades,* the first hospital in the world to be devoted entirely to children, established in 1802. After visiting various other European capitals to study similar hospitals, they returned to Edinburgh and campaigned for the foundation of a children's hospital here. The need was certainly great. In 1860 the first Sick Children's Hospital was opened in a house at 7 Lauriston Lane (now Lauriston Terrace), immediately beyond what is today the mortuary of the Edinburgh Royal Infirmary.

In 1865 Dr Henry Littlejohn published a report on the health of Edinburgh's population for the year 1863. The census of 1861 had recorded the population as numbering 170,444. In 1863 the total number of deaths in the city was 4,412, including 2,010 children under the age of ten years. Children's deaths thus accounted for 45.5% of the death rate, and just under half of the children who died were under one year of age.

Such children as were hospitalised were admitted to Edinburgh's only such establishment in the mid-nineteenth century, the old Royal Infirmary in Infirmary Street. The opening of the little hospital in Lauriston Lane was a beginning, but the need for increased facilities was urgent. Amongst those who supported Dr Henny Littlejohn's campaign was Charles Dickens who had written much in support of proper medical care for children. In 1857, speaking at a dinner in London in aid of funds for the Sick Children's Hospital in Great Ormond Street, Dickens described a pathetic scene he had witnessed in one of Edinburgh's congested, over-crowded closes: a sick child lying in an old wooden egg box. The famous novelist wrote in 1864: "We want to move Johnny to a place where there are none but children; where the good doctors and nurses pass their lives with children, talk to none but children, touch none but children." This was also the plea of the pioneers of Edinburgh's Sick Children's Hospital.

The original intention of the directors of the little hospital in Lauriston Lane was to admit sick rather than injured children, but even so the hopelessly inadequate accommodation and facilities meant that it was impossible to deal with the vast number of children suffering from infectious diseases. Fortunately the restrictions of 7 Lauriston Lane were soon to end; a much larger building was acquired. This was the four-storey Meadowside House at the foot of Lauriston Lane, facing south-wards across the Meadows. Alterations allowed for the segregation of fever cases in twelve beds and provided for twenty-eight cots and four special beds. Surgical treatment was, however, still available only in the old Royal Infirmary. The scene in the children's ward there in 1873, when Lister was Professor of Clinical Surgery, was graphically described by William Ernest Henley in a poem, "Children: Private Ward", written when he, an adult patient, was accommodated next to the children's ward.

In 1879 the Royal Infirmary moved from Infirmary Street to its present site, adjacent to Meadowside House in Lauriston Place. In 1890 there was an outbreak of typhoid fever amongst the children in Meadowside House and it was decided to evacuate and demolish this building and erect a new children's hospital on the same site. Temporary

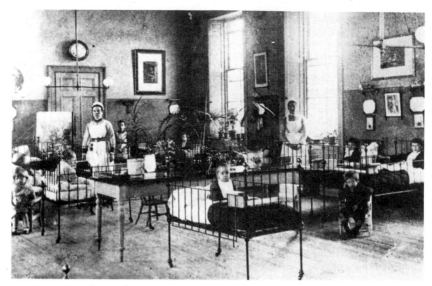

A ward in the Royal Hospital for Sick Children at Plewlands House

By courtesy of Dr F. H. Robarts

premises had to be found. The annals of the hospital record: "A conveniently sized building was found in the Morningside Academy. The Sick Children's Hospital was transferred to it in 1890. The annual rent was £500 and the building was re-named Plewlands House."

The Sick Children's Hospital was to remain within the precincts of Morningside for five years. Soon after its establishment in Plewlands House it was agreed that the site of Meadowside House should be sold to the Royal Infirmary which urgently required to expand. The present-day Royal Hospital for Sick Children in Sciennes Road was opened in October 1895, at a cost of £40,000. The architect was George Washington Browne.

While it was temporarily located at Plewlands House, the name most closely associated with the Sick Children's Hospital was its first Ordinary Surgeon, Dr Joseph Bell, great-grandson of Dr Benjamin Bell. One of Edinburgh's earliest and most distinguished surgeons, and one of Professor James Symes "two bright boys", Dr Joseph Bell was also perhaps the source of a wider fame. He was long believed to have been the prototype for Conan Doyle's immortal detective, Sherlock Holmes. Conan Doyle had studied medicine in Edinburgh under Dr Bell, for whom he developed a deep admiration. It was the surgeon's great gift of quick perception and rapid deductive reasoning, displayed in the diagnosis of cases, which, it was believed, was the inspiration for Sherlock Holmes. In recent years this assumption has been questioned and Dr Joseph Bell's grandfather has been suggested as the more likely prototype.

Whatever the facts may be, there was certainly a similarity between Dr Joseph Bell's acute powers of observation and those of Sherlock Holmes. One of many examples of Bell's keen perception is found in his *Notes on Surgery for Nurses*. "Children suffering from diarrhoea of a wasting type", he wrote, "sometimes take a strong fancy for old green-moulded cheese and devour it with the best effect. Is it possible that the germs in the cheese are able to devour in their turn the bacilli tuberculosis?" In 1887 this was a remarkable anticipation of the effect of antibiotics, confirmed nearly fifty years later by Sir Alexander Fleming's observations of the anti-bacterial effect of penicillin, although the penicillin produced in Dr Bell's green-moulded cheese would have been unlikely to have had an antibiotic effect on the bacilli of tuberculosis.

During its short existence at Plewlands House, the Sick Children's Hospital became more and more overcrowded. Dr Joseph Bell's arrival there each morning in his horse-drawn Victoria was eagerly awaited: he endeared himself to children and staff alike on account of his great

Dr Joseph Bell, said to be the prototype of Sherlock Holmes

kindness and generosity. A man of deep religious conviction, he also served as a "father confessor".

A few years after the departure of the Sick Children's Hospital to its new premises in Sciennes Road in 1895, Plewlands House, which in short succession had housed a Hydropathic, an expensive boys' college and one of Edinburgh's great hospitals, was demolished. Much of its stonework was used to build the villas between 28 and 38 Morningside Grove which now occupy its site.

CRAIGHOUSE

At the top of Morningside Drive, Craighouse Road turns northwards. On the left are the venerable stone pillars at the entrance to the driveway leading up to the ancient mansion of Craighouse. The great avenue of trees which once enhanced the approach has long since gone. Behind the mansion-house, now known as Old Craig, on the slopes of Easter Craiglockhart Hill, towers the administrative block of this part of the Royal Edinburgh Hospital, one of the great landmarks of Edinburgh when approaching from the north-west.

The lands of Craighouse appear in the Scottish Records as early as the reign of David II. There is some evidence that they belonged to the Abbey of Newbattle as there is a charter by Edward, "Abbot of Newbottle", dated 1528, which refers to a land transaction with Hugh Douglas, burgess of Edinburgh, and Mariota Brown, spouse, who owned the "lands commonly called Craighouse, between the lands of the Laird of Braid called the Plewlands. . ."

As several other of the ancient mansion-houses on the Burgh Muir still remain, restored and serving modern purposes, so too does Craighouse. Bruntsfield House, the old Whitehouse and Merchiston Tower have been integrated into modern educational establishments; the Old Craig now provides comfortable accommodation for patients of the Royal Edinburgh Hospital.

MacGibbon and Ross, in *Castellated and Domestic Architecture of Scotland,* describe the architecture "of this old-fashioned mansion-house" and provide a sketch plan indicating its two portions, one nearly one hundred and fifty years older than the other. The original portion is a long narrow structure, approximately seventy-two by twenty-six feet, which faces south. It has a projecting tower near its west end, at the base of which is the entrance doorway and a wheel-staircase leading to the first and second floors. Because of the peculiar position of the tower, MacGibbon and Ross found it difficult to decide whether the house had been built to an "L" or "T" plan. In this original part of the mansion-house, the whole ground floor is vaulted. The kitchen is at the west end, well illuminated by two large windows. There is also a cellar with small windows or slits. In certain sections of the vaulted ground floor the walls

The sixteenth-century Craighouse

A view of Craighouse from the west
From "The Castellated and Domestic Architecture of Scotland" by MacGibbon & Ross

are ten feet thick. Much of the original corbie-stepped gabling has been rendered flat during repairs and restorations.

Visitors to the Old Craig may pause at the old doorway which gives entrance to the wheel-stair. On the stone lintel above the door are carved the initials, "L.S. C.P. 1565". These are of Laurence Symson (or Simpson) and his wife Catherine Pringle who came to reside at the old mansion at this date. It seems from records that they may possibly have inherited or purchased the house from their parents or grandparents, which suggests that it was built prior to 1565.

The extended wing, at right angles to the original mansion on the north-west side, was added in 1746, probably by Sir James Elphinstoun. Over the entrance to the extension are carved the arms of Sir James, impaled with those of his wife, Dame Cicele Denholm of the Denholms of West Shields. Sir James Elphinstoun was one of the commissaries of Edinburgh and a Writer to the Signet, and his coat of arms alludes, as was common, to his profession. It incorporates a hand holding a pen and the motto, "Sedulitate". The new wing provided a suite of three additional rooms on each floor. These were also served by the original wheel-stair in the tower but on the ground floor there was a separate entrance leading to a large room at the north end used as the master's office, where he could transact his affairs with servants and visitors without having to bring them into the house itself.

Much has been written about Craighouse and its successive owners or tenants, of which a great deal appears more legendary and romantic than factual. Many such accounts are contradictory. While there is some evidence that the Symson family were still in residence at Craighouse during the first quarter of the seventeenth century, Pitcairn's *Criminal Trials* reports an event which counters this. Pitcairn gives the owner of the mansion in 1600 as John Kincaid, who on December 17th of that year earned a certain notoriety by abducting a widow, Isobel Hutcheon, from her home "in the village of the Water of Leith and proceeding to bring her forcibly to Craighouse." "King James VI", the account continues, "happened to be passing near the Water of Leith at the time of the incident and, being informed of the outrage on the lady, dispatched to Craighouse the Earl of Mar, Sir John Ramsay, and others to demand the release of the distressed lady. After threats by James' emissaries to set fire to the mansion-house, Isobel Hutcheon was set free. Kincaid was brought to trial and suffered a very large fine." Five years after this incident, Kincaid is on record as inheriting the nearby lands of Craiglockhart.

Another incident which appears in certain chronicles of Craighouse is difficult to substantiate historically. In 1569, four years after Laurence Symson and his wife had taken up residence in the mansion, it became associated with the name of Stephen Bruntfield (who had no connection with the district of that name, although certain writers have suggested that he had), a staunch supporter of Mary, Queen of Scots. While the Queen was being kept prisoner at Lochleven Castle, Sir Robert Mowbray of Barnbougle (an old castle on the Earl of Rosebery's estate, between South Queensferry and Cramond), a supporter of the Earl of Moray against Mary, laid siege to Craighouse. In due course Stephen Bruntfield was captured. Having been promised protection, he was being escorted prisoner from Craighouse to Edinburgh Castle when Mowbray, breaking his promise, slew his charge on Bruntsfield Links (an event erroneously, in the account of some writers, said to be the origin of this area's name).

This story has been responsible for one of the romantic legends of Craighouse. Bruntfield's widow, it was said, was Marie Carmichael (one of Mary, Queen of Scots' "four Maries"). Further, it is said, her husband's tragic death having brought unrelenting grief, she, with her three infant sons, shut herself up in Craighouse in a special appartment hung with black cloth and lit only by a dim lamp. One obsession possessed her: revenge against Mowbray for her husband's murder, and to this end she reared her three sons. Stephen, the eldest, eventually charged the Laird of Barnbougle in combat and was slain. The second son, Roger, met the same fate. Henry, the youngest, coming upon his father's slayer on Cramond Island, at last avenged his death. Bruntfield's widow, however, died full of remorse for the revenge that had been achieved, and inevitably, according to the tradition of old mansion-houses, became the phantom lady haunting the Old Craig, seen when the moon is full.

While the two episodes related are of doubtful origin, it is possible that Kincaid and Bruntfield did reside at one time at Craighouse, probably as tenants. What is more certain is that Laurence Symson's descendants were in possession until 1636, although they did not always reside there. There is also evidence that the last of the Symson owners was succeeded by James Nasmyth, who was apparently given the Craighouse lands by Charles I. Nasmyth's ownership was brief and he was followed by a series of other owners in rapid succession. These included Alexander Lowis, Robert Inglis and Elizabeth Spence.

More detail returns to the mansion's chronicles in 1642. In that year the lands were added to the already extensive possessions of one of Morningside's most notable families, the Dicks of the Hermitage of Braid and later of the Grange of St Giles. In May 1642 Charles II granted to Andrew Dick "the lands and Manor place of Craighouse, in the shire of Edinburgh, anciently by union in the Baroney of Newbotle". Andrew Dick, for some time Sheriff of Orkney, was the second son of Sir William Dick of Braid, one of Edinburgh's wealthiest merchants of all time, who purchased the Braid estate in 1631 and was Lord Provost of Edinburgh from 1638 until 1640.

By 1711 Craighouse had passed from the Dick family to the Herald Painter George Porteous, who is said by some writers to have built the new north wing, which he let to tenants at £100 Scots per annum. MacGibbon and Ross, however, give the date of the new wing as 1746 as this date was once carved on one of the window-sills. In 1726 the mansion had been acquired by Sir James Elphinstoun, and, as already suggested, it was probably he who built the new wing.

From Sir James Elphinstoun, Craighouse passed to Sir Alexander Lockhart (later Lord Lovington), Dean of the Faculty of Advocates, whose family, during an earlier period, had owned the adjacent lands of Craiglockhart which had superiority over Craighouse. A rapid succession of owners and tenants followed Sir Alexander Lockhart. The first of note were the Gordons of Cluny, who later, through Charles Gordon in 1771, acquired the estate of Braid and rebuilt the mansion-house. The only other resident of note at Craighouse in relatively modern times was Dr William Lizars, an important artist and engraver known chiefly for his anatomical studies.

In 1861 Craighouse came to be associated with two of Scotland's most distinguished historians. In that year Dr John Hill Burton presented to his wife, Katherine Innes, as a birthday present, the keys of the dream home of her childhood, the old mansion of Craighouse. Katherine Innes was the daughter of Professor Cosmo Innes, one of the great source writers of Scottish history.

Dr Hill Burton was a native of Aberdeen who, after graduating at Marischal College, took up law and became an advocate. Seeing little prospect of progress in this profession, he turned to the study of history and political economy. Best known for his standard work on Scottish history, written at Craighouse, he also wrote lives of David Hume, Lord Lovat and Duncan Forbes of Culloden. He was appointed the Queen's Historiographer Royal for Scotland.

Burton wrote much of his own work at Craighouse and was also visited there by many other writers seeking advice. One of these was Captain Speke, who, while a guest at Craighouse, worked on the outline of *The Discovery of the Source of the Nile*.

A Liberal in politics and a close friend of Richard Cobden, Burton was actively involved in the repeal of the Corn Laws. The library which he built up at Craighouse numbered some ten thousand volumes, for which he himself constructed all the shelving. One of many anecdotes concerning the historian related that, so well was his library organised, he could find any book within minutes, even in the dark.

Dr Hill Burton, during his seventeen years at Craighouse, became a well-known "character" in Morningside, seen walking daily to the offices of the Prison Board in George Street, of which he was a member. One Morningside resident recalled that he was "a bent figure clad in rusty black, his large pockets stuffed with books and papers". Burton's son William was also well known in the district. Familiarly referred to as "Little Willie Burton", he had long flaxen hair falling over his shoulders. He travelled to and from Craighouse in a carriage drawn by a very small

Administrative block and wards of Craighouse Asylum, built in 1894

Photograph by Mr W. R. Smith

pony, driven by his sister Mattie. William Burton eventually became a consultant engineer to the Japanese government and died in Japan. He was said to have contributed considerably to the technical skill of the Japanese.

The advent of a new era brought Dr Hill Burton's attachment to Craighouse to a deeply regretted end. The old mansion-house and surrounding estate was sold in 1878 to the Commissioners of the Edinburgh Lunatic Asylum, who planned to develop the slopes of Craighouse Hill. Burton's tenancy ended suddenly, and, it seems, unexpectedly. The distinguished historian moved to Morton House in the village of Winton near Fairmilehead, where he died in 1881.

Morningside's tradition of attracting historians to its quiet seclusion was to continue into recent times. Professor P. Hume Brown, Queen's Historiographer Royal for Scotland, lived at Corrennie Gardens, while, until his death in 1958, Dr Henry Meikle, Historiographer Royal for eighteen years, also resided in Morningside.

The man responsible for Dr Hill Burton's departure from Craighouse was Dr (later Sir) Thomas Clouston, who has a prominent place in the annals of the study and treatment of mental disorders. He was appointed Physician Superintendent of the Edinburgh Asylum at Morningside Park in 1873 and held the office for thirty-five years. Five years after his appointment he became disturbed by the inadequate facilities offered at East House and West House and turned his eyes towards the sixty acres of pleasant woodland on Craighouse Hill. He eventually persuaded the Board of Directors to purchase the property, which he described as being "on the most beautiful site in Edinburgh", and, with the help of an architect patient prepared sketch plans from which Sydney Mitchell, the architect eventually engaged, created the massive complex that came to be known as Craighouse Asylum.

Before completing his plans, Dr Clouston had toured the United States and Europe to study the design of similar institutions in those countries. The foundation stone of the administrative block of Craighouse Asylum was laid by the 10th Earl of Stair, the Deputy Governor, on July 16th, 1890, and new premises were opened by the Duke of Buccleuch, the Governor, on October 26th, 1894. The total cost of the buildings, which offered unique facilities, was more than £150,000, considered a large sum at that time.

As a result of his study tour Dr Clouston had decided to plan the new asylum as a series of separate villas: Queen's Craig, East and South Craig, Bevan Villa and the restored mansion-house of Old Craig. From its establishment and until relatively recent times, Craighouse was exclusively for private paying patients. It attempted to offer surroundings of the utmost comfort to patients, who were wealthy and often of aristocratic background. Some paid as much as £1,000 per annum for treatment and accommodation, which frequently included a suite of rooms, with personal servants and a carriage to convey them into the city. Each detached villa was to be a little community. Decor was of the brightest, in conformity with Dr Clouston's often expressed belief that "Truly the light is sweet". Sunlight and cheerful colours, he sensibly believed, were therapeutic. The present-day Thomas Clouston Clinic at Craighouse commemorates his long and distinguished direction for over thirty-five years.

Dominating the skyline above Craighouse, the administrative block, with its great tower, is one of Edinburgh's most prominent and pleasant landmarks. Entering this building, the original grandiose conception of Dr Clouston is sensed immediately. The wide marble staircase seems to lead back to days when life was lived in the grand manner. On the oak-panelled wall above the first steps of the staircase is a carved plaque which fittingly commemorates the man to whose concern and tenacity of purpose the hospital owes its origins, Dr Andrew Duncan. Added to this tribute is one to the generous support of an early patron of the hospital, Elizabeth Bevan, after whom one of the villas is named. On the left at the top of the staircase is the magnificent oak-panelled Grand Hall, in Tudor baronial style, eloquently exemplifying Dr Clouston's grand design. Among the most notable features of the hall are the large canopied twin fireplaces, one of which is surmounted by Dr Andrew Duncan's Coat of Arms and the other by those of Dr Thomas Clouston. Several portraits of those prominent in the history of the hospital include one of Dr Andrew Duncan by a pupil of Sir Henry Raeburn. The fine barrel-vaulted ceiling may be studied more closely from the Minstrel Gallery, from which, in the hospital's earlier days, musicians played during grand balls graced by the noble surroundings. Orchestral recitals were also once a regular feature of the patients' entertainment. Today the Grand Hall recaptures some of its former atmosphere during the medical staff's annual dinner-dance and the staff-patients' Hallowe'en parties. Adjoining the hall is a very fine drawing-room with period furniture where patients meet regularly for group therapy.

In Old Craig itself, whose walls brooded over stirring events in centuries long before the Grand Hall was built, a few interesting relics remain. On the first floor, reached by the narrow wheel-stair, is a small oak-panelled room where the oldest item of interest is probably the wooden chest inscribed "1693 MB". This, tradition has it, belonged to Mary Beaton, one of Mary, Queen of Scots' "four Maries". It is now impossible to verify either this or the claim that Mary, Queen of Scots herself once visited Old Craig, although the mansion-house certainly existed during her reign. It is also said that another of the Maries, Marie Carmichael, once resided here. In this room there are also three murals set in the oak panels. These, and others which originally surrounded the room, depict Grecian scenes. Certain writers have attributed them to George Porteous, the Royal Portrait Painter, who resided in Craighouse in the early eighteenth century.

The other room of interest, also on the first floor and leading off from that already described, was originally a small dining-room. Here, above the fireplace, is the inscription, "R.A.E. 1565-1878" (or, as the sequence of the numerals is not obvious, perhaps the later date is 1788). It is difficult to associate the initials with any particular succession of residents. Also in this room is an old mural, now barely discernible, and a framed oil painting of Old Craig signed by J. M. Dodds.

Amongst the archives of the Royal Edinburgh Hospital is a water-colour panoramic impression of Morningside and the surrounding district including Plewlands farm, with Arthur's Seat in the background. This undated work was probably done by a patient.

Dr Hill Burton, during his long occupancy of Old Craig, firmly believed that part of the house dated back to Roman times. He also noted an underground passage leading from the thick-walled basement and believed that this eventually emerged at Edinburgh Castle. Various opinions as to the ultimate destination of this tunnel were expressed. In fact, foundation excavations many years ago revealed that the tunnel, now largely blocked up, emerged only a short distance from the old mansion-house, in the overgrown northern slope of the grounds. The chronicles of Craighouse have been so colourfully and enthusiastically embroidered with legends that the task of presenting authentic historical fact is no easy one.

The magnificent panoramic view from the Craighouse administrative block tower, encompassing Edinburgh and far beyond, reveals two places

A stone pillar from the original entrance is all that remains of Meggetland House

Photograph by Mr W. R. Smith

in the foreground which merit reference. At the foot of the north-east slope of the hill, just beyond the point where the railway lines are bridged by Myreside Road and just within the boundary wall of the Royal Edinburgh Hospital, was the ancient village of Myreside, the name of which was derived from the considerable expanse of marshland which in early centuries existed at this western fringe of the Burgh Muir. It is in this once waterlogged area that, as already related, the Jordan Burn has its origin. Myreside Cottage, the last remains of the old village, became the property of the Royal Edinburgh Hospital in the 1860s and was used as a hospital annexe until its destruction by fire a century later. A number of stones from the old cottage remain near its site. In the early records of the old schoolhouse at Morningside it is mentioned that one of the members of the small Parish Council responsible for the little village school was Adam Curor of Myreside. A number of old maps indicate the site of the village, describing it as "Old Myreside", and also show, a short distance to the north, "New Myreside", located near the present-day Watsonians' rugby football pitch and little grandstand close to George Watson's College.

The other place of interest is the old district of Meggetland which lies just west of the University of Edinburgh recreation field adjacent to the former Craiglockhart Station. While this district is outwith the scope of South Edinburgh, the original Meggetland House, long since gone, merits attention. By the early eighteenth century it was owned by Thomas Sievewright and, with the adjacent estate of Plewlands, it remained in his family's possession for some time. Indeed the area became known as "the Plewlands Patrimony" and in a *Plan of the Barony of Braid* produced in July 1772 by John Home, the district of Plewlands is indicated as "Mr Sievewright's Lands". All that now remains of the old Meggetland mansion-house is a solitary stone pillar at the entrance gates to a large villa at the north-east corner of Lockharton Gardens, off Colinton Road.

The chief interest of Meggetland House lies in the dark deeds once perpetrated therein, filling the people of Edinburgh with such horror and panic that it is said that many people were deterred from leaving the city to reside in the district for at least a decade.

In 1743 a wealthy East India merchant, Thomas Sievewright, retired from service and settled in Meggetland House with his wife (a member of a family of notable Edinburgh goldsmiths, the Gordons) and his daughter Mary, a girl of rare beauty and vivacity. Small wonder that her ardent admirer, cousin Tom Gordon, was a frequent visitor to Meggetland House. On October 21st, 1743 Tom Gordon was about to leave the house when his uncle called him into his study. Mary and her mother perhaps assumed that Sievewright wished to speak to Tom about a noticeable coolness which had lately developed in his dealings with Mary.

Next morning Thomas Sievewright was found by his butler dead in his study, lying back in his chair as though resting, but with a look of horror and amazement frozen on his features. He had been stabbed through the heart with a long, narrow and sharp weapon which scarcely left a trace.

Tom Gordon and his father were at their house in Bank Close in the High Street when the news reached them. On their arrival at Meggetland House the procurator fiscal, a close friend of the Gordons, had the difficult task of suggesting to young Tom that he had been the last person to see Thomas Sievewright alive. Furthermore, the servants had already testified that they had heard Tom Gordon and Sievewright arguing heatedly late that night in the study. In fact, Susan Dickson the housemaid, a girl of considerable beauty herself, had asserted that she had heard her master declare, "You are a scoundrel, Sir, to suggest such a thing!" followed by, "It is a foul lie, and if you repeat it I shall shoot you where you stand!" Young Tom Gordon had retorted just as angrily, "It is no lie, as I shall prove!"

But more damning evidence was yet to come. It was elicited from Mrs Sievewright that, just before retiring, she had crept to her husband's study door, having heard raised voices, and heard Tom Gordon say in an angry tone, "I would have killed anyone a week ago who dared to say that!" Sievewright, in a mocking tone, had replied, "Then you had better kill me." In the face of such evidence, and largely because Tom Gordon would say nothing to answer the accusations made against him, things looked black indeed for Mary Sievewright's young suitor.

Nancy Joyce, Mary Sievewright's maid, said she had heard nothing at all. As she apparently knew no-one in the neighbourhood, her contribution to the evidence was negative. The most baffling aspect of the case was, however, yet to come. Mary Sievewright, on being questioned by the procurator fiscal, was confronted by Tom also, but would say nothing. Suddenly Tom whispered to her, "What were you doing in the south-wing corridor at half past ten last night, Mary? For God's sake, speak!"

Mary looked at Tom, astounded. "I? In the corridor last night? I was never near it!"

"But Mary, I saw you," said Tom sadly, "and someone else saw you as well."

"Someone else?" echoed Mary incredulously, "Who was that?"

Tom's reply came like a bombshell to the harassed girl, "Your father, Mary, who is now dead."

Mary Sievewright was astounded at Tom's statement. Nancy Joyce, Mary's maid, who was present, let out a cry of horror and, white-faced, crept from the room.

In further cross-examination, suspicion of Tom Gordon's part in the murder deepened. Maxwell, the procurator fiscal, found his task exceedingly difficult: Robert Gordon was one of his closest friends and for his son Tom he had the highest regard. A final, urgent appeal to the young man to confide in him or in his father had no effect. Tom declared that he would handle his own case. Maxwell, painfully, then issued a warrant for his arrest.

Next day, however, new horror swept the city. Before Tom Gordon's arrest, another murder was committed at Meggetland House. This time Mrs Sievewright was found dead, stabbed, as her husband had been, by a very thin dagger. On the night of her death Tom Gordon had been seen in the vicinity of Meggetland House. Now charged with the murder of both uncle and aunt, he was remanded in custody in the Tolbooth.

The next morning further sensational news spread through Edinburgh like wildfire: the night before, young Mary Sievewright had been found, stabbed in the same manner as her father and mother. At first it was thought she too was dead, but, by the slenderest thread, though seriously injured, she still clung to life. The dagger had been diverted from her heart by a whalebone support in her underclothes. Now the investigations being conducted by the procurator fiscal had to take a different course: on the night of Mary Sievewright's attempted murder Tom Gordon had been safely locked up in the Tolbooth. "The Plewlands Panic", as it was called, now spread rapidly. Many people left the neighbourhood of Meggetland House and went to stay with relatives in the city.

The procurator fiscal was baffled by the new developments. He called for the assistance of George Williamson, the King's Messenger, and his brother, the leading detectives of the time. When Mary Sievewright had recovered slightly from her injuries and shock, they questioned her closely, but she was still so distressed by the death of her parents and her own ordeal that she could offer no assistance. Her condition was critical, but her young lover's life depended upon the evidence she could provide. Further attempts to question her were fruitless. Becoming almost hysterical when asked to recall the circumstances of her assault, she would cry out, "The eyes of Siva! Oh, the eyes of Siva!"

As the sessions of the Justiciary Court were due, Tom Gordon was prepared to face his trial. His defending counsel was Robert Dundas, afterwards Lord Dundas, Dean of the Faculty of Advocates. He could elicit nothing from young Gordon which might make a case for his defence: the young man would not talk. Dundas then tried something which was quite unusual at that time. Normally a prisoner was not told of any further developments which had occurred relating to his case, but his counsel received permission to break with precedent. Dundas visited Tom Gordon and informed him that Mary Sievewright had been stabbed and remained critically ill. Young Gordon was horrified. With a note of fatalistic resignation in his voice, he made but one comment: "Then that black-bearded Hindu has murdered her after winning her love!"

Robert Dundas immediately grasped this first and vitally important clue. He pressed Tom Gordon for more information, leading him to believe that something about the Hindu was already known to him and the others handling the case. The young accused believed that Mary Sievewright no longer loved him but had given her affections to the man who had stabbed her. He then at last gave his counsel a useful line of investigation for his defence, saying, when asked about the Hindu's whereabouts, "Well, if you want to get information see Nancy Joyce and frighten her into telling you all."

Robert Dundas acted immediately. Meggetland House was visited without delay. But Nancy Joyce, Mary Sievewright's maid, had disappeared. She had not been seen since the morning following the attempted murder of her young mistress. The day of Tom Gordon's trial duly came. Despite his counsel's attempts in his defence, in the absence of the key witness, the young man was convicted of murder and sentenced to death.

The court proceedings had just ended when the detective George Williamson arrived from London, where he had gone in search of Nancy Joyce and had found her. She produced a signed testimony which at the eleventh hour exonerated Tom Gordon. Her statement, still preserved, revealed that she was twenty-five and a native of Yorkshire. Her master, Mr Thomas Sievewright, had lived long in India, where he had been very wealthy. One reason for his wealth, the maid alleged, had been his robbing of shrines in Hindu temples. One such theft had been of two very valuable diamonds which formed the eyes of an Indian god called Siva in the temple at Burdwan. Sievewright, she said, had substituted small balls of wood for the god's precious eyes. When this was eventually discovered, the priests of the Burdwan temple swore an oath to recover the diamonds. Eventually suspicion fell on Thomas Sievewright and his residence in Edinburgh was traced. One of the priests, Kharul Hankya, set out for Edinburgh, disguised as an Indian gentleman. Finding Meggetland House, he made the acquaintance of Nancy Joyce and they began to meet regularly. He professed to be in love with her and, saying he was very wealthy, promised to marry her after he had accomplished his mission. This, he revealed to her, was the recovery from her master's possession of the eyes of Siva. He persuaded her to help him in this task. In her nightly meetings with the Hindu priest outside Meggetland House, she wore a cloak of Mary Sievewright's so that any passer-by would think it was the young lady of the house who was meeting the Hindu.

On several occasions young Tom Gordon had been thus deceived. This had been the cause of the argument between him and Thomas Sievewright on the night of the first murder. When questioned about his recent coldness towards Mary, Tom had informed her father of her secret meetings, but he had constantly refused to reveal this secret during all his cross-examinations, being prepared to die rather than cast aspersions on her good name. Thomas Sievewright, taken aback, had remained in his study, brooding over Tom's revelations. This was the very night that, at last, Nancy Joyce had been able to arrange entry into the house for her Hindu friend. The latter, intending simply to search Sievewright's study, had unexpectedly found him there. To silence him, the Hindu had stabbed him. Next night he visited the study again: this time he was disturbed by Mrs Sievewright. He stabbed her. On his third attempt to find the eyes of Siva the distressed Mary Sievewright, no doubt unable to sleep, had gone to her father's study. Thrusting at the girl with his dagger, the Hindu then made off, leaving her for dead. He had still not found the eyes of Siva. Nancy Joyce, horrified at the murders, had promised to find the stones herself and, having succeeded, she set off for a secret rendezvous in London where the Hindu joined her and demanded the stones. Not until he had married her, insisted Nancy. The Hindu's ready dagger was again produced: stabbing her, he retrieved the diamonds and left her unconscious. When George Williamson the detective found her. Nancy, fearing she was about to die, was only too ready to prove the innocence of Tom Gordon.

Tom read the maid's testimony with amazement. He was reconciled with Mary Sievewright. They were married and lived on in Meggetland House. Here Tom Gordon's father died in 1767. There were still Sievewrights associated with Meggetland House in 1888. The young man once nearly hanged for murders he had never committed rose to a high place in the legal profession. The eyes of Siva were taken back to their shrine in India but the priest who had retrieved them with such brutality and amidst such mystery was never traced. In Edinburgh the horror, the Plewlands Panic, for long remained.

CHAPTER 3

Greenbank · Craiglockhart

GREENBANK

While today recognised as a distinct and spacious district, Greenbank was, in the earliest records, never clearly defined, being most commonly described as a part of or an appendage to the estate of Plewlands. Today Greenbank may be defined as extending from Greenbank Drive to Greenbank Crescent, the major road which forms its southern frontier, and from Comiston Road westwards as far as Greenlea and the City Infectious Diseases Hospital. On the fertile land of Greenbank Farm, a substantial building programme begun in the 1930s created a most pleasant district of bungalows and villas.

Greenbank appears in the records in quite early times. In 1719 there was a transaction involving "Mr Andrew Brown of Greenbank, Wester Plewlands" who purchased a large area of land near Grange House and Blackford. Wester and Over Plewlands along with Blackford eventually became part of the extensive estate of Mortonhall. Cannonball House at the corner of Castlehill and Castle Wynd North, once the residence of the famous Scottish family, the Gordons of Huntly, and later of the Gordons of Braid, became the property of the Browns of Greenbank in the early eighteenth century. Brown's Close, from which the old mansion-house was once entered, was named after Andrew Brown's two sons, Colonel George Brown and Captain James Brown, commander of the ship *Alfred* of the East India Company.

Perhaps the first house to appear in Greenbank was Greenbank farmhouse, a stately and substantial two-storey villa surrounded by a pleasant garden. Resident in this house in about 1880 was Robert L. Alexander, R.S.A., an artist of some fame noted for his animal subjects. By 1884 he had moved to Canaan Grove in Newbattle Terrace. The farmhouse remained occupied until the early 1930s, when it was swept away by the growth of modern Greenbank. One relic of the old farm which many Morningside residents still recall, and of which many still have postcards, was the last of the old thatched cottages which stood beside the little lane which still leads from Greenbank Crescent to the pathway that runs high along the top of the western slope of the Braidburn Valley Park.

One of Morningside's more modern churches is Greenbank Parish Church, situated at the south corner of Comiston Road and Braidburn Terrace. Its opening in October 1927 signified the steady expansion of Morningside to the south. While St Matthew's Parish Church was

Greenbank Farmhouse, c. 1900
By courtesy of Miss G. M. Hood

originally an extension of Morningside Parish Church at the corner of Newbattle Terrace, the establishment of the original Greenbank United Presbyterian Church was fostered by Braid Church which was of the same denomination. The first worshippers met in the hall, opened on May 13th, 1900. In July of that year the thirty-five Greenbank members were formally declared a congregation. The first Kirk Session included Joseph Bennet and William Forrest, two Elders from Braid Church who had been appointed to take charge and act as founder Elders of Greenbank. Two years after the union of the United Presbyterian Church and the Free Church of Scotland in 1900, the Reverend Norman Fraser, B.D. of Hamilton was appointed the first minister of Greenbank United Free Church. Under his charge the congregation steadily increased until his departure for Liverpool in 1913.

In January 1914 the new minister inducted was the Rev. T. Ratcliffe Barnett, called from St Andrew's Church, Bo'ness. Dr Barnett was to earn a high reputation not only as a powerful preacher and devoted parish minister but also as a distinguished and prolific author of a long series of scholarly and entertaining books on various parts of Scotland, from the Borders to the Western Isles. He was awarded a Doctor of Philosophy degree by Edinburgh University. Soon after his appointment, Dr Barnett began pressing for the building of a church. The Great War, however, intervened. During the war years and in the period immediately afterwards, the congregation contributed to a building fund and, when the foundation stone was laid on April 24th, 1926, £11,000 was already available. The final cost of the church was £18,000, the additional amount being raised by further generous gifts. The architect, Lorne Campbell, designed the church in simple style but with an impressive dignity. Seating was for six hundred. The opening service of dedication took place on October 8th, 1927.

After a ministry of nearly twenty-five years, Dr Ratcliffe Barnett resigned in 1938 to make way for a younger successor. He died in 1946. Under his vigorous pastoral ministry, the original congregation of thirty-five in 1900 had become eight hundred.

Another notable name in the succession of ministers of Greenbank Church is the Rev. David Reid who was mobilised as a chaplain in the Second World War almost immediately after his call to Greenbank. After being a prisoner in Germany for five years, he returned to his ministry at Greenbank in September 1945, where one of the first of his many enterprises was the foundation of "Quest", a challenging and stimulating organisation for the young people of the parish, inspired by a discussion group he had formed in the German prisoner-of-war camp. Ever since, Quest has remained a lively and imaginative feature of the life of Greenbank Church and of Morningside itself. The well-presented annual

South Morningside Primary School in Comiston Road, opened in 1892

Photograph by Mr W. R. Smith

Quest entertainments in the Churchhill Theatre draw large audiences. The organisation has inspired a wide variety of service by its young members. The Rev. David Reid left Greenbank in 1949 to become Chaplain at Edinburgh University, and a few years later he became minister of the notable Madison Avenue Presbyterian Church in New York. Under the present ministry of the Rev. Donald Mackay, Greenbank Parish Church, now with a congregation of over a thousand, continues, after more than three-quarters of a century, to serve this pleasant southward district of Morningside which, in the course of time, has been transformed from a landscape of farmland and isolated cottages into a populous residential area of villas and classical bungalows.

The construction of Comiston Road, by which we approach other features of Greenbank, was not completed until about 1910, relatively late compared with its more ancient parallel highway to the south, Braid Road. South Morningside School was opened in 1892. The date 1891 carved on the commemorative plaque on the facade was probably that of the building's completion.

The school's carefully kept log-books reveal much of interest concerning the development and rapid expansion of Morningside towards the close of the nineteenth century. They also contain much significant social comment. From 1823 until the opening of South Morningside School nearly seventy years later, the little schoolhouse of Morningside village had become a cherished institution. For long it had been the only source of education for the children of the district, many of whom travelled a considerable distance to it. During most of its existence, attendance at the school had been voluntary. There is scant evidence of financial resources, which for a considerable period came largely from a few public-spirited Morningside residents, pre-eminently from George Ross of Woodburn House in Canaan Lane. At one time small fees were charged according to parents' circumstances, but no doubt many children were admitted free.

It was not until soon after the Disruption of 1843 and the establishment of Morningside Free Church that this congregation opened their own little school, which, according to the Ordnance Survey Map of 1852, was near Denholm's smiddy, where Morningside Public Library was later built. When this school ceased to function is not on record. Between 1870 and the early 1880s other private schools began to spring up in the Morningside district, catering for children with parents of some means. These included Mr Baillie's school at Marmion Terrace in Churchhill, its site probably being the present-day 92 Morningside Road. Morningside College was established in Morningside Drive in 1882, transferring to Rockville House in Napier Road in 1889 and finally to Falcon Hall in 1890 until its closure two years later.

In 1872 came the Education (Scotland) Act, which proclaimed: "Education is to be made available to the whole people of Scotland." The Act made it "the duty of all parents to provide elementary education in

301

Programme of the Opening Ceremony of South Morningside Primary School, October 1892

By courtesy of Edinburgh City Libraries

reading, writing and arithmetic for their children between the years of five and thirteen." Primary education had become compulsory. To enable parents to fulfil their obligations, the authorities had to provide facilities. The Act created a new central authority, the Scotch Education Department, with nearly one thousand local authority committees responsible for education. These corresponded with parishes and burghs. Education in each district was to be organised by a School Board. Former parish and privately managed schools such as Morningside's village schoolhouse had to be transferred to the appropriate local School Boards. While the latter could prosecute parents for failing to send their children to school, it was some time before this could be fully enforced as in many places facilities were inadequate.

The School Board responsible for Morningside was that of St Cuthbert's and Dean. For nearly twenty years it apparently regarded the little village school as adequate, or perhaps found that financial resources were not forthcoming to enable a new larger school to be built. A note in the St Cuthbert's and Dean School Board minutes for 1876, referring to the old schoolhouse, emphasises that, whereas prior to that year parents were merely urged to send their children to school, now if they failed to do so they would be prosecuted. It was not until September 5th, 1892 that South Morningside School in Comiston Road was opened. By this date much new building had taken place in Morningside and the surrounding district and the population had greatly increased, a fact reflected by the first enrolments at South Morningside School.

The old village schoolhouse must have been limited to accommodating a maximum of some one hundred children in its two small classrooms. On the opening day of South Morningside School, the headmaster had before him a list of 522 names of children for enrolment, 344 of which actually appeared at the school. Four days later, the total number attending had grown to 572.

While the school had opened on September 5th, 1892, the formal ceremony did not take place until a month later, on October 3rd. There was considerable Press coverage of the event, possibly on account of the many distinguished persons present. The principal guests were Professor David Masson and the celebrated Andrew Carnegie. Professor Masson, who delivered the opening address, held the Chair of Rhetoric and English Literature at Edinburgh University. An active pioneer of higher education, he enjoyed great distinction in the world of literature and was a close friend of Thomas Carlyle and many other literary giants of his time. Masson Hall, one of Edinburgh University's halls of residence, was named after him. Andrew Carnegie, the other principal speaker, who was accompanied by his wife, was of course to achieve world renown for his practical efforts to spread literacy and education through his generosity towards the establishment and support of public libraries. Edinburgh's Central Public Library on George IV Bridge was but one of these gifts. Amongst the Morningside ministers present at the opening ceremony was the elderly Dr Thomas Addis, who, whilst minister of Morningside Parish Church during the Disruption of 1843, had led a large number of his congregation in "coming out" from the established church and founding Morningside's first Free Church with its own small school.

In his address Hew Morrison, Chairman of the St Cuthbert's and Dean School Board, stressed that the new school would not charge fees, at the same time repudiating the assertion "that free education was worth just what it cost". The education offered by the school would, he claimed, be just as good in character and substance as any that was paid for. To illustrate his point he stated that, in addition to the teaching of reading, writing and arithmetic, the school curriculum would include mathematics, Latin, Greek, French and German.

This historic occasion in the annals of Morningside was followed by a short concert given by pupils. A copy of the programme is still in existence. Colour was added to the day's events by floral decorations from Seth's Nurseries, then in Ethel Terrace, where they were a most pleasant feature of the district which a great many Morningside people will recall.

The school's original teaching staff of seven included John King, M.A., B.Sc., the first headmaster, A. Myrtle Cockburn, a former "maister" of the old village schoolhouse, appointed to the staff as "second master", and Miss Mary McAllister, a pupil-teacher, and Mr Cockburn's former colleague at the schoolhouse. Later Miss McAllister was required to carry out further training at Moray House. The school's first janitor was James Cameron. Teacher's salaries during 1893-4 were: "Mr King, Headmaster: £310 p.a.; Infant mistress: £135 p.a.; and Mr Cockburn: £125 p.a."

The log book entry for September 9th, 1892, four days after the opening of the school, comments: "Unexpectedly large number of 572. Many of these, especially amongst infants and younger juveniles, have come from numerous private schools in the district kept by ladies. This factor increases the difficulty of proper classification throughout the school. The other schools which have contributed most largely to our roll are the old Morningside School (which is now closed). Gorgie Public School and Gillespie's." The latter was James Gillespie's which in 1892 was situated in Gillespie Crescent.

Pupils were classified into six standards according to age and educational level already reached. Soon after the school's opening, three additional teachers were appointed. Subsequent entries in the log book reveal the difficulties encountered as more and more children sought enrolment. By October 1892, 612 pupils had been accepted, 259 in the "infant" classes. One teacher had a class of eighty pupils and another of one hundred and five, described as "beginners". Already many pupils had been "put down a class" as their standards became more accurately assessed, to the resentment of many parents. By November 1892 more pupil-teachers had been appointed. The log book notes, among miscellaneous developments, that the boys were given "Drill" by the janitor. By December 1892 French was being taught to older pupils. Accommodation proved a problem and a vacant shop at 143 Comiston Road was acquired for use as an additional classroom.

Early in 1893 log book entries begin to reveal the prevalence of infectious diseases among the children: a measles epidemic caused many absences. A note of snowstorms in March 1893 is followed by another recording a widespread outbreak of scarlet fever. In October 1894 the prevalence of diphtheria is noted; the school's ventilators were sprayed with carbolic acid and books from affected households were disinfected. By January 1895 the absence of pupils due to various illnesses had become a major problem. It may be noted that, during this decade after the establishment of the new school when diseases such as scarlet fever, diphtheria and whooping cough, then serious conditions, were so prevalent, the City Fever Hospital at Greenbank Drive had not yet been opened, and was not to be until 1903.

Some indication of the development of social life in Morningside in the 1890s is indicated in the school records: in 1892 the newly formed Morningside Young Men's Mutual Improvement Association unsuccessfully applied for evening use of the newly opened school, and a year later the Morningside Choral Society was granted evening use of a classroom.

In May 1895 the school came under the Edinburgh School Board, into which the St Cuthbert's and Dean Board had been incorporated. Later that year it is recorded in the log that pupils were being sponsored for George Heriot's School bursaries. Entries continue to refer to absence through illness, the teaching staff also being seriously affected. German, French and Latin were by this time established subjects in the school curriculum. Soon afterwards, physics and chemistry were added. In June 1897 pupils brought contributions towards the cost of planting trees in front of the school to mark Queen Victoria's Jubilee. In lighter vein, an entry a year later records a school holiday to allow the children to attend the famous Barnum and Bailey's circus.

By January 1899 South Morningside School, then with a roll of 737 pupils, had been selected by the Edinburgh School Board as one of Edinburgh's twelve schools to have an "advanced department". In the same year the school had set up well-appointed workshop facilities for the teaching of woodwork and technical subjects. On March 2nd, 1900 the school was given a half-holiday to celebrate the relief of Ladysmith by General Buller. Before being dismissed, the whole school assembled to give three rousing cheers! In May of the same year the relief of Mafeking was similarly celebrated and the decision made to purchase a school flag at the cost of £2 2s 3d. On June 5th this was unfurled for the first time to mark the taking of Pretoria by Lord Roberts. An entry for September 1900 notes that the school had by this time gained many passes in the Higher and Lower Grade Leaving Certificates. A year later a sadder note is struck when the death of Queen Victoria is recorded; the reaction of the pupils was "a touching and never-to-be-forgotten sight".

In January 1902 it is noted that a teacher, James Ritchie, resigned to take up a teaching post in "a concentration camp in South Africa". A year later the whole school was disinfected following a case of smallpox in a pupil's family. In September 1904 thirty pupils qualified for admission to Boroughmuir Secondary School, then recently built at Bruntsfield Links. The following year it is noted that a child from Comiston Farm was refused enrolment at South Morningside as Comiston was outwith the city boundary. At the end of 1905, several senior pupils who had distinguished themselves left for Boroughmuir School and George Watson's College. Two years later the school roll numbered one thousand, and there were twenty-five teachers. A subsequent log entry records that 138 pupils were working with various shops and dairy-keepers, thus contravening current bye-laws.

Soon after the outbreak of the First World War, the military authorities announced that the school would be required for occupation by troops and pupils were transferred to Craiglockhart School. Soon afterwards, however, the order was cancelled, Craiglockhart School becoming the army billet. In December 1915 many pupils were in the City Fever Hospital suffering from scarlet fever and diphtheria. In July 1919, a Peace Service took place in the school to mark the end of the war.

In 1926 Bruntsfield School began to enrol many pupils who previously would have attended South Morningside and the latter's roll decreased considerably: many other children who would earlier have attended South Morningside were being sent to fee-paying schools. Up to 1934 absence through infectious diseases was still being noted. Upon the outbreak of the Second World War in September 1939, plans were made for the evacuation of many pupils from Edinburgh.

After the school's return to normal at the end of the war, the pattern of a modern educational system begins to emerge as South Morningside continued to prepare pupils for entry to Boroughmuir Senior Secondary School in Viewforth and various fee-paying schools. Towards the end of the 1960s, the building of large new housing estates at Firrhill, Comiston and Oxgangs, which came to be occupied mainly by young parents with primary school children, meant an increased need for educational facilities in addition to those provided by the Oxgangs and Hunter's Tryst primary schools. The Comiston annexe of South Morningside School was therefore opened at Oxgangs Green, and in 1971 it became independent as Comiston Primary School. Headmaster during the mid-1960s was Forbes MacGregor, author of several books on Scottish life and customs.

The catchment area of South Morningside School remains wide, extending to the boundaries of what might be termed "Greater Morningside". It includes, to the south, the Winton Village district in Frogstone Road, Buckstone and Greenbank, and extends westwards as far as Myreside, eastwards to South Oswald Road and northwards to Newbattle Terrace. In the 1930s the school prepared pupils for entry to Boroughmuir Senior Secondary School, though in later years it tended to become a "feeder" for Firrhill High School. Today a close association has again developed with Boroughmuir, now a comprehensive school.

As with most modern schools, there is a continuing demand for increased accommodation to develop new subjects and activities. The recent demolition of the old sheds and outhouses in the little lane leading from the south side of Craiglea Drive to the school boundary wall will permit expansion, while the projected establishment of a new primary school at Buckstone should relieve pressure on space at South Morningside. Surviving reminders of the school's early days which must mystify the pupils of a new era are the triangular stone wedges built into the playground walls, which were used for sharpening slate pencils long before the advent of the ball-point pen.

Original main entrance to the City Poorhouse, now Greenlea

Photograph by Mr W. R. Smith

The terraced villas of Comiston Drive, immediately beyond South Morningside School, were among the last to be constructed in accordance with the Plewlands Estate building programme of 1882. Much of Comiston Drive was built by William Forrest, J.P., quarry-master and Morningside councillor who himself resided at No. 1. Also in Comiston Drive lived Joseph Laing Waugh, author of the Scottish classic *Robbie Doo. Thornhill and Its Worthies* and *A Little Child Shall Lead Them* were among his other titles.

While historically and geographically within the districts of Colinton Mains and Craiglockhart, the City Hospital and Greenlea may be considered as part of present-day Greenbank. A still extant reminder of the origins of Greenlea, which just over a century ago was built as the City Poorhouse, is the little grey stone gate-lodge immediately beyond the railings on the south side of the entrance to Comiston Drive, once 144 Comiston Road. Beside it are the long-locked gates which once formed the entrance to the now disused and overgrown Poorhouse Drive, running parallel to Greenbank Drive and the back of Comiston Drive, with the Comiston Burn in between.

The new City Poorhouse, or Craiglockhart Poorhouse as it came to be known, was opened in 1870 on the pleasantly situated southern slopes of Wester Craiglockhart Hill. Part of the Craiglockhart estate, comprising some two hundred and fifty acres, had been purchased for the new institution some three miles from the city. The origins of the Poorhouse were in an environment very different from sunny, if at times wind-swept, Craiglockhart. They had been the old Charity Workhouse, with its two wings on either side of Forrest Road. The east wing stood in the Bristo Port-Teviot Place triangle and part of it had, for a period, been the City Bedlam for pauper lunatics in which the brilliant poet Robert Fergusson had died in 1774. Some time after the new Poorhouse was opened at Craiglockhart, the Bristo Port buildings were sold to Edinburgh's Royal College of Physicians, becoming medical research and diagnostic laboratories. Certain of the original buildings still stand, slightly altered, now forming part of the University Department of Endocrinology, established here when the Royal College of Physicians' laboratories closed soon after the introduction of the National Health Service in 1948.

The west wing of the old Charity Workhouse, the poorhouse proper, stood just east of Greyfriars Church. Towards the end of its existence, inmates were accommodated in whichever wing was more suitable. Beside the west wing was the Ragged School.

The proposal to build a new City Poorhouse was first made in 1861 but its implementation was delayed by disagreement among members of the Parochial Board which managed the Charity Workhouse and, later, by a dispute between the Board and Edinburgh Town Council concerning the ownership of the land at Forrest Road. The Parochial Board won. While there was now agreement to build a new Poorhouse, however, a dispute arose over its site. In 1865 part of the Craiglockhart estate was purchased at a cost of £29,000 and a contest was organised to obtain suitable plans, twenty-two submissions being received and exhibited at the Corn Exchange. The contract was awarded to George Beattie of 13 Grove Street. Each plan had been required to bear a motto for the project, Mr Beattie's being "Comfort for the Poor and care for the Ratepayer." Beattie estimated the cost of building at £41,000, but various alterations to his plan were requested, resulting in a higher estimate of £57,000.

The foundation stone was laid by the Grand Master of the Orange Order of Masons on July 4th, 1867. The Rev. David Aitken saw fit to include the event in his diary: "Thursday, July 4th, 1867, walked by Dalry and Canal to Craiglockhart", he noted, "and saw the foundation stone laid of the new Poor House." A volunteer band and special guard of police were conveyed to the foundation ceremony by a special train running to Slateford Station. As building proceeded, costs escalated to something like £90,000 — more than twice the original estimate. Much of the stone used was provided locally by the builder Robert Hutchison of Craiglockhart Farm, who opened a quarry on Wester Craiglockhart Hill. The Craiglockhart Poorhouse was opened on May 2nd, 1870 and the inmates of the old Charity Workhouse at Forrest Road were transferred to the new institution which provided accommodation for six hundred. In 1856, 1,275 people had applied for admission at Forrest Road; in 1869, a year before Craiglockhart was opened, applications numbered 3,454. The accommodation originally estimated for Craiglockhart had been twelve hundred, but when it opened only half that number could be admitted. By 1894 provision could be made for nine hundred and fifty. As had been the practice during the existence of the Old Charity Workhouse, people in poor circumstances who could not be admitted, or who preferred to remain at home, were given "outdoor relief" by the Parochial Board, being then described as living "on the parish". An indication of the conditions in some homes in Edinburgh five years before the new poorhouse was opened is given in the *Report on the Sanitary Conditions of the City of Edinburgh, 1865* which was published by Dr Henry D. Littlejohn, the city's Medical Officer of Health. In Middle Meal Market Stair, a tenement off the High Street, there were fifty-nine rooms in which fifty-six families lived; there was no water and no sinks or lavatories for a hundred and ninety-seven adults and fifty-one children under the age of five. Dr Littlejohn, advocating a radical approach to the problem of poverty, was critical of the Parochial Board's system of outdoor relief.

A Plan of the Estate of Craiglockhart: The Property of the Parochial Board of the City Parish of Edinburgh 1870, signed by John C. Hay, illustrates the various features of the new poorhouse and also many points of interest in the surrounding landscape. The design was of a well-constructed stone building, most of which remains today, in the baronial style common to such institutions at that time. The different types of accommodation are indicated, including the original corrugated iron infirmary wards running parallel to the eastern boundary wall of the poorhouse. These still stand today, though long since used for other purposes. During the First World War they served as a small military hospital, while in the 1920s they housed destitute tuberculosis sufferers. The institution's original sources of water are indicated in the plan. The catchment area was the valley between the Wester and Easter Craiglockhart Hills, also one of the sources of the Comiston Burn. For some time water was drawn from this area by steam-driven pumps, piped up to large storage tanks and distributed to various parts of the poorhouse by a double-action pump. The sources from which the water was drawn are still indicated by gratings on the north side of the Merchants of Edinburgh Golf Course. The source of water from this area, however, soon proved inadequate, and the plan of the poorhouse indicates "an Edinburgh Water Pipe" entering the property just west of the main entrance and clock-tower. This water is reputed to have been piped from Swanston springs. Another source of water, which was not drawn upon, was a stream flowing beside the little quarry on the eastern base of Wester Craiglockhart Hill. This stream prevented the poorhouse governors from using this site as a cemetry as originally planned.

The new poorhouse provided accommodation for adults and children, including "lunatic paupers" and the destitute sick. Initially each new inmate was placed in a probationary ward until his health and character had been assessed. He was later transferred to an appropriate section of the poorhouse. "Tramps and imposters were soon discovered" according to one report. The original intention had been to have separate wards which would allow segregation according to sex, character and physical and mental ability, but arrangements had frequently to be changed. One place where all could mix was the dining-hall, which also served as a chapel. A plan which was never carried out was the construction of cottages for married couples.

The statutory conditions for admission were destitution and disability, which lent themselves to various interpretations. In his pamphlet, *The New City Poorhouse, Craiglockhart,* the architect George Beattie described the organisation and regulations governing the new institution in great detail. Scottish poorhouses were not workhouses as in England: inmates could not be forced to work. Those who conformed to the rules were given a good basic diet, reasonably comfortable sleeping quarters and an allocation of tobacco and sweets. Those willing to carry out various tasks during a working day of from 7 a.m. to 5 p.m. six days a week enjoyed better amenities. A firewood factory was established in the 1880s and male inmates, dressed in the institution's grey tweed suits, were a familiar sight in Morningside, selling bundles of sticks. Others sold vegetables and manure. Those of more robust physique helped to cultivate the surrounding land.

When Craiglockhart Poorhouse was first opened, access from the city was by way of the tree-lined drive branching off from Comiston Road, constructed by the Parochial Board as the exclusive route to the poorhouse. Access from the west was by way of a picturesque avenue, now Glenlockhart Road, with a lodge and large gate. While the lodge has long since been demolished, the original gate-posts may still be seen. In the 1880s, Edinburgh Corporation pressed the Parochial Board to permit their drive to be used as a public road from Morningside to Colinton, but the request was refused. When the new Fever Hospital was opened at Colinton Mains in 1903, access was permitted via the drive, though eventually many town councillors came to feel that there was a certain stigma attached to using what was traditionally known as "the poorhouse drive", and in due course Greenbank Drive was constructed parallel to the old drive, with a red sandstone gate-lodge on Comiston Road. The long-standing ill feeling between the Parochial Board and Edinburgh Town Council, expressed in the former's reluctance to allow Poorhouse Drive to be used for public traffic and the latter's decision, later, to build a separate drive, often gave rise to incidents. The Parochial Board accused the Town Council of not allowing them to be represented at public functions, notably the famous Holyrood Review and the opening of the restored St Giles Cathedral.

Many people, although destitute and eligible for admission to

"Uniforms" of male and female inmates of Craiglockhart Poorhouse

By courtesy of Dr Audrey Paterson

Craiglockhart Poorhouse, never applied. There were several reasons. The rules were strict and entry entailed a loss of liberty. The poorhouse was three miles from the city and, at the time of its establishment in 1870 public transport was infrequent and went only as far as the old toll-house at the foot of Morningside Road. The remaining distance had to be covered on foot. Relatives were able to visit the institution only on Saturdays; inmates felt isolated. Institutionalisation affected many of them mentally. Those who could not endure the isolation absconded, only to be driven back by desperate home circumstances. On re-admission they were placed in less amenable wards.

When the site of the new poorhouse had first been discussed, many Parochial Board members had anticipated the problems of its isolation, but the Board's chairman, having climbed Wester Craiglockhart Hill to survey the new institution, had waxed lyrical in praise of the situation. One member of the Board who expressed reservations was rebuked by the retort that at Craiglockhart there was the prospect of changing "the present dungeon of idleness into a village of industry . . . health and happiness.''

In the late nineteenth century there was much public debate on the lot of the poor, largely prompted by Darwin's *Origin of Species*. Some protagonists of the evolutionary theory argued that the poor, weak and diseased should be allowed to die out, thus reducing their numbers in society. Those who survived would prove more useful. Paupers were regarded as "degraded, vicious characters who lacked honesty and the ability to budget, spending more than they possessed" until, "lacking in self respect, they applied for Parish Council help." The argument that poverty was not a crime or a disgrace "since Christianity is based on the life of a poor man" was heard less frequently as the nineteenth century drew to a close. At this period Charles Dickens was one of the great champions of the poor. The poorhouse at Craiglockhart developed in the midst of such debate.

Eventually the poorhouse sold much of its surrounding farmland to the Merchants of Edinburgh Golf Club. Glenlockhart Road was opened to public transport in 1908. The poorhouse as such, as established under its original provisions, was eventually phased out. In 1944, after the passing of the National Assistance Act, it became known simply as Glenlockhart. Twenty years later, the name was changed to Greenlea, when Edinburgh's first purpose-built home for the elderly at Muirhouse was named Silverlea. Greenlea's address is 1 Glenlockhart Road, the original address, 144 Comiston Road, having long since been replaced. This latter number, attached to the old gate-lodge in Comiston Road, had once served a useful purpose. Many children had been born in Craiglockhart Poorhouse and, rather than indicate this unfortunate place on a child's birth certificate, the place of birth was entered as "144 Comiston Road." A writer to the Press some years ago, having returned from the United States of America, decided to visit the house of her birth at 144 Comiston Road. Though some tried to discourage her from doing so, she persevered, only to discover she had been born in the City Poorhouse.

Today, the comfortable amenities of Greenlea, now organised in accordance with the enlightened approach of the Edinburgh District Council Social Work Department, make it difficult to recall the austerity in what was virtually the same building just over a century ago. How remote now seem the appalling social conditions of nineteenth-century Edinburgh which forced so many people, young and old, to make their sad, ominous journey along Poorhouse Drive, many never to return to the far-off city.

In his *Report on the Sanitary Conditions of the City of Edinburgh*, published in 1865, Dr Henry D. Littlejohn, Edinburgh's first Medical Officer of Health, provided a stark description of the grossly overcrowded housing conditions in the older parts of the city, particularly in Middle

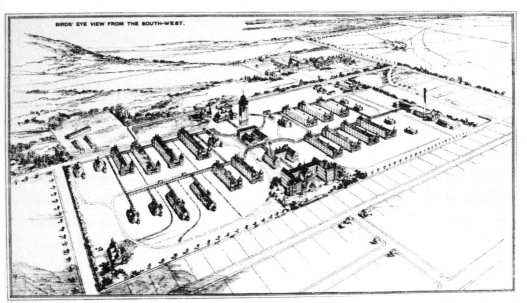

BIRDS' EYE VIEW FROM THE SOUTH-WEST.

Architect's plan of the City Fever Hospital, showing the surrounding district

From "Care of the Public Health and the New Fever Hospital in Edinburgh" by James Pollard

Meal Market Stair off the High Street. The widespread lack of running water in homes, and of sinks and lavatories, led Dr Littlejohn to comment significantly: "Disease is spreading like wildfire."

At the time of this report, infectious diseases were treated in certain wards of the old Royal Infirmary in Infirmary Street off South Bridge. Here, at the time when Professor (later Lord) Joseph Lister was on the staff, one of his colleagues became Edinburgh's first bacteriologist. In a side room, following the recently published techniques of Louis Pasteur, this doctor attempted to identify the bacteria in specimens from patients suspected of suffering from infectious diseases. Accommodation and facilities for the isolation, diagnosis and treatment of such cases were, however, hopelessly inadequate.

In 1843, when "fever" was prevalent in the city and the Royal Infirmary was unable to cope, a public meeting was held in the Assembly Rooms in George Street. Resolutions were passed appealing to the Town Council to open a separate Fever Hospital. Amongst those leading the campaign was Professor James Syme of Millbank in Canaan Lane, the distinguished surgeon, father-in-law of Joseph Lister and his immediate predecessor in the Chair of Clinical Surgery in Edinburgh's Medical School. Twenty years were to pass after this meeting which saw no progress towards a Fever Hospital, then Dr Henry Littlejohn's revealing

313

report again stirred public opinion. As Dr Andrew Duncan had found in his attempts to bring about the establishment of "a proper asylum for the insane", the transformation of public opinion into practical response is a slow, painful process. It was not until 1894 that the first steps were taken towards building a separate hospital for infectious diseases.

In 1867 the Public Health (Scotland) Act had placed the responsibility for providing for the isolation and treatment of patients during epidemics of infectious disease upon local authorities. The Royal Infirmary managers had attempted to meet these requirements, first in the old hospital and later in the new Royal Infirmary in Lauriston Place. In 1885, however, the hospital authorities informed Edinburgh Town Council that they could no longer meet the increasing demand for the treatment of fever cases. Dr Littlejohn's report had also revealed that in a population of some 330,000 in Edinburgh in 1865 "the number of infectious disease cases, including those treated at home, is seldom below 600 at any given time". As Medical Officer of Health he therefore urged that a new fever hospital should provide for at least that number. He further recommended that it should be built on the outskirts of the city. In this he was supported by Edinburgh's Royal College of Physicians. However, in the early 1890s, when the Town Council had at last come to accept the proposals for a new hospital, they were divided on where it should be built. Some councillors favoured a site adjacent to the Royal Infirmary in Lauriston Place or incorporating the old Infirmary buildings in Infirmary Street. Obviously aware of the debates in the country at that time on the inadvisability of situating infectious diseases hospitals in city centres, those who favoured the Infirmary Street site were at pains to point out that it was not far from the open space of the King's Park, that it was capable of having an excellent drainage system, that mortality from infectious disease in the old Infirmary had been lower than in many other hospitals in Britain and that the confinement of such patients in Infirmary Street had never led to the spread of infection in the surrounding district.

The proposal to build outwith the city nevertheless prevailed. At first there was difficulty in finding a site, but in 1894 Edinburgh Corporation purchased the seventy-two-acre farm of Colinton Mains for the modest sum of £20,500. Colinton Mains was in 1894 still considered far from the city, as had been the adjacent City Poorhouse. The Corporation replied to public concern about its remoteness by saying that "the distance does not matter, since ambulance waggons will carry patients quite safely". Plans for the new Fever Hospital to accommodate at least six hundred patients were drawn up by Robert Morham, the City Architect. In May 1897 the first sod was cut by Edinburgh's Lady Provost, in the presence of her husband, Lord Provost Andrew McDonald, and a large number of bailies, councillors and citizens. Amongst the most ardent campaigners for the new hopsital had been Bailie Pollard, who wrote a

314

valuable history of it and of the events which lead up to its establishment.

The plans for the Edinburgh City Fever Hospital, or Colinton Hospital as it was for long known, incorporated the most modern facilities. The location of the hospital was considered ideal. An early report noted: "There are no buildings of any kind at present to intercept the space between the grounds and the Pentland Hills, about one and a half miles southwards." Great stress was placed on fresh air and sunlight and the hospital wards were built on the peninsular-plan with some sixty to eighty feet between each, and running north-south so as not to over-shadow each other. Toilets were installed at the south ends of wards to be subject to the maximum amount of sunlight. Red sandstone was used in the construction to give a sense of warmth.

The hospital was eventually designed to accommodate seven hundred and fifty patients. The number and allocation of the wards indicate the infections most prevalent at the end of last century. Provision for scarlet fever cases required the construction of seven large two-storey wards, allowing for three hundred and thirty beds. These were on the east side of the hospital. West of the main gates there were separate wards for diphtheria, typhoid fever, erysipelas, measles, chicken-pox and whooping cough. Single-storey wards and cottage-type pavilions located some distance from the main hospital accommodated cases of typhus and other highly infectious diseases such as smallpox, which sometimes required the strict isolation of single patients. During outbreaks of smallpox, a small group of timber wards were set up outwith the hospital boundary on the southern slopes of Wester Craiglockhart Hill, to the north of the little lane leading from the hospital to Firrhill. When such outbreaks were over, the buildings were burned to destroy all vestiges of infection.

The Nurses' Home provided separate bedrooms for one hundred and fifty nurses. A special hospital drainage system was installed, and a disinfection plant. The pipe led to one of the main city sewers half a mile away, passing under Morningside Road parallel to the Jordan Burn at the site of the old Briggs o' Braid. The new hospital with its excellent facilities cost £350,000 to build, at the time considered a very large sum, but not begrudged for the provision of a hospital unsurpassed in the United Kingdom. On May 13th, 1903, almost exactly six years after building had commenced, the new Fever Hospital was officially opened by King Edward VII, accompanied by Queen Alexandra. The day was an occasion for the citizens of Edinburgh: the route of the royal procession from the city was thronged. Special viewing stands had been built at the best vantage points. Some Morningside residents will recall the great cavalcade of mounted Life Guards passing down Morningside Road and turning into Poorhouse Drive, then the only road leading to the new hospital. It is on record that ten thousand people gathered around the hospital gates and on the lower slopes of Wester Craiglockhart Hill to view the opening ceremony. Presiding over the proceedings was Lord Provost James Steel,

The arrival of Edward VII to open the City Fever Hospital, May 1903
By courtesy of the City Hospital Administrative Officer

Edward VII is received by Lord Provost James Steel at the opening of the City Fever Hospital, May 1903
By courtesy of the City Hospital Administrative Officer

knighted by Edward VII immediately after the ceremony. Two elm trees were planted beside the main entrance to mark the occasion.

Strict isolation soon became a feature of the new hospital. For nearly half a century after its establishment, infectious diseases were prevalent and epidemics occurred regularly. Each patient was allocated a reference number and tabulated progress reports were published daily in the Edinburgh newspapers with reports such as: "Making satisfactory progress" or "Condition serious: relatives requested to come out." Visitors to the hospital were for long conveyed by special bus from the entrance to Greenbank Drive and were subject to strict regulations. Parents of children suffering from scarlet fever and diphtheria were permitted only to look through the glass-panelled ward doors in the hope of glimpsing them. Visitors admitted to certain wards were required to wear overalls. In the 1930s the relatively high incidence of tuberculosis in the city led to two bungalow-type wards being built within the grounds of the adjacent Glenlockhart Old People's Home. These remain, long since vacated, and are now part of the facilities of Greenlea.

Over the last twenty years, dramatic advances have been made in the prevention, diagnosis and treatment of infectious diseases. Immunisation, antibiotics and therapeutic drugs, radiography, food inspection and hygiene, and vastly improved housing and working conditions have all contributed to the substantial reduction and control of infectious diseases. While soon after the opening of the new Fever Hospital, some four hundred beds were required for tuberculosis patients, by the mid 1950s this number had been reduced to fifty. Today cases of tuberculosis requiring hospital treatment are rare.

Edinburgh's Fever Hospital, now known as the City Hospital, has, since its establishment, undergone great changes in function. It now bears a vastly different image from that of the strictly controlled, isolated and forbidding Fever Hospital of 1903. However, it seems to be a permanent feature of health statistics that, as former scourges are eliminated, the very social developments which have helped to do this usher in other conditions to maintain a balance. Wards once used for infectious diseases such as scarlet fever and diphtheria are now adapted to provide for contemporary conditions such as chronic bronchitis and virus infections, and perhaps the occasional case of enteric fever or dysentery. Within the hospital in recent years have been built modern units for cardiothoracic surgery and the treatment of ear, nose and throat cases, while further developments may yet reach the architect's drawing board. Despite the constant pattern of change and adaptation, and the expansion of Edinburgh to its boundary walls, the City Hospital retains its pleasant setting and maintains its proud traditions.

CRAIGLOCKHART

A detailed account of the history of the Craiglockhart estate is outwith the scope of this book but some reference to those parts of the district which adjoin Craighouse and the outer fringes of Greenbank may be appropriate. The pleasant residential district of Craiglockhart, originally within the wide parish of St Cuthbert's, in 1630 became part of the parish of Colinton. The revision of Edinburgh's boundaries in 1920 brought it within the confines of the city. Grant, in *Old and New Edinburgh*, gives the origin of the name Craiglockhart as "Craig-loch-ard", bearing reference to the great sheet of water, once known as Cortorphin

Plan of the lands of Craiglockhart

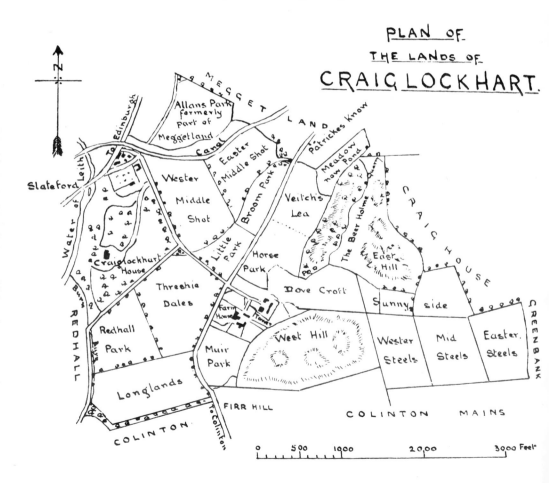

PLAN OF
THE LANDS OF
CRAIGLOCKHART.

Loch, which extended to the northern slopes of the Craiglockhart estate. The estate spans the Easter and Wester Craiglockhart Hills, taking in all of the latter and the southern slopes of the former. To the north it descends steeply to Craiglockhart Dell Woods, the Water of Leith and the old village of Slateford. Wester Craiglockhart Hill rises above the Convent of the Sacred Heart to a height of five hundred feet above sea level. On account of its prominence, in far-off times it must almost certainly have been the site of fortifications. Some years ago archaeologists discovered ancient pottery and iron-age remains. Both hills above Craiglockhart were once known as "the Craggis of Gorgin". Stewart, in *Notes for a History of Colinton Parish,* cites a reference to this name in records of 1226. The name Gorgie is said by other writers to have been derived from "Gorgine" or "Gorgyne", in turn derived from the Welsh "Jor Cyn" meaning "a spacious wedge". What is now Gorgie lies in "the spacious wedge" between Craiglockhart and the Water of Leith at Roseburn.

Those interested in the history of Craiglockhart have frequently centred their attention on the apparently ancient ruined tower or castle which still stands on the south side of Glenlockhart Road next to the old farm cottages at the side entrance to the convent. Referred to by many writers as Craiglockhart Castle, the ruin is considered to be of a thirteenth-century keep associated with the Lockhart of Lee family. While the 1929 Edinburgh volume of the Royal Commission on Ancient Monuments made a brief reference to the building, describing its architectural features, the volume of 1951 does not mention it. Its origins must be left largely to conjecture. It has been suggested that it was one of a chain of medieval signal or outlook towers on which beacons were lit to give warning of the approach of English invaders. To Grant the Craiglockhart ruin seemed to be "totally without a history" but he nevertheless considered it of more ancient origin than the nearby sixteenth-century mansion of Craighouse. He gives the ruin's dimensions as 28' 6" by 24' 8", the walls being 6' 3" in thickness. John Munro Bell's *Castles of Lothian* provides a sketch of Craiglockhart Castle, confirms the measurements given by Grant and notes that it had an entrance door at one corner and a wheel-stair. The vaulting of the ground and first floors Bell considered unusual for such a small keep, which, he suggested, was reminiscent of many which the Normans built in Scotland to maintain their tight rule. He also notes that "the castle is without a history but somehow linked with the Lockharts of Lee". McGibbon and Ross have nothing of significance to add. Close study of the Craiglockhart ruin has revealed that its original residential quarters may have been quite attractive. In the nineteenth century ruins in Scotland became greatly prized for their romantic associations and this was no exception. When the Craiglockhart Hydropathic was built at the base of Wester Craiglockhart Hill in 1880, it had a sketch of the old ruined castle on its headed notepaper.

Like the origins of Craiglockhart Castle, details of the earliest ownership of the estate are shrouded in uncertainty. One reason for this is that, when Edward I of England took the Stone of Destiny from Scone to London, he took with it three chests of ancient Scottish records. It is recorded that, on August 27th, 1324, King Robert the Bruce granted a Charter of Confirmation, noting a donation made by Helen Lockhart to John of Cowie, and Marion his spouse, of the lands of Craiglockhart. Among the missing charters of David II was one relating to "James Sandilands of Craiglockhart and Stonypath in Edinburgh" and another to "James Sandoks [?] of the same lands".

In Sir James Dalrymple's *Collections Concerning the Scottish History* (1705) there is mention of a charter in the Newbattle Abbey Register during the reign of Alexander III (1249-85), which refers to "lands lying betwixt Bred [Braid] and Merchistoun which Sir Simon Loccard held there: these lands seem to be Craigloccard". It is known that, during the Wars of Independence, Sir Stephen Lockhart in 1306 swore allegiance to Edward II of England "for lands in the shire of Edinburgh". The Lockharts, like many of the Scottish nobility, were not consistent in their loyalties, being influenced frequently by opportunism. We find, however, that Sir Symon Lockard of Lee and Cartland (and presumably still connected with Craiglockhart), was Knighted by Robert the Bruce for his services against England, and, after Bruce's death in 1329, Sir Symon was one of the Scottish Nobles who accompanied Lord Douglas when taking the King's heart to the Holy Land. It was while returning from this expedition, it was said, that Lockard captured a Saracen prisoner whose wife gave him, as part of her husband's ransom, the magic "Lee penny", the talisman which Sir Walter Scott immortalised in his novel. It is also recounted that, long after the Reformation, the Kirk Sessions in Lanarkshire were still deploring the widespread popular faith in the magical power of this charm.

In about 1460 the lands of Craiglockhart passed to the Kincaid family and remained theirs for nearly a century and a half. During the latter half of the sixteenth century the Kincaids also owned the neighbouring mansion and lands of Craighouse. Because members of this family were so frequently involved in disputes and feuds with various Edinburgh citizens, their lands at Craiglockhart were eventually forfeited, and reverted to the Crown.

From this point onwards the successive owners of Craiglockhart are well documented. In 1609 the purchaser was one whose family occupies a prominent place in the chronicles of the neighbouring district of Colinton, George Foulis, a wealthy goldsmith who had lent large sums of money to James VI, reputedly some £180,000 Scots. He had thus gained great influence at Court. In 1610 George Foulis made over the property to his brother James, who already owned all the land of Colinton parish ("the lands of Collingtoune, Swanston, Dreghorn, Bonyley, Baddis, Pitmure, Oxgangs, Comiston, Reidhall" — a very substantial inventory of possessions). Like Sir William Dick of Braid, James Foulis, having been a devoted and generous supporter of the Royalist Cause, suffered greatly when Cromwell came to power. In 1649 Foulis had pledged his Craiglockhart lands to Sir John Gilmour of Craigmillar in return for a loan of £10,000. When Cromwell occupied Edinburgh, his troops burned down Sir John's property at Craigmillar and in other parts of Edinburgh. At the Restoration in 1661, Gilmour recovered possession of Craiglockhart, Foulis being required to make over his titles. Sir John Gilmour also became Lord President of the Court of Session in 1661. He had been defence counsel for the Marquis of Montrose before the latter's imprisonment in 1641. He also became a Member of Parliament from 1661 until his death ten years later. Despite his Royalist devotion, he had advocated leniency towards the Covenanters taken prisoner not far from Craiglockhart after the Battle of Rullion Green.

Following Sir John Gilmour's ownership, Craiglockhart estate reverted to the Lockhart family, whose allegiance during the recent Civil War had been divided. One of the Lockharts, George, became an ardent Jacobite and adviser to James II and VII. In 1689 what might have proved an interesting career was dramatically ended. On a Sunday morning, returning from St Giles Church to his home in Bank Close, he was shot dead by a neighbour, John Chiesley of Dalry and Redhall, who greatly resented a verdict on alimony which had gone against him. So ended the brief second Lockhart ownership of Craiglockhart.

In 1691 the estate passed to George Porteous, the Royal Herald Painter, also for some time the owner of Craighouse. He was succeeded by his two brothers. During their possession improvements were made to the estate: a new two-storey dwelling-house was built and the farmlands were let to profitable tenants. Soon after the third Porteous brother's acquisition, however, the house and lands were put up for sale. Edinburgh's *Caledonian Mercury* on November 17th, 1726 described the property and its attractions:

> There is to be exposed to voluntar Roup and Sale on Thursday the 15th of December 1726 in the house of Partrick Herdman, Vintner, betwixt the Hours of 3 and 4 after Noon, the Town and Lands of Craiglockhart, Tower, Fortalice, Mannor-Place, houses, biggings, yards and pertinents thereto belonging, being a good fertile soil, pleasantly situate, having large conveniency for pasturage on the hills belonging thereto; with the Houses and Stone-Quarry pertaining to the same in Sclateford. There is a large handsome House, two-storey high, lately built on the said Lands, possessed by the Tenant, besides several other Conveniences; such as a Brewery, possessed by a Sub-tenant, a convenient seat in the Church, and the like; lying about two miles west of Edinburgh, in the Sherriffdom thereof, Parish of Hails, alias Colington.

The purchaser attracted by this detailed advertisement was a merchant, John Parkhill, who served as Treasurer of the Merchant Company of the City of Edinburgh from 1708 until 1751. The property later passed to Parkhill's son and in 1773 was sold by him to a remarkable Edinburgh medical family, the Monros. The period of 128 years during which Dr Alexander Monro, *primus,* his son Dr Alexander Monro, *secundus,* and his grandson, Dr Alexander Monro, *tertius,* each successively occupied the Chair of Anatomy in the Edinburgh Medical School was known as "the Monro dynasty". Dr Alexander Monro, *primus,* father of the Dr Monro who purchased the Craiglockhart estate in 1773, was the first Professor of Anatomy in the Medical School and, indeed, when appointed in 1720, was virtually the School's founder. It was he who was largely responsible for the Edinburgh Medical School earning in his day, and for some time to come, a world-wide reputation. Realising that a teaching hospital was essential to a medical school, he was, with Lord Provost George Drummond, the co-founder of the Edinburgh Royal Infirmary.

Professor Alexander Monro, *primus,* when his retiral from the Chair of Anatomy was imminent in 1750, took the unusual step of proposing to Edinburgh Town Council, administrators of the University and Medical School, that his son should succeed him. At the time his son, aged twenty-two, had no medical degree or other relevant qualifications. After some years, and no doubt much debate, the proposal was accepted. Alexander Monro, *secundus,* having pursued intensive medical studies abroad, returned to Edinburgh suitably qualified, first to assist his father and then, in 1759, to succeed him. In many respects he was eventually to outshine him.

The fame and distinction of the Monro father and son attracted many medical students to Edinburgh. After his father had retired, it was said of the son that "He was a complete master of his subject. . .his eloquence was of an unusual sort, lucid, impressive and earnest". He made a point of stressing to Edinburgh Town Council, which may originally have had reservations regarding his appointment, that it had proved to be of considerable economic benefit to the city. During his teaching career which lasted over forty years, no fewer than 14,000 students had attended his lectures, including 5,831 from outside Scotland. The latter, Dr Monro claimed, had brought into Scotland a total of £466,480. With the revenue from Scottish students, the financial advantage to the city had reached a million pounds.

Large classes were not without personal benefit to Dr Monro. His salary as a professor was no more than £15 per annum until 1798, but each of his students paid £3 in class fees, collected by him. At the peak of his career, his students averaged an annual total of 436, ensuring him a quite considerable income. With several important discoveries in anatomy to his name, Dr Alexander Monro, *secundus,* enhanced even further the

The farmhouse at Craiglockhart, c. 1853

By courtesy of Sister Valerio of the Convent of the Sacred Heart

high reputation of the Edinburgh Medical School earned for it by his father.

He himself never resided at Craiglockhart. His home was at 30 St Andrew Square, in the then recently completed New Town. Nevertheless, he took a keen interest in the large estate he had acquired and did much to beautify it. It was he who planted the trees which now form the woods on Easter Craiglockhart Hill "as a pleasure ground with winding paths and shady bowers", to which residents of Craiglockhart still have right of access. Dr Monro fitted up a two-roomed cottage on the Craiglockhart estate, alongside the house of his gardener, and here, during Edinburgh's Golden Age of intellectual gatherings, wining and dining, entertained his guests. Dr Andrew Duncan in an address to the Harveian Society in 1818, honoured his close friend and colleague by paying tribute to the excellent hospitality he extended to his friends at Craiglockhart. "Without transgressing the bounds of the most strict sobriety, he afforded us demonstrative evidence of the exhilarating power of wine."

Dr Alexander Monro, *tertius*, who inherited the Craiglockhart estate in 1817, had, twenty years earlier, also inherited his father's Chair of Anatomy. His occupancy of the latter was, however, not entirely popular or congenial. The long "Monro Dynasty", brilliant as it had been during the first two generations, had not been without its critics and rivals,

323

notably Dr John Barclay and Dr Robert Knox. A new era was approaching in the Medical School and the third of the Monros resisted change. He could not claim to equal the high standards set by his father and grand-father: they had taken their teaching responsibilities seriously, while he seemed indifferent to the progress of his students. By 1840 his in-competence was giving rise to violent verbal reactions in the lecture theatre. The University authorities became alarmed and Dr Monro's resignation in 1846 was welcomed with a sigh of relief. The 128-year-long dynasty was at an end.

If the third of the Monros of Craiglockhart failed to earn for himself a memorial in the annals of the Medical School, he did create one on his estate. It was he who, in 1823, built Craiglockhart House, a twenty-two-roomed mansion on that part of the estate now lying between Colinton Road and Slateford, overlooking the Water of Leith. Here Dr Monro, in his seventies, lived with his three sons, two daughters, their families and a large household staff. Eventually the mansion was deserted by Monro's family. Some time after his death in 1859 the house passed to his trustees. In 1863 the estate was sold to the City of Edinburgh Parochial Board and on it was established the new City Poorhouse in 1867.

One of Dr Monro's sons was to perpetuate the name of Craiglockhart far from Scotland. This was David, who, it is said, perhaps to escape carrying on the "Monro Dynasty", emigrated to New Zealand. There he became a successful sheep farmer and named two of his properties Craiglockhart. The mansion-house which his father built still stands in Craiglockhart Dell Road, now hemmed in by more modern villas and bungalows.

The part of the Craiglockhart estate set aside for the new poorhouse was that formerly occupied by the farm and three large fields to the east. The City Parochial Board, with an eye to future revenue, had envisaged that most of the remainder of the estate purchased would before long become desirable to prospective builders of residential property. The Board's hopes were soon fulfilled. In 1873 much of the land to the west was sold to the Craiglockhart Estate Company. The substantial villas on the east side of Colinton Road under the shadow of Easter Craiglockhart Hill were the first to be built. This company in 1877 feued the thirteen acres or so between Colinton Road and Wester Craiglockhart Hill to the Craiglockhart Hydropathic Company.

The feu contract contained several stringent provisos. The Hydro-pathic Company was required to erect for their purpose within three years buildings worth not less than £10,000. The old castle could not be pulled down, nor could factories or public houses be built. Any separate dwelling houses which might be built were not to be worth less than £1,000 each. In 1877 the farmhouse and steading of Craiglockhart Farm were cleared away to make way for the erection of the hydropathic which was built by Peddie and Kinnear between 1878 and 1880. A majestic, almost

Craiglockhart Hydropathic

palatial, building with a central Italianate block arose and the irony of the situation was duly commented upon in Groome's *Ordinance Gazetteer of Scotland* (1882): the rich and poor of the city (the wealthy residents of the luxurious hydropathic and the paupers in nearby Craiglockhart Poorhouse) could now reside on the same hill.

At this time hydropathics began to spring up across Scotland. The cult of "electricity and hydropathy" became the popular secret of good health. The Craiglockhart establishment was unique in being so near a great city. Most hydropathics were in country districts. An illustrated brochure or prospectus from Edinburgh's new hydropathic, now in the National Library of Scotland, makes great play of this special feature, especially stressing the spiritual advantages: "Visitors can, with small inconvenience, enjoy the ministrations of the leading preachers of Edinburgh — no small matter in a city so long and justly famed for its pulpit eloquence." Another advertisement for the hydropathic in 1891 describes it as the nearest residence to the International Exhibition, and emphasises that visitors have all the benefits of residence in the country with the amenities and enjoyments of city life.

Many photographs exist indicating just how attractive was the site of the new hydropathic, commanding a magnificent panoramic view over Edinburgh, the Forth and the Fife coast, and towards the High-

PRAYERS in Lounge every morning after Breakfast, and on Sundays at 9 P.M.

MEALS.—Breakfast (8 A.M. for those requiring it) at - - - - 9 A.M.
Luncheon at - - - - - - - 1.30 P.M.
Afternoon Tea - - - - - - - 4 P.M.
Dinner - - - - - - - - 7 P.M.
Tea and Coffee - - - - - - - 8 P.M.
Dinner at 8 P.M. on Sundays.

Serving Meals in Parlour or Bedroom 6d. extra each meal per visitor. Visitors may entertain their friends at the following rates:—Breakfast, 2/6; Luncheon, 2/-; Dinner, 3/6; Plain Tea, 1/-. Afternoon Tea is served from 4 to 4.30, after which time it is charged extra.

The Warning Bell is rung at 8 A.M., and also 15 minutes before each meal. The Gong is sounded at the hours of meals.

BATHS.—In the Basement—Turkish, Russian, and Swimming Baths are open for Gentlemen from 6.30 to 8 A.M. and from 3 to 5.30 P.M. daily, except Tuesdays; for Ladies from 10 a.m. to 1 p.m. daily, except Tuesdays. On Tuesdays for Gentlemen from 6.30 to 8 a.m., and 10 a.m. to 1 p.m.; for Ladies, 3 to 5.30 p.m. Plunge, Spray, etc., Baths, from 6.30 to 8 a.m., 10 a.m. to 1 p.m., and 3 to 5.30 p.m., for both Ladies and Gentlemen.

A charge is made for Baths in Bedrooms and in Bathrooms in Corridors, and for Medicated Baths. Swimming Lessons, 7/6 per dozen. Massage Treatment, 2/6 per visit.

LIGHTS AND ATTENDANCE.—Gas must be extinguished in Bedrooms during the night. Night Lights can be obtained at the Office if required. Lights in the Public Rooms are extinguished at 10.30 p.m.; in the Smoking and Billiard Rooms at 11 p.m. No attendance to be expected from servants after 10 P.M.

WASHING.—Lists of Clothes sent to the Laundry must be made on the Duplicate forms provided, and all articles must be marked, otherwise the Management will not be responsible.

FARES TO STATIONS.—Waverley, 4/-; Princes Street, 3/-; Haymarket, 2/6; Merchiston, 2/-.

ACCOUNTS are rendered weekly from the day of arrival. Cheques cannot be taken in payment unless presented three days before departure.

NOTICE OF DEPARTURE to be given at least one day previous, and in July, August, and September three days when possible.

VALUABLES.—The Management will not be responsible for any Valuables lost in the Establishment, unless they are left at the Office accompanied with a written memorandum.

MOTORS are kept and parties will be arranged. Full particulars given at the Office.

AFTERNOON VISITS can be made to Forth Bridge, Roslin, Craigmillar, Hawthornden, Dalkeith, Palace, Hopetoun, Dalmeny, Linlithgow, and day excursions to Abbotsford, Peebles, Melrose, Dryburgh, The Trossachs, and to Forth and Clyde for Marine Trips. Swanston Cottage, the birthplace of R. L. Stevenson, is within walking distance.

FEATURES.—Splendid Croquet Lawns, the largest and finest in Scotland. The Scottish Championship Meeting is held here annually, also numerous Competitions and Tournaments. Excellent Golfing in the neighbourhood. Tennis Courts. Bowling Greens.

PRINCIPAL CHURCHES IN EDINBURGH:—

Established Church of Scotland.—St Giles, High Street; St Cuthbert's, Lothian Road; St George's, Charlotte Square.

United Free Church of Scotland.—St George's, Shandwick Place; Barclay, Bruntsfield Links; St Mary's, Broughton Street; Palmerston Place Church; Morningside Church.

Episcopalian.—St Marys Cathedral, Palmerston Place; St John's, West End of Princes Street; St Paul's, York Place.

Roman Catholic.—St Mary's (Pro-Cathedral), Broughton Street.

PLACES OF INTEREST IN EDINBURGH:—

The Castle; University, South Bridge; United Free Church College, The Mound; Surgeons' Hall, Nicolson Street; National Gallery, Princes Street; Scottish National Portrait Gallery, Queen Street; John Knox's House, High Street; Greyfriar's Churchyard (Martyr's Monument); Antiquarian Museum, Queen Street;

Prospectus of the Craiglockhart Hydropathic

By courtesy of Sister Valerio of the Convent of the Sacred Heart.

lands. The grounds were pleasant and varied in layout, with fine lawns, shrubberies and ornamental plantations. There were excellent facilities for tennis, archery, croquet and bowls. Behind were pathways to the summit of Wester Craiglockhart Hill. If certain aspects of the facade of the building were forbidding, the interior was pleasant and impressive, especially the long parquetry-laid ground-floor corridor with its avenue of square pillars and the handsome drawing and dining rooms leading from it. There were also billiards, reading and card rooms, a heated swimming pool and a large recreation hall, suitable for balls, concerts and theatrical performances. For personal comfort, servants abounded. In 1881, one attended every two guests. Most of the guests were Scots; many came in family groups; there were few old people. Many had private means, but professional and commercial people seemed equally able to enjoy the luxuries of the hydropathic. Of guests' occupations listed in the visitors book, perhaps the most unusual was that of a Greenock gentleman entered as "Theologian, electrician and engineer". Many students came to enjoy pleasant respite from their studies, probably occupying, as advertised in 1891, "A few Upper Rooms at 35/- for young gentlemen." Permanent guests were accommodated for £100 *per annum*.

A booklet preserved in the National Library of Scotland, entitled "Craiglockhart Hydropathic Establishment Edinburgh. An Illustrated Brochure. Edinburgh 1903", observes that : "The special attention of Ladies and Gentlemen at present living alone in the Town, and of those who may wish to get rid of the cares and expenses of housekeeping, is directed to the foremost most favourable terms from the Superior and Residence of 'Craiglockhart' with its many advantages."

The "General Regulations and Arrangements" printed in the brochure show that the hydropathic was designed to appeal to middle-class respectability:

The bell is rung every morning at 8 o'clock. Family Worship in the Drawing Room every morning immediately after breakfast and every evening at 9.15 p.m. A short service on Sunday evening at 8.30 p.m. Children under eight years of age will have their meals provided for them in the children's nursery. Gas is turned off from the Public Rooms at 10.30 p.m. and at the Meter at 11 p.m., at which hour all are expected to have retired to rest. Visitors to be absent after 11 p.m. are expected to give notice at the Office of their intention to be late, as special arrangements have to be made for their admission.

With a view to assuring the comfort of all, the Directors reserve to themselves the power of excluding from the Establishment or Baths such parties as they may consider objectionable. Smoking is not allowed in any part of the establishment except in the room set apart. Dogs strictly prohibited. . .

Despite the establishment's attractions, the management of the Craiglockhart Hydropathic encountered difficulties even before its opening. In 1881 the directors were forced to negotiate a loan of £25,000, giving the property as security. When they failed to maintain the interest repayments, the insurance company which provided the loan, along with other creditors, succeeded in calling for the winding up of the Craiglockhart Hydropathic Company. In 1888 the Directors attempted to sell the property but had still failed after five attempts. The upset price of £20,000 was then reduced to £13,500, although the buildings alone had cost £46,000 in 1880. A further auction in 1889 again resulted in no sale. Finally, in March 1890, at a further reduced price of £12,500, the hydropathic was bought by James Bell, lessee of the Dunblane Hydropathic Company Limited, of which he became Secretary. By 1891 he was in charge of the Craiglockhart Hydropathic and under his experienced management it became a more viable enterprise.

In 1920 the hydropathic was sold to the Society of the Sacred Heart, becoming a convent and, soon afterwards, a training college for Roman Catholic teachers.

While it has not been possible to discover what prominent persons enjoyed the health-giving facilities of the Craiglockhart Hydropathic there is ample documentation concerning two distinguished men of letters who graced the fine ground-floor corridor when the building came temporarily to serve another purpose. This was during the First World War, when the hydropathic became a military hospital. Here came to reside those seeking to escape not from the cares of life in the city but from the stress of war. From 1917 till 1919 the establishment was the refuge of officers suffering from nervous disorders, and here were sent those two great poets of the First World War, Siegfried Sassoon and Wilfred Owen.

In the House of Commons on July 30th, 1917, an item on the Order Paper must have caused embarrassment to the military authorities: the attention of the House was drawn to the refusal of Second-Lieutenant Seigfried Sassoon to serve further in a war which he had come to regard as futile and unjust. The case was unusual in that Sassoon could not be dismissed as a coward: his military career had been distinguished by exemplary courage which had earned him the Military Cross, though it was well known that he had thrown his coveted medal into the Mersey. He now refused to serve. The Under-Secretary for War attempted a neat solution to an awkward situation: Sassoon was declared to be suffering from a nervous breakdown. No need then for him to face a military tribunal and disciplinary action; he should be sent to a Military Hospital for psychiatric treatment. Towards the end of July 1917, therefore, he was placed in the charge of Dr W. H. R. Rivers, who was responsible for a hundred patients suffering from shell-shock. A psychiatrist of wide experience, interested particularly in dreams and the complexities of shell-shock, Dr Rivers found Sassoon a stimulating and

Siegfried Sassoon and Wilfred Owen, famous patients at the Craiglockhart Military Hospital

challenging patient. They would talk in depth, Dr Rivers with spectacles pushed up on his forehead and hands clasping one knee, as fading light in the autumn of 1917 gradually reduced the parlour in which they sat to darkness. Dr Rivers recorded these conversations with Sassoon in a book he wrote at the time and Sassoon in turn immortalised Dr Rivers in *Sherston's Progress.*

Dr Rivers' work at Craiglockhart, under his Chief, Dr W. H. Bryce, was concerned with the interpretation of dreams as symptoms of his military patients' nervous disorders, and here he enhanced his already high reputation in this field. While, in his frequent sessions with Siegfried Sassoon, the doctor sought to find in his patient significant indications of a nervous disorder resulting from the ordeal of his war experiences, it is a reflection of the poet's integrity and persuasiveness that Dr Rivers, in his own comments on the case, expressed concern lest his patient convert him to pacifism.

In prose and poetry Sassoon related the influences which he experienced at Craiglockhart. In his collection *Counter-Attack,* written in the hospital, the poem "Sick Leave" dwells upon the comfort of his own situation, while thoughts of the men living and dead under his former command bear in upon him:

> When I'm asleep, and dreaming and lulled and warm:
> They come, the homeless ones, the noiseless dead.
> While the dim charging breakers of the storm
> Bellow and drone and rumble overhead,
> Out of the gloom they gather about my bed.
> They whisper to my heart; their thoughts are mine:
> "Why are you here, with all your watches ended?
> From Ypres to Frise we sought you in the line."
> In bitter safety I awake, unfriended;
> And, while the dawn begins with slashing rain,
> I think of the battalion in the mud.
> "When are you going out to them again?
> Are they not still your brothers through our blood?"

In a passage in *Sherston's Progress,* the same theme occupies his mind. He describes the autumn gale buffeting the towers of Craiglockhart while he is safely indoors. In the trenches, his men suffer from the storms of war. In late November 1917, Siegfried Sassoon informed Dr Rivers of his decision to return to active service. In December he closed the door of his room in the hospital for the last time, gazed upon the stately building and across the wide panorama of Edinburgh, and beyond the sea to France. He returned to the war. His stay at Craiglockhart he always remembered, and the deep understanding of Dr Rivers. Years later, the war over, Sassoon was to write, in the poem "Revisitation (W.H.R.R.)":

What voice revisits me this night? What face
To my heart's room returns?
From that perpetual silence where the grace
Of human sainthood burns,
Hastes he once more to harmonise and heal?
I know not. Only I feel
His influence undiminished
And his life's work, in me and many, unfinished.
Our fathering friend and scientist of good,
Who in solitude, one bygone summer's day,
And in throes of bodily anguish passed away
From dream and conflict and research-lit lands
Of ethnologic learning — even as you stood
Selfless and ardent, resolute and gay.
So in this hour, in strange survival stands
Your ghost whom I am powerless to repay.

While at Craiglockhart, Sassoon was not constantly in a mood of guilt-stricken remorse. He enjoyed the pleasant environment of the hospital and all the recreational facilities formerly available to residents in the hydropathic. He enjoyed walking in the Pentland Hills, and he played golf regularly on many local golf courses, becoming a member of Mortonhall. He also spent much time relaxing in the Conservative Club in Princes Street.

Sassoon was one war poet unforgotten in the annals of Craiglockhart, and there was another, who was to become his closest friend, and also the greatest of the writers of the First World War. This was Wilfred Owen.

Owen arrived at Craiglockhart from the front-line on June 25th, 1917, a month earlier than Sassoon, suffering from neurasthenia. Weakened by the rigours of a winter campaign on the Somme followed by an arduous spring offensive, his nerves were finally shattered by a fall into a cellar in the trenches and twelve days in "No-man's land". Owen spent his first weeks at the hospital resting, then gradually began to explore the attractions of Craiglockhart and Edinburgh. "I saw Holyrood", he wrote, "on Sunday afternoon (being alone on Salisbury Crags), a floating mirage in gold mist — a sight familiar enough in dreams and poems, but which I never thought possible in these islands." He must have been aware of Sassoon's arrival at the hospital a month after his own, but being of an unassuming and retiring nature it took time before he plucked up courage to introduce himself to his fellow-poet. On a sunny morning in August 1917, Owen knocked at his door. Entering, he found Sassoon polishing his golf clubs. From their first meeting, a deep, mutually stimulating friendship began.

The pre-war backgrounds of the two poets were very different. Sassoon has been described as having been better known in the hunting-field and cricket ground than in the literary world. Although he had, before the war, begun to attract some attention with his poetry, he was little noted. There was something of "the happy warrior" approach in his entry to the war, though disillusion soon followed. Owen, before his enlistment, had held a teaching post at the Berlitz School of Languages in Bordeaux. He was more serious and introspective than Sassoon, but both soon came to share a profound sense of the futility and wastage of war, which threw Owen into deep depression.

Owen's friendship with Sassoon at Craiglockhart soon brought him the encouragement and sense of purpose he desperately needed. For his fellow-poet, he had the deepest respect and admiration. He regarded him as "the master", and wrote: "I am not worthy to light his pipe." When Sassoon received Owen's draft of "Anthem for Doomed Youth", written at Craiglockhart in October 1917, he immediately recognised his friend's genius. The final draft of this work, written on the hospital's headed notepaper and bearing Sassoon's pencilled corrections, still survives:

> What passing bells for these who die as cattle?
> Only the monstrous anger of the guns.
> Only the stuttering rifles' rapid rattle
> Can patter out their hasty orisons.
> No mockeries for them; no prayers nor bells,
> Nor any voice of mourning save the choirs —
> The shrill, demented choirs of wailing shells;
> And bugles calling for them from sad shires.
> What candles may be held to speed them all?
> Not in the hands of boys but in their eyes
> Shall shine the holy glimmers of goodbyes.
> The pallor of girls' brows shall be their pall;
> Their flowers the tenderness of patient minds,
> And each slow dusk a drawing-down of blinds.

Much of Owen's best work was written in Craiglockhart during the late summer and autumn of 1917. In one week he wrote six poems, including *Dulce et Decorum Est,* a graphic, almost aggressive description of conditions in the trenches and "its cynical sarcastic comment on 'the old lie': Dulce et decorum est pro patria mori." He was to write also, as a result of observant visits to Edinburgh, "Six O'Clock in Princes Street":

> In twos and threes they have not far to roam,
> Crowds that thread eastward, gay of eyes;
> Those seek no further than their quiet home,
> Wives walking westward, slow and wise. . .
> Or be you on the gutter where you stand,
> Pale rain-flowed phantom of the place,
> With news of all the nations in your hand,
> And all their sorrows in your face.

"The Hydra", magazine of the Craiglockhart Military Hospital which published work by Siegfried Sassoon and Wilfred Owen

By courtesy of Sister Valerio of the Convent of the Sacred Heart

Those first to read the considerable output inspired by the mutual influence of Sassoon and Owen were their fellow-patients at Craiglockhart, Owen having taken over the editorship of the hospital magazine, *The Hydra*. Originating in April 1917 as a modest leaflet with a photograph of the hydropathic on the front page, including a great-coated soldier on the bowling green, and serving simply to report hospital news and the activities of its various clubs, *The Hydra* circulated also among patients' relatives and friends. The magazine's name did not refer to the military hospital's having previously been a "hydro", but was drawn from the classical legend of the giant, Antaeus, who retained his strength only as long as his feet were firmly on Mother Earth. The philosophy underlying the legend had appealed to the hospital's medical director as illustrating the basic principles of psychotheraphy as applied to military patients.

The hospital magazine might have remained a leaflet of little importance, its back numbers consigned to city refuse carts after the hospital's closure, had not the contributions of Sassoon and Owen given it great literary importance. By November 1917, the status of the magazine was such as to merit a coloured cover, on which was portrayed the many -

headed hydra, with a thumb-nail sketch of the hydropathic glimpsed over one of its heads. In addition to literary contributions, much interesting day-to-day detail of the life of the military hospital was recorded in its pages. One of the most entertaining contributions was a humorous article by Wilfred Owen entitled "Extract from ye Chronicles of Wilfred de Salope, Knight". "The Castle that is called Craiglockhart", it began, "doth stand perilous near unto two rival holds, the House of the Poor and eke the Asyle of the Loony Ones, so that many seekers of the latter abodes have oft been beguiled into this castle uninviting; some of whom as soon as they perceived their error, departed hastily away, and some of whom yet remain." After the war hospital's closure in 1919, twenty-six back numbers of *The Hydra* became treasured possessions of Owen's family and remained in their keeping until the death of his brother Harold a few years ago, after which they passed to a lecturer at All Souls College, Oxford who has recently written a new biography of Owen.

While Sassoon at Craiglockhart continued his protest against the futility and inhumanity of the war through his poetry, yet nevertheless found release, mental and physical, on the golf courses of Edinburgh, especially Mortonhall (where on one occasion Owen took Robert Graves over to meet him), Owen's excursions into Edinburgh and the countryside around Craiglockhart always had an underlying intellectual motive. He was one of the founders of the Natural History Society at the hospital and wrote to his mother of his pleasure in exploring the nearby Pentland Hills. After such excursions he would frequently write on philosophical themes in the manner of Hilaire Belloc, whom, with G. K. Chesterton, he greatly admired.

For a short period Owen taught English Literature at Tynecastle School in Gorgie, and he greatly enjoyed taking groups of pupils "from the Braid Hills tram terminus to Swanston Cottage". "It is a beautiful thing", he wrote, "that children of Tynecastle School are able to get nearer to the romantic heart of Stevenson." His class had been studying St Ives, some of the events in which, Owen noted, took place "even on the road just outside the Hydro". At Swanston Cottage, Owen met Lord Guthrie, the distinguished High Court Judge and close friend of the Stevenson family who succeeded them as the tenant of Swanston Cottage, and had tea with him in Robert Louis Stevenson's room. Owen, in a letter to his mother dated October 21st, 1917, describes Lord Guthrie as "my old idea of a judge, tall, long-faced, with solemn hanging jowls, scrupulously shaven, and dazzlingly clean in his tall collar, blue clothes, cravat and tie pin." He continues: "But he led me into a trap. He wants me to do some historical research work for him in the Edinburgh libraries. I was not at all keen and pleaded in vain my ignorance and my hatred of legal matters. But I had to meet him this morning in the Advocates' Library and have now my work cut out."

At the end of October 1917, Owen was discharged from the

Craiglockhart War Hospital. On November 3rd he dined with Sassoon in the Conservative Club in Princes Street and his dear friend saw him off on the night train to London. He carried with him letters of introduction from Sassoon to Arnold Bennett, H. G. Wells and Osbert Sitwell, whose sister Edith was the first to publish his poems in 1919. Owen returned to Edinburgh on December 20th, 1917, staying at the North British Hotel. He went straight to Craiglockhart, although Sassoon had gone back to the war, and then to Tynecastle School, where he found his former pupils writing Christmas letters to him. On December 22nd he left Edinburgh for the last time, but did not return to the front line until August 31st, 1918. Two months later, on November 4th, he was killed on the banks of the Oise-Sambre Canal, one week before Armistice. His family did not learn of his death until the Armistice bells were ringing. Through Sassoon's influence, much of Owen's work was published posthumously and his fame as the greatest of the war poets soon spread. Sassoon's work was also increasingly recognised; he was awarded the Hawthornden Prize in 1929, honorary degrees from several British universities and the Gold Medal for Poetry by the Queen in 1957. He died in 1967. Some years earlier, he had been converted to the Roman Catholic Church.

After the war the Craiglockhart Hospital was handed back to its owners, but the Edinburgh Hydropathic Company now doubted the establishment's chance of success in a new era of economic hardship and changes in life-style. It was briefly re-opened but the cost of repair and redecoration was so great as to force the company in 1920 into voluntary liquidation. Later the same year James Bell sold the hydropathic, with all its contents, surrounding land and properties, to Rev. Mother Walsh, Mothers Kennedy and D'Alton, Trustees of the Roman Catholic Religious Order, the Society of the Sacred Heart. This transaction was first reported in the *Glasgow Herald*. The reaction in Edinburgh to the news was one of indignation. On account of the site and its history, the proposed new convent, it was strongly felt, would be too conspicuous. If another Catholic religious order must be established in the city, then let it be in a much less ostentatious manner. When they had first arrived in Edinburgh to establish a Catholic teachers' training college, the nuns had, however, in addition to religious prejudice, met with interest, and they had received practical help from the two other training colleges already functioning in Edinburgh, Moray House and the Episcopal Training College at Dalry House. The establishment of a college on a much larger scale was facilitated in September 1918 by the passing of the Scottish Education Act which granted Catholics the right to their own schools, and thus their own teacher training colleges. By March 1919, the Scottish Education Department had authorised the nuns of the Society of the Sacred Heart to establish a college providing for one hundred student teachers. This they attempted first at Moray Place and, soon afterwards, because of accommodation problems there, by renting another house at 9 Ainslie Place, the back gate of which opened into the property in Moray Place. However, increased applications for admission created a problem. The nuns' first attempts to purchase the hydropathic at Craiglockhart were unsuccessful, but by July 27th, 1920 negotiations for its acquisition were completed and the religious community and its students moved to Craiglockhart.

The task of making the former hydropathic merely habitable, let alone suitable for a training college, was a formidable one. The building was infested with rats and beetles. The group of women employed to clean the premises soon resigned: the state of the kitchens seemed beyond remedy. In the hydro's one hundred and fifty bedrooms, every carpet was nailed to the floor, as also on the stairs and in the spacious corridors. The nuns themselves set about lifting them, removing curtains, stripping beds, scrubbing, staining, waxing and polishing.

Although at first the vast accommodation of the former hydropathic seemed excessive for the needs of the college, so that it was decided to shut off certain wings, by the second half of the 1920s most of the space was in use, housing a boarding and a day-school in addition to the training college. Before long extensions were built. The boarding-school was transferred to the order's Convent at Kilgraston in Perthshire in 1930. and the day-school was closed a few years ago. The convent chapel with its cloister corridor was opened in 1933 and extended in 1963. The Demonstration School was built in 1957. The building of a new lecture block, hall, gymnasium and a six-storey hall of residence was completed in 1965. All these have been skilfully integrated architecturally with the original building, still forming the centrepiece, suitably redecorated and restructured.

While, over its long history, the pleasant environment of Craiglockhart has remained virtually unspoiled — indeed at times it has been enhanced — in more recent times protests have been made, through letters to the press and in a pamphlet, against developments considered undesirable. The pamphlet, published privately in 1889 by a Craiglockhart resident, expressed concern over the proposed extension of the asylum at Morningside by the purchase of the old mansion-house of Craighouse, the possible erection of other buildings and the closure of much of Easter Craiglockhart Hill to residents of the district, granted right of entry by Dr Alexander Monro *secundus* when he planted the trees on this hill. The author strongly urged that, if the asylum required to expand, it should remove to the outskirts of Edinburgh. Following the acquisition of much of Easter Craiglockhart Hill and the erection of new asylum buildings on the western and southern slopes in 1894, access to the hill is, however, still available to the public. In 1879 Adam Curor of Myreside was involved in the sale of land at Craiglockhart, which included the pond at the base of Easter Craiglockhart Hill which eventually became very popular for skating, curling and boating. In more recent times this pond, in what became "The Happy Valley" recreation complex, has been the property of Edinburgh Corporation. Here the tennis courts became the venue of East of Scotland championship events and tennis stars of world renown have played here. In the spring of 1976, after substantial alterations, Edinburgh Corporation opened the Craiglockhart Sports Centre with a new block, costing £300,000, forming the centrepiece of a sports complex serving the city, and Craiglockhart in particular, a special feature of which are the facilities for water sports on Craiglockhart Pond.

CHAPTER 4

Blackford · Braid

BLACKFORD

Since, from ancient times until relatively recently, the Jordan Burn at the foot of Morningside Road formed the southern boundary of the city, the early chronicles of the lands beyond the Jordan such as Plewlands, Craighouse and Greenbank are strictly outwith the history of South Edinburgh. So, too, the lands of Blackford and Braid. Nevertheless, their origins and development are relevant to its growth.

Blackford of the present day is associated by most Edinburgh citizens with the unspoiled slopes of Blackford Hill, one of the city's pleasantest public parks, with a magnificent panoramic view of Edinburgh and the distant Lothians, Fife and the Highland hills. Below, Blackford Pond and its colony of ducks provide happy hours of relaxation. Blackford has been immortalised by Sir Walter Scott, whose vivid appreciation of its charm as he knew it in his younger days is still easy for the modern visitor to share:

> Blackford! on whose uncultured breast
> Among the broom and thorn and whin;
> A truant-boy I sought the nest,
> Or listed, as I lay at rest,
> While rose, on breezes thin,
> The murmur of the city crowd,
> And from his steeple, jangling loud,
> St Giles' mingling din.

As related in an earlier chapter, it was from Blackford's "uncultured breast" that Scott depicted Lord Marmion surveying the great muster of the Scottish army on the Burgh Muir before its ill-fated march to Flodden.

Blackford first appears on record in 1631, when the lands were known as Champanye, Champunzie or, elsewhere, as Hampany. At that period it was fashionable to give French names to places in the Lothians, especially in West Lothian. It is not known why this name was given to Blackford, or by whom. The place-name Blackford occurs in other parts of Scotland. In 1598 the Magistrates of Edinburgh passed an Act reserving the passage of "twelve ells broad to and from the Pow Burn [later the Jordan Burn] for the use of the town in time of pest and other times as has been of auld". This passage became Blackford Avenue. In 1719 Archibald Brown of Plewlands purchased from Dr James Forrest, M.D. thirty-eight acres of land to the south of the mansion-house of Wester Grange, on the north bank of the Jordan Burn, overlooked by Blackford Hill. Four years later Brown gifted his lands at Greenbank and Plewlands, along with those at Blackford, to his nephew Archibald Brown and these together were for a period known as the wider estate of Blackford. In 1760 Brown's nephew sold his thirty-eight acres below Blackford Hill to Henry Trotter of Mortonhall and this part of Blackford, along with the hill itself, remained in the possession of the Trotter family for many generations. Present-day Mortonhall Road commemorates the Trotters' ownership of land in this district. Oswald Road, bisecting Mortonhall Road and once forming the western boundary of the Trotter lands at Blackford, marks the marriage of Richard Trotter to the daughter of General Sir John Oswald of Dunniker in 1836.

A *Plan of Part of Lands of Blackford* drawn by Robert R. Raeburn in 1875 designates Lt. Colonel Henry Trotter of Mortonhall as the owner at that time. The plan indicates the probable site of Blackford House, although it is not named, which may have been built by Lt. Col. Trotter at a much earlier date as a dower house of his family of Mortonhall. Blackford House stood on the south bank of the Jordan Burn and a photograph

Blackford Farmhouse, showing bridge over the Jordan Burn
Photograph by Thomas Keith; by courtesy of Edinburgh City Libraries

of an ink drawing of it by "J.P." is preserved in the Edinburgh Room of the Edinburgh Public Libraries. The drawing, "Presented by Colonel Trotter of Morton House" (the dower house of Mortonhall House) is undated. It shows the original two-storey house with a plain doorway and, adjoining this at right angles, a more modern and elegant two-storey Georgian extension. The Edinburgh Room also has a valuable collection of photographs of Blackford House and farm (part of the Hurd Bequest) by Thomas Keith, a mid-nineteenth century Edinburgh surgeon of world-wide distinction and a colleague of Professor James Syme of Edinburgh's old Royal Infirmary, who resided at Millbank in the Canaan estate bordering on Blackford. Keith was also pre-eminent in his time as an amateur photographer who worked with the paper negative process, formerly known as the "calotype" process, and associated particularly with the distinguished Edinburgh photographer, David Octavius Hill. One of Keith's Blackford farm photographs is particularly interesting as it illustrates not only the farmhouse itself but also the little stone bridge over the Jordan Burn, which may still be seen today, tastefully covered with flowerbeds. In another photograph, the gable-end of Blackford House itself on the opposite bank of the Jordan Burn from the farmhouse is just discernible.

Apart from the interesting description of Blackford House by Sir Thomas Dick-Lauder in *Scottish Rivers,* and the pleasant reminiscences of his friend and neighbour, the serene elderly Miss Meenie Trotter, daughter of Thomas Trotter, 7th Laird of Mortonhall, who for long resided in Blackford House, other authors have also recalled the house on the banks of the Jordan and its gracious owner. Lord Cockburn in his *Memorials,* a classic autobiography of life in Edinburgh in the latter half of the nineteenth century, pays tribute to the "Singular race of excellent Scotch old ladies" of his time. Those whom he describes range from titled ladies to Mrs Siddons the famous actress and among them is Miss Meenie Trotter. "She", wrote Lord Cockburn, "was of the agrestic order." Unlike those he knew who were most becoming in the drawing-room in rustling silks and who travelled by sedan chair, "Her pleasures lay in the fields and long country walks. Ten miles at a stretch, within a few years of her death was nothing to her. Her attire accorded. But her understanding was fully as masculine. Though slenderly endowed, she did unnoticed acts of liberality for which most of the rich would expect to be advertised. Though lonely, she enjoyed her friends for whom she always had diverting talk and 'a bit of denner'." "Indeed," wrote Lord Cockburn, "she generally sacrificed an ox to hospitality every autumn, which, according to a system of her own, she ate regularly from nose to tail; and as she indulged in him only on Sundays, and with a chosen few, the animal lasted her half through the winter." He remembered her urging Sir Thomas Dick-Lauder to dine with her soon: "For, eh!, Sir Tammas, we're terribly near the tail noo!" One of Miss Trotter's most frequent guests was

Miss Meenie Trotter and Blackford House

By courtesy of Major Trotter of Mortonhall

Mrs Grant of Laggan. Cockburn, in characteristic turn of phrase, described Blackford House as "a melancholy villa".

Margaret Warrender of Bruntsfield House in her *Walks Near Edinburgh* described Miss Trotter as "one of the last of the race of old Scottish ladies, so clever, so original, almost to eccentricity. So idiomatic and plain spoken in their expressions and yet such perfect gentlewomen. Every morning, she bathed in the Jordan which ran pure and sparkling through her garden, and afterwards she walked all over Blackford Hill before breakfast. She was about ninety when she died."

Blackford Hill Station on the Edinburgh and South Side Junction Railway was opened in 1884, and until 1940, when the service stopped, passengers halting here might well have thought they were in a rustic Highland station: the bleating of sheep could be heard from the cluster of pens behind the south platform, Blackford House was in view, pleasantly situated on sloping ground, and on the north side stood the old farmhouse and stone bridge over the Jordan Burn.

Last relic of this bygone rural scene is the sturdy farmhouse, for sixty years the home of two former workers on Blackford farm. Glenisla Gardens, built in 1868, from which the farmhouse is reached, may have been named from the fact that this street descends into the small glen or hollow of the former farm or it may have been named by one of the Trotters of Mortonhall after Glenisla in West Angus to mark the marriage of one of the family to the 3rd Duke of Atholl whose seat, Blair Castle, is near Glenisla. Charterhall Grove, built in 1960, where Blackford House once stood, as also Charterhall Road, take their names from the Trotters' estate in Berwickshire. Looking over the east side of the railway bridge at the foot of Blackford Avenue, the Jordan Burn may be seen running parallel to a large sewage pipe, modestly reduced to ditch-like proportions and no longer exhibiting the rural charms of its earlier course at Woodburn House in Canaan Lane, which recalls how it must have looked in the garden of Blackford House.

Over the busy crossroads of Blackford Avenue, Charterhall Road and West Savile Terrace, several little streets running steeply up the slope of Blackford Hill recall the Trotter ownership of these lands. Maurice Place, built in 1897, commemorates Maurice Raymond Elton, son of the 2nd Baron Gifford and brother of Eva Elton (hence Eva Place), who married Major General Henry Trotter of Mortonhall. In this district Ladysmith Road marks the South African town's heroic defence in the Boer War.

Before proceeding south-east up Blackford Avenue, the impressive architecture of the Reid Memorial Church immediately attracts attention. It was built between 1929 and 1933 under the will of the late William Crambe Reid, in memory of his father William Reid, who for many years was closely associated with the late Dr Guthrie's church. The architect, Leslie G. Thomson, A.R.I.B.A., F.R.I.A.S., built the cathedral-like church in a free and modern Gothic style unrelated to period or locality. The

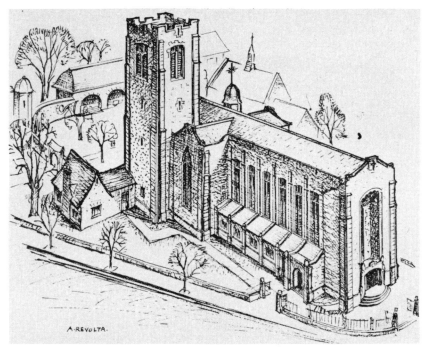

Reid Memorial Church, Blackford

Drawing by Dr A. Revolta

emphasis on vertical lines and the height give a sense of aspiration and loftiness, in keeping with the interior artistic work, illustrating Christ's Ascension into Heaven. The fine exterior sculpture is by Alexander Carrick, R.A. The hewn stone was from Doddington, the facing stone from Craigmillar and the roofing slates from Caithness. The three great stained-glass windows to the east are the work of James Ballantyne, F.S.A. Scot. They illustrate the three basic Christian themes: the Nativity, the Crucifixion and the Ascension. The continued effectiveness of these windows was ensured by the architect's skilful positioning of the church at the busy Blackford crossroads so that the eastern wall of the chancel was sited where no future building could overshadow them, obscuring their source of daylight. Again, on account of the busy and noisy thoroughfare around the church, the cloister court was designed to provide an area of peace and quiet within the church precincts. Around the court are grouped the vestries, session house, hall and the Church Officer's house. On the east side a loggia provides a quiet area of retreat. Within the court's centre arch, a rostrum makes it possible for a speaker to address a gathering assembled in the open. The courtyard was planted with almond trees and Italian cypresses. The wrought-iron work of Thomas Hadden completes the varied features of the grounds. Inside the church is a striking picture of the Last Supper by William R. Lawson, framed in oak. The organ, concealed from the view of the congregation, was designed by the eminent organist Dr Alfred Hollins.

Proceeding south-eastwards up the continuation of Blackford Avenue to its meeting point with West Mains Road, Observatory Road branches steeply to the right. At its entrance is the Harrison Arch, designed by Sydney Mitchell and constructed of red ashlar, with Ionic columns, a pediment and smaller side arches. While this is no longer the most popular entrance route to Blackford Hill, save for cars, historically it is the most appropriate beginning to the chronicles of Blackford. On the arch, inscriptions summarise the salient facts. On the apex of the pediment is a sculpted bust of Lord Provost Harrison, with a Latin inscription below. On the right-hand arch is inscribed: "Blackford Hill was acquired and opened to the public by the Corporation of the City of Edinburgh 1884. The Rt. Hon. Sir George Harrison, LL.D. L.P.", and on the left: "This arch is erected 12.9.1888 to commemorate the work and

The Harrison Arch, Observatory Road, Blackford

Photograph by Mr W. R. Smith

character of George Harrison, Kt, M.P., U.D., whose life was devoted to the public good. Born: 1812. Died 1885."

While Lord Provost Harrison was to have another park and a street named after him in the west of the city, Blackford might well have been named Harrison Park, such were the untiring and determined efforts of this Lord Provost to acquire it for the recreation of Edinburgh's citizens. Harrison's dreams were not easily realised. There was considerable opposition to his repeated proposals to Edinburgh Town Council. The price required by its owners, the Trotters of Mortonhall, for the one hundred and seven acres of Blackford Hill was £8,000. This may now seem a relatively low call on the city's financial resources but Treasurer Boyd strongly argued that it "was not a bargain". Citizens who wished to enjoy Blackford Hill's amenities, he said, should simply pay the annual £1 fee for a key to its various gates rather than gain free access at the city's expense. Harrison, however, won the day, and Edinburgh acquired one of the most attractive public parks in Britain.

Lord Provost Sir George Harrison had much public service to his credit when he died. It had begun with his secretaryship of the Chamber of Commerce in 1856, and later Chairmanship. Representing Newington Ward on Edinburgh Town Council, he became City Treasurer in 1879. During his short term as Lord Provost, he was involved in the restoration of St Giles Cathedral and the opening of the University's new Medical School in Teviot Place. During the tercentenary celebrations of the University in 1882, he was awarded an honorary LL.D. He was knighted in August 1884. Sir George Harrison had wide interests, including connections with France and Italy. In 1860 he founded an Edinburgh branch of the Friends of Italy. He was also much involved in the passing of the important Education Act of 1872. After retiring as Provost he served briefly as a Member of Parliament until his death in 1885. His son John also became City Treasurer, and received a knighthood. When the controversial architect James Gowans went bankrupt and had to sell his unique creation, Rockville, Sir John Harrison purchased it after its short period as a boys' college. The Harrison family lived in Rockville for fifty-eight years.

Soon after its acquisition, Edinburgh Corporation, in 1890, sold three and a half acres on the east slope of Blackford Hill to the Government Office of Works for the building of the Royal Observatory, transferred from Calton Hill in 1894. Today, the Royal Observatory is one of Blackford's, and Edinburgh's, most familiar and colourful landmarks. There is evidence that in 1607 astronomy was being taught at Edinburgh University. Early Master of Arts theses of astronomy students preserved in the University Library reveal that, in 1618, several students observed a phenomenon like that of a comet, subsequently confirmed by Kepler's treatise of 1619. In 1674 James Gregory, of the academically distinguished Aberdeenshire family, was appointed to the Edinburgh University Chair

The Edinburgh Royal Observatory, Blackford Hill

By courtesy of the "Scotsman"

346

of Mathematics at the early age of thirty-seven. He was the inventor of the Gregorian reflecting telescope. He died suddenly soon after his appointment and it was not until fifty years after his death that serious astronomical work is again reported from Edinburgh. The new impetus came from James Short, a telescope maker of international repute. Short's work encouraged his teacher, the Edinburgh University Professor of Mathematics, Colin MacLaurin, to press for the establishment of a properly equipped astronomical observatory in Edinburgh. However, despite the raising of funds, principally through special lectures given by Professor MacLaurin, it was not until thirty years after his death, and eight years after that of Short, that the foundation stone of the observatory was laid on Calton Hill. This first establishment did not flourish. The building originally proposed by James Craig, famous architect of the New Town, had not been followed, and the observatory had not been adequately equipped. As one of the many fruits of Edinburgh's Golden Age in the latter half of the eighteenth century, an Astronomical Institute of Edinburgh was founded, the first British Society devoted entirely to the pursuit of astronomy. Many of the capital's most distinguished citizens joined this Institute and soon sufficient funds had been accumulated to found a new observatory. In 1818 Edinburgh's second observatory was founded on Calton Hill, close to the site of the original one. William Playfair was the architect and the building, a striking cruciform structure, remains one of Edinburgh's most prominent landmarks. This new establishment was very well equipped.

In 1786 a Regius Chair of Astronomy had been established in Edinburgh University and James Blair, a Scottish naval surgeon, was appointed to it in the same year. Important developments followed Blair's death. During George IV's visit to Edinburgh in 1822, the establishment on Calton Hill became the Royal Observatory. In 1834 the post of Regius Professor of Astronomy at the University was combined with that of Her Majesty's Astronomer Royal for Scotland, the dual responsibility remaining to the present day. Scotland's first Astronomer Royal was Professor Thomas Henderson, appointed in August 1834. He carried out much important work from Calton Hill, as did his successors. Professor Charles Piazzi Smyth, appointed in 1846, instituted the link between the Royal Observatory at Calton Hill and the firing of the one o'clock gun from Edinburgh Castle, controlled from the Royal Observatory since 1861. Professor Smyth's successor in 1889, Professor Ralph Copland, was responsible for planning the transfer of the Royal Observatory from Calton Hill to Blackford Hill. Calton Hill had become too enclosed by the city, with its problems of smoke and light, A site was required outwith the city but not too far from the University. After much study, Blackford Hill was chosen and three and a half acres of land purchased from Edinburgh Corporation. The new observatory was opened by Lord Balfour of Burleigh on April 7th, 1896. It was able to meet the requirements of an observatory equal to the world's greatest at that time. The stately stone building with its large green copper turrets and embellished stonework, and its commanding position, was regarded as a major architectural contribution to Victorian Edinburgh. Invaluable to the new establishment was the famous Crawford Collection of telescopes and early books and manuscripts gifted by Lord Lindsay, the 26th Earl of Crawford, brought from his own observatory of Dunecht. This generous gesture is commemorated by a plaque on the exterior wall of the observatory.

The history of the Royal Observatory at Blackford Hill is an important chapter in any account of modern astronomy. During the reign of successive Astronomers Royal, important contributions have been made to the subject. A major expansion of the observatory took place in the early 1960s with the building of a new laboratory and office block, the installation of a novel sixteen-inch twin telescope and a substantial increase of staff. In more recent times the administration of the Royal Observatory has passed from the Scottish Office to the Science Research Council. There are now some eighty members of staff. The expansion has occurred in collaboration with the University's development of its own Department of Astronomy providing for undergraduate and postgraduate students. The work of the observatory is at present mainly devoted to studies of the physical constitution and chemical composition of stars and of inter-stellar matter, and to investigation of the evolution of stars and galaxies. Research work and systematic observation are co-ordinated with that carried out at the Edinburgh establishment's observatory at Monte Porzio Catone near Frascati in Italy. The observatory is also involved in research made possible by rockets and satellites.

As a result of the growth of the city southwards, close to the observatory, resulting in interference with its delicate instruments, and the infrequency of clear nights suitable for telescopic studies, the Edinburgh establishment, in common with its counterparts in other parts of the world, has been forced to collaborate in the setting up of international observatories in more suitable parts of the world. Edinburgh is involved in the choice of such sites.

A joint Edinburgh Royal Observatory team is at present working with a sixty-inch infra-red telescope at Tenerife. The observatory has also recently been made responsible for the construction of a one-hundred-and-fifty-inch infra-red telescope, the largest in the world, to be mounted at Marma Kee in Hawaii at an altitude of nearly fourteen thousand feet. Thus the Royal Observatory on Blackford Hill maintains its traditions in the forefront of the world-wide advance of astronomy.

From the Royal Observatory a broad pathway gives easy ascent to the summit of Blackford Hill, from which, five hundred feet above sea-level, interesting features of the immediate landscape may be observed. On the highest point of the hill itself is a striking contrast between ancient and modern. Under the shadow of the gigantic television relay station have been found cup-and-ring markings from the second millennium B.C. Some evidence has also been found of an ancient fortification. There are, however, so many stone remains here of more recent installations (including the base of an anti-aircraft gun) that it takes a skilled archaeologist to identify those of earliest times. Below the north face of the hill, Blackford Pond may be seen to advantage. Maps which show the seven ancient lochs of Edinburgh, such as Corstorphine, Lochend and the South or Burgh Loch (the Nor'Loch once on the site of Princes Street Gardens was dammed artificially in relatively recent times), also reveal two smaller ones of some interest in the history of Morningside. These are Jordanville Loch, referred to in an earlier chapter, on the Jordan Burn and Blackford Loch, which lay on the course of this burn, north east of Blackford Hill within the area today bounded by Blackford Avenue, Mayfield Road, West Savile Terrace and Relugas Road. Henry M. Cadell in *Some Ancient Landmarks of Midlothian,* which contains a special map, considered Blackford Loch to have existed in prehistoric times. Cadell suggests that in ancient times Blackford Loch would alternatively have drained and filled the Jordan Burn. The burn still flows along what was the southern boundary of Blackford Loch. Despite its name, the loch had no connection with Blackford Pond, which may be presumed to be simply the catchment area of water draining from Blackford Hill. Some years ago there was a small stream running into the south-east end of the pond but this now seems to have dried up. One report of the purchase of Blackford Hill by Edinburgh Corporation refers to the pond as being part of "Egypt

Blackford Pond skating scene

349

field". This would seem to be extending the district of Egypt further eastwards than shown on maps of its location such as the *Barony of Braid* drawn in 1772. There is nothing in the records to indicate that Egypt was ever the property of the Trotters of Mortonhall.

Over thirty years before the citizens of Edinburgh acquired free access to Blackford Hill, the pond had become the home ground of the thriving Waverley Curling Club, established in 1848. In the Edinburgh Almanack for 1885, the curling club is referred to as at "Blackford, Grange". The President at that date was J. Smart, R.S.A., and the Vice President, William Scott. In the not too distant memory of many Morningside residents, Blackford Pond was also frequently the scene of winter skating and the news quickly spread when the pond was "bearing". At night it was "floodlit" by gas flares, with very many families enjoying the sport. It was on Blackford Pond, Lord Cockburn relates in his *Memorials,* that he first learned to skate and where he "practised with unfailing ardour ever since".

On the steep south-western aspect of Blackford Hill, facing the allotments and Midmar Drive, were once the shooting targets used by the Edinburgh Volunteers, whose rendezvous was the Volunteers Rest (now the Volunteer Arms) at the corner of Canaan Lane. The route to the shooting butts, before the villas of the Cluny-Midmar district had been built, was by what is now Braid Road and then through a gap in the hawthorn hedge on the east side and across open fields. The rallying place of the Volunteers was the field at the junction of Midmar Drive and Hermitage Drive. In more recent times this green space with its picturesque little island of trees was a pasture for sheep brought to the Morningside Road Station goods yard at the end of Maxwell Street and, to the consternation of motorists, shepherded across Morningside Road and thence to Hermitage Drive.

The summit of Blackford Hill is also a good vantage point from which to note the pleasant situation of the Braid Estate Recreation Club. Located as it is within the district of Blackford, the question arises of why the club should bear the name of Braid. The reason is historical. The site of the bowling green and tennis courts, while bordering on the boundaries of Blackford Pond, was in fact originally within the estate of Braid. In 1890 the Superiors of the Braid Estate, the Trustees of the Gordons of Cluny, introduced a bowling green and lawn-tennis courts "for the use and enjoyment of feuars in a specified area of the estate". The feuars concerned eventually repaid the cost of the recreation ground and in due course received a feu-charter from the Gordon Trustees. The recreation club which came to be formally established held its first meeting in premises in Morningside where many schemes were first mooted — Torrance's Tea Rooms at the corner of Belhaven Terrace and Comiston Road. Here in April 1892, at a well attended gathering of "the reconstructed clubs" (which suggests a slightly earlier actual origin), presided

350

over by Mr Cargill, a number of decisions were taken: non-feuars on the Braid Estate were to be eligible for admission (hence "reconstructed clubs"), although feuars would be given preferential consideration. In 1892 the memberships of the bowling and tennis clubs numbered fifty-eight, of whom thirty-nine were Braid feuars. Forty years later, the club records reveal that, of its one hundred and ten members, only seventeen were resident in Braid. In 1974 only three members were feuars in Braid, and it is these who still bear the special responsibility for maintenance of the grounds.

At the first meeting in 1892, it was also resolved to apply for admission to the Association of Bowling Clubs of Edinburgh and Leith. The first bowling match took place on Saturday, May 7th, 1892. For the first few years the only clubhouse accommodation was in the Bowl House on the west side of the bowling green, now used as a tool-shed and shelter. In 1900 a fund-raising concert was held in Morningside Public Halls (now the Dunedin Hall in Morningside Drive) and a year later the present handsome pavilion was opened. Extensions were added in 1930. Many important international bowling matches have taken place on the Braid green and members of Braid have represented Scotland on several occasions.

While the magnificent panoramic view to the north of Blackford Hill reveals the expanse of the city, that to the south presents a very different scene. The eye ascends from the "furzy hills of Braid" to the higher backcloth of the Pentland Hills. To the left the ancient district of Liberton is seen, with Liberton Tower at the eastern end of Braid Hills Drive providing a prominent landmark. Below is the great gorge dividing Blackford Hill and the Braid Hills, through which, emerging from the Hermitage of Braid, flows the Braid Burn, passing the old Blackford Quarry, the lower slopes of Craigmillar Park Golf Course and the modern skyline of the King's Buildings of Edinburgh University, and proceeding onwards to Liberton Dams. From the heights of Corbie's Craig, south-west of the Royal Observatory, on the lower scree of which an ancient cup-and-ring marked stone was discovered in 1926, it is not difficult to imagine from the dramatic appearance of the gorge below that this was cut out by a great land glacier as it slowly slid eastwards towards the sea. The valley from Comiston by the Hermitage of Braid to Liberton Dams was further deepened by the powerful flow of waters from the melting ice. Conclusive evidence of the part played by a glacier in the shaping of this gorge is to be found on a rock at the entrance to the former Blackford Quarry. This cave-like structure, known as the Agassiz Rock, was so named in 1840 when Charles MacLaren, the editor of the *Scotsman,* brought it to the attention of his friend, the distinguished Swiss geologist Louis Agassiz of Neuchatel. After careful study of the grooves on the rock, Agassiz made the emphatic comment commemorated on a plaque on the rocks, now protected by railings: "This is the work of the ice." While various writers

351

The Agassiz Rock

By courtesy of the Department of Geology, Edinburgh University

have questioned the opinion of Agassiz, the more recent research of Professor Gordon Davies of Trinity College, Dublin, has confirmed that, in fact, the Swiss geologist's statement was correct. The grooves in the rock were cut, not by a floating iceberg but, in the far-off ice age, by a glacier. Agassiz's observations at Blackford stimulated research in Scotland on the effects of land ice in various parts of the country. They also gave rise to much controversy in geological circles in London. From the Swiss geologist's comments, it has also been concluded that the great valley from Comiston, along the Braidburn Valley, the Hermitage of Braid and on to Liberton Dams, was carved out by glacial action and, later, by the powerful waters from melting ice.

Blackford Quarry was first opened in 1826. Prior to this, from 1815 to 1819, stone had been quarried from Salisbury Crags, which yielded one hundred tons a day. Seven years after the closure of the work at Salisbury Crags, Blackford Quarry was established. About 1816 MacAdam had introduced his method for strengthening road surfaces, which required certain types of stone. The dark grey andesite lava rock of Blackford Quarry proved ideal for this purpose and for twenty-five years the quarry was a major source. In 1951 the quarry owners sought permission to extend their operations. Many local residents, however, felt strongly that, during the twenty-five years of the quarry's existence, Blackford Hill had already become badly disfigured and that grave danger was threatened to children playing on this part of the hill. Furthermore, the various scientific departments of Edinburgh University, rapidly developing at the King's Buildings complex at West Mains Road, had found that their instruments were seriously affected by vibrations from explosives used in Blackford Quarry. In 1952 a Public Inquiry was initiated which, a year later, resulted in the Secretary of State for Scotland's ruling that not only was the extension of the quarry's work not permissible but also that it was to cease its operations. This was done soon afterwards. Opposite the quarry, an attractive pathway on the banks of a virtually dried-up stream, traditionally known as "the dry waterfall", climbs steeply up to Braid Hills Drive. This is known as the Howe of Dean path. No account of Blackford in more recent times would be complete without reference to the man who earned the title of "the bishop of Blackford Hill". This was the late Edinburgh Town Councillor George Horne, who for very many years conducted open-air mission services in the natural amphitheatre on Blackford Hill above the pond.

BRAID

A systematic study of the ancient lands of the Braid Estate is best begun by returning from Blackford by Cluny Gardens and entering Braid by the original route to the south, Braid Road. Before proceeding to the Hermitage of Braid, with which the earliest recorded history of the estate begins, several features of more recent times merit attention. A watercolour by E. Michie, A.R.S.A. of the little iron building which was the original Braid Church, built near the junction of Braid Road and Cluny Gardens, reveals the pleasant, rural charm of Braid in 1883. The little church is surrounded by open fields, with no houses standing between it and the Braid Hills. Braid Road, the old Wester Hiegait skirting the ancient Burgh Muir, or, as it appears in early maps, the "Road to Moffat" or the "Road to Biggar", was lined with hawthorn hedges. Down this road into Edinburgh travelled a succession of historical figures — men of the Roman legions, Edward I of England, the Regent Morton, Cromwell, the Covenanters and Bonnie Prince Charlie.

Cluny Parish Church, until 1974 St Matthew's Parish Church, on the south corner of Braid Road and Cluny Gardens, stands near the site of the Braid iron church. The history of St Matthew's, a parish church of the established Church of Scotland, opened on May 4th, 1890, has at least one feature in common with that of Braid Church, opened on July 10th, 1887, which was of the United Presbyterian denomination: it had also originated in a little iron church opened on November 11th, 1883 on the site of what is now 2 Cluny Avenue. Braid's iron church had been opened nearly eleven months earlier on January 27th, 1883. While Braid was established independently of any other church in the Morningside district, St Matthew's was originally a "mission station" of Morningside Parish Church at Churchhill. On May 22nd, 1883, a meeting of the congregation of Morningside Parish Church discussed the need for increased accommodation. The alternatives were either to enlarge the church or to erect an iron church further down the hill, in Morningside. The latter proposal was adopted. A site was obtained in Cluny Avenue and in November 1883 the iron church was opened, having cost £650. The first minister of the embryonic St Matthew's was the Reverend George Milligan, B.D.

In October 1886, the congregation of Morningside Parish Church again discussed the problems of accommodation, deciding that a permanent church should be built, to be named St Matthew's. The site at the corner of Braid Road and Cluny Gardens was purchased. A notable Edinburgh architect of the time was engaged, Hippolyte Blanc R.S.A., who had designed Christ Scottish Episcopal Church at Holy Corner. The foundation stone of St Matthew's was laid by the then Lord High Commissioner of the General Assembly of the Church of Scotland, the Earl of Hopetoun, on June 1st, 1888. Two years later the new church was dedicated, on May 2nd, 1890, the special preacher being the Reverend J. Marshall Lang, D.D., then of the Barony Church in Glasgow, and formerly minister of Morningside Parish Church. The opening service took place on May 4th. The cost of the cathedral-like church was eventually in the region of £20,000. After the opening of St Matthew's, the vacated iron church in Cluny Avenue was transferred to Bruntsfield Gardens, to become the nucleus of St Mark's Church, later called St Oswald's Church, eventually built at Montpelier Park. In his notes, the architect of St Matthew's describes his work, modelled on late-thirteenth-century church architecture. Of large proportions, the nave measures eighty by forty-two feet, and presents a skilfully conceived effect of great height. The fine timber ceiling is decorated with coloured ornament. Side aisles were provided to enable members of the congregation to enter or leave less conspicuously. The north and south transepts provide additional accommodation without requiring disproportionate elongation of the church. A congregation of one thousand can be seated comfortably. The choir, chancel, and vestry were completed some time after the official opening of the church. The church has many fine stained-glass windows. Those on the east, illustrating the authors of the four Gospels, were designed by Sir Edward Burne-Jones, while those on the west, added in 1905 to mark the twenty-first anniversary of the formation of the congregation, are the work of Messrs Percy Bacon & Co. in London. They illustrate four scenes in the life of Christ and were donated by members of the congregation. The marble steps to the chancel were

St Matthew's Iron Church, Cluny Avenue

Laying the Foundation Stone of St Matthew's Church, June 1888

By courtesy of Rev. Dr Robert Mathers

gifted by domestic servants who were members of the congregation and of whom there were very many in the "big houses" of Morningside from the end of the nineteenth century until the 1930s. The pulpit, baptismal font and very fine brass lectern, along with many other church furnishings, were gifts from individual members of the congregation. In the architect's original plan, the church was to have had a tower and spire rising to a height of one hundred and fifty feet above the present ventilating fleche, but these were never completed. In April 1896 the well-appointed church halls were opened.

The beautifully designed and equipped church was regarded as unique among Edinburgh churches of the latter part of the nineteenth century. The chaste yet ornate chancel is in particular still most highly regarded. On the wall of the north transept, a large panel of Pericot marble, embellished with gold and in the form of a Celtic cross based on that of St Martin at Iona, the creation of Pilkington-Jackson who resided in Jordan Lane, fittingly commemorates the minister who, during his twenty-nine years of service, endeared himself to the people of St Matthew's. This was the Rev. Frank Hale Martin, B.D., called to his parish ministry at St Matthew's in 1912, and who died in 1941. In January 1974 a large congregational gathering in St Matthew's Church bade farewell to the Rev. Robert C. M. Mathers, D.D., who had succeeded the Reverend Martin and continued as parish minister for thirty-two years. He retired at this time in the interests of the imminent union of St Matthew's with South Morningside Church to form Cluny Parish Church. In addition to his long, dedicated service to St Matthew's, Rev. Robert Mathers had also convened many important Church of Scotland committees.

Since its establishment, the activities of the many St Matthew's organisations have not been confined by parish boundaries. For over twenty years, practical service has been given to the Simon Square Centre of the Edinburgh and Leith Cripple Aid Society, to handicapped children through supporting the work of Challenger Lodge, and in arranging short holidays for crippled men at Wiston Lodge near Biggar. Some years ago, the success of a special fund-raising campaign enabled the congregation to purchase a commodious villa at 3 Cluny Gardens. This became St Matthew's Church House, serving the needs of church organisations, and being used also as a daily lunch club for Morningside's senior citizens. St Matthew's played an important part in developing closer understanding between the various religious denominations in Morningside in what is now known as the Ecumenical Movement. In 1969 a well attended joint service was held when the special preacher was the late Right Rev. Columban Mulcahy, O.C.R., Abbot of the Roman Catholic Cistercian Abbey at Nunraw in East Lothian.

In January 1974 St Matthew's and its near neighbour, South Morningside Church, entered into union to become Cluny Parish Church, under the ministry of the newly appointed Rev. George A. M. Munro. The traditions of each of the former churches are preserved. The first example of this occurred in February 1975 when the former 55th (St Matthew's) Company of the Boys' Brigade, now the 55th (Cluny) Company, celebrated its Diamond Jubilee with a dinner in the church hall on February 22nd and a Thanksgiving Service in the church on the 23rd, conducted by the Rev. G. A. M. Munro, the special preacher being the Rev. Bill Whalley, former St Matthew's assistant minister and Boys' Brigade chaplain. During its sixty years, the 55th has become more than just one of St Matthew's many youth organisations: it has become one of Morningside's most valuable institutions, a countless succession of boys from widely varying social and educational backgrounds having passed through its ranks, learning a unique sense of comradeship, tradition and loyalty, as the Diamond Jubilee reunion demonstrated.

South Morningside Parish Church, at the corner of Braid Road and Cluny Drive, following the union with St Matthew's has remained unused while a decision is being made concerning its future. Its history provides interesting insights into the growth of Morningside itself. Originally, when opened in June 1892, it was known as Braid Road Free Church, but soon afterwards the name was changed to South Morningside Free Church, to avoid confusion with Braid Church. The date of the first informal meeting of its pioneers is not on record. While Mair gives this as some time in 1879, the official records of the church cite the first meeting as having been held on January 14th, 1889, in the house of the Rev. Alexander Martin of the Free Church at 4 Nile Grove. Those present decided "to open the services of Morningside Free Church in the Hall, South Morningside Drive on the Sabbath, 20th curt". Bills were to be printed and displayed in various shops in Morningside to publicise the service. The hall referred to, also known as Morningside Hall, later became the Dunedin Hall. At this opening service, proposals to build a new Free Church were well supported. A site was obtained from the Gordon of Cluny Trustees on the Braid Estate, at the corner of what was then Egypt Avenue, now Cluny Drive, and Braid Road. Dr R. Rowand Anderson was appointed architect and a provisional committee campaigned to raise funds. An interim Kirk Session was recruited from the first Morningside Free Church then occupying what is now Morningside Baptist Church near the corner of Colinton Road and Holy Corner. A legacy of £7,000 left by a Morningside resident to build a Free Church "on the outskirts of Edinburgh" was applied for but was given instead towards the building of a new church at Parsons Green. The building of the new South Morningside Free Church, therefore, had to be financed locally. The church hall was opened first, in September 1889, and a few months later the Rev. Charles A. Salmond, D.D. was appointed the first minister, a manse being provided at 9 Cluny Drive, which was later moved to 8 Midmar Gardens. The foundation stone of the church itself was laid on January 22nd, 1891 and the opening service held in the completed building on June 16th, 1892. The church is Gothic in style, built from stone from Hailes Quarry in Dumfriesshire, and has seating accommodation for eight hundred. The total cost of church and hall, originally estimated at £8,500, was finally £11,030. Even at this increased cost, long periods of bad weather and rising costs of raw materials caused the builder to lose heavily. Contributions toward completing the church were made by Morningside Free Church at Holy Corner, and other Free Churches at Grange and Viewforth, the Barclay and in north Edinburgh. A steady increase in the congregation of South Morningside Church was due, as in the case of Braid and St Matthew's, to the development of transport from the city out to Morningside, especially the Suburban Railway in 1884, and the rapid growth of the suburb. While the pioneer congregation in 1889 had numbered a mere fourteen, by 1890 it was sixty-seven, and four hundred five years later. Amongst the many active organisations which arose was the Morningside Literary Association, revived in 1895 from an earlier society founded in 1879, which, with undulating support, flourished until 1933. South Morningside Free Church took part in the Union of 1929 and was re-named as of the Church of Scotland. In joining with St Matthew's, South Morningside Church brought to this union its own traditions in the religious life of Morningside.

When South Morningside Free Church Hall was opened in 1889 it was the first building in what is now Cluny Drive. Opposite the church, on the south-west corner of Cluny Drive and Braid Road, were for many years the tennis courts of the Pentland Club. A few yards uphill, in the middle of Braid Road, opposite No. 66, there may still be seen the two celebrated Braid Road "hanging stanes". During recent road repairs the two stones were reset. They were found to be five inches thick and, strangely, exactly one metre square. Many writers have given their versions of the highway robbery which took place at this spot on November 23rd, 1814, amongst these Robert Louis Stevenson in *Edinburgh: Picturesque Notes,* and Miss Margaret Warrender in *Walks Near Edinburgh.* Stevenson recalled how, as a child, he had been shown a flat stone on the roadway where "there stood in old days a crow-haunted gibbet, with two bodies hanged in chains. People of a willing fancy were persuaded, and sought to persuade others, that this stone was never dry. And no wonder, they would add, for the two men had only stolen fourpence between them." Miss Warrender tells a similar story.

That there was much more to the case than that "the two men had only stolen fourpence between them" may be studied in great detail in the report of the High Court trial which appeared in *The Edinburgh Evening Courant* for December 22nd, 1814. The two men in the dock were Thomas Kelly and Henry O'Neil. They were being tried on three charges of highway robbery, the first two in places outwith Edinburgh. The third

The single "Hanging Stone" in Braid Road prior to the uncovering of a second one

Photograph by Mr W. R. Smith

charge was the Braid Road robbery. The case for the prosecution was that on November 23rd, 1814, David Loch, a carter in Biggar, travelling along the road about 6 o'clock in the evening from the Briggs of Braid or Braid's Burn, was pulled from the horse he was bringing to Edinburgh by the accused, who struck him on the head with the butt end of a pistol to the effusion of his blood, threatened to knock out his brains if he made any resistance and then and there robbed him of four one-pound banknotes, twenty shillings in silver, a tuppeny loaf of bread and a spleuchan or leather tobacco pouch. The accused pleaded not guilty and the trial proceeded by jury. In the context of the trial's account, the Briggs of Braid referred to was not the bridge over the Jordan Burn at the foot of Morningside Road, commonly called the Briggs o' Braid, but the bridge over the Braid Burn at the entrance to the Hermitage of Braid.

During the assault and robbery, David Loch's cries for help were heard by Andrew Black, a smith and farrier at Braidburn dairy farm opposite the entrance to the Hermitage of Braid, who, with his friend Samuel Payne hurried to Loch's assistance. They found him bleeding badly, quite seriously injured, and took him to the house of a Mr Scott at Myreside. Both witnesses so testified. The jury, unanimously and without retiring, found Kelly and O'Neil guilty. The judge, the Lord Justice Clerk, the Honourable David Boyle, in pronouncing sentence, emphasized that, in view of the prevalence of such crimes, stern measures were required. He concluded: "You are to be executed, not at the ordinary place (the Tolbooth Prison) but on the spot where you robbed and assaulted David Loch, or as near as possible to that spot." The judge appealed to the condemned men to "pray fervently that you may come to a state of heart-felt sorrow and contrition and hope for access to the favour of God in that world to which you are soon to go." The condemned men then made their last confessions to a priest and, "after spending twenty minutes at their devotions below the gallows", were hanged at Braid Road on January 25th, 1815. *The Edinburgh Evening Courant* reported that "we never on any occasion witnessed so great a crowd, who had walked out in a snowstorm the three miles from the High Street." The procession accompanying the condemned men left the High Street at 1.15 p.m., led by a large contingent of police, High Constables of Edinburgh, City Officers with halberds, Magistrates, ministers of the church and priests. A horse-drawn cart bore the two prisoners, surrounded by the City Guard. While Grant in *Old and New Edinburgh* states that the two robbers were buried near an old thorn tree in the hedge opposite the gallows, other more recent writers have reported that, in fact, they were buried in Greyfriars churchyard. This was the last execution in Scotland for highway robbery.

A few yards further up Braid Road, on the right, a garage occupies the site of the third of Morningside's early iron churches. In 1887 the congregation of Christ Scottish Episcopal Church at Holy Corner considered establishing a mission chapel at Blackford, but this was not pursued. In 1893 the Morningside Hall in Morningside Drive was hired for £52 per annum to provide services for Episcopalians living south of the Jordan Burn. In 1896 a site was obtained at the south corner of Braid Road and Comiston Terrace and, on July 2nd of that year, the little iron church, known familiarly in Morningside as "the tin Kirk", was opened. It accommodated two hundred and fifty people and was dedicated to St Fillan, the eighth-century Scottish saint. By 1900 the tin Kirk's roll numbered two hundred and eighty-five. Six years later the site was required for the completion of the great house-building programme in this area and the little church was closed. It was sold to a purchaser in St Boswells, where it stood for long on the west side of the road passing southwards through this border town. A small Scottish Episcopal Church dedicated to St Fillan was opened at Buckstone Drive in 1937, thus thirty years later succeeding the original tin Kirk in Braid Road.

Immediately beyond its intersection with Braidburn Terrace and Hermitage Drive, Braid Road descends steeply and crosses over the Braid Burn. On the right, the triangular site of the Mortonhall Tennis Club, in earlier times a curling pond, was once the location of Braidburn dairy. It was here that Andrew Black, the farrier, heard the cries of David Loch during the Braid Road robbery and hurried to his assistance. A number of

Braidburn Dairy Farm, opposite the entrance to the Hermitage of Braid

By courtesy of
Mr Gilmour Main

The Curling Pond, which became Mortonhall Tennis Courts

By courtesy of
Mr George Anderson

Morningside residents still have postcards of the dairy which stood opposite the entrance gates to the Hermitage of Braid, and was for long owned by a family named Duff.

In Joseph Laing Waugh's classic Scottish tale, *Robbie Doo,* something of the atmosphere of the old village of Morningside is captured. The most haunting incident in the story occurred near the original stone bridge over the Braid Burn at the entrance to the Hermitage. The Braid Road, originally referred to as the road to Biggar or Moffat, was the main route of farmers and carriers from the south coming in to Edinburgh. In Waugh's tale, Robert Dow (Robbie Doo), a Biggar carrier, is returning from Edinburgh with his young son, who tells the story: "We were amaist clear o' the toon and gaun doon a lang steep hill into Morningside when my faither noticed that Darlin's off hin' shoe was a bit loose, so we had to stop at a smiddy at the Toll-bar to get it made siccar. The smith was an auldish man wi' a waddle in his walk, and when he cam oot and lookit at my faither he put his hand on his broo and said 'Sir' to him...When we were crossin' a brig ower what's caa'd the Braid Burn — a bonnie wimplin stream it was, I mind — my faither, wha was walkin' by the front cairt wheel had just dune tellin' me about a thief wha had been publicly hanged near the spot, when, on lookin' up, we baith saw a great big mastiff comin' doon the brae in front o' us. A lady came doon the brae ahint the dug..." The lady, named Elsie, of great beauty and obvious fine breeding, turned pale at the sight of the lad's "faither". The strange, moving encounter and brief conversation between "the lady and my faither" is best read in this passage of *Robbie Doo.* It was this lady's name which the lad's father breathed amongst his last words on his death-bed.

Before passing through the gates of the Hermitage of Braid to explore the more ancient history of this large estate, we should consider the old toll-house which once stood at the Briggs o' Braid at the foot of Morningside Road. As related in an earlier chapter, in 1888 this house was removed from its original site and re-erected stone-by-stone where it now stands. Proof of its origin may still be seen on a lintel at the rear of the house which still bears the number "269", as it did when it stood in Morningside Road. If we proceed along the pleasant path beside the Braid Burn, into the grounds of the Hermitage, the mansion-house soon comes into view. In relation to the earliest history of this estate, the house, built in 1785, is relatively modern, The recorded chronicles of the lands of Braid began nearly five centuries before, when the original owner's residence was a castle. Sir Henry de Brad, Brade or Breda (the forms of his name vary in the records), who owned these lands during the reign of William the Lion (1165-1214), probably inherited them from his father, the first owner, a Flemish Knight who came north to Scotland during the reign of David I, from whom he may have received their superiority. Other knights of this Scottish King were awarded the lands of Pentland, Gilmerton, Liberton, Craiglockhart, Inverleith and Restalrig. The name of the lands of Braid perpetuates that of Sir Henry de Brad, though other origins of the name have been suggested. Some say that it is derived from the Gaelic *braghaid,* meaning "upper park", or from the Irish *braid* meaning "a narrow gorge".

Sir Henry de Brad enjoyed a high office of state: he was Sheriff of Edinburgh and a judge in the courtroom of Edinburgh Castle. He was also responsible for collecting all rents due to the Crown and for leading the King's army into battle. His two sons, Richard and Ralph, were graduates of a European University and entered the service of the Church, Richard in the diocese of Glasgow. By 1250 another Sir Henry de Brad had succeeded to the Braid estate. The records associate him with the foundation of the Chapel of St Catherine on Pentland moor and with the ownership of the estate of Bavelaw, situated on the Pentlands just south of Balerno. The family of de Brad appears to have become extinct in Scotland by about 1380.

The next name associated with ownership of the Braid estate was that of Fairley, but this was not until the reign of Mary, Queen of Scots. While Mary was held prisoner in Edinburgh Castle by Kirkcaldy of Grange, Sir Robert Fairley, a supporter of the Queen, suffered attacks on his property at Braid by soldiers from the Castle. In 1571 a band of these set about the miller of Braid and were looting his house when the noise brought Sir Robert to the rescue. By nature a peaceful, quiet man, he requested the soldiers to depart. Merely amused, they continued to remove the miller's possessions, whereupon Sir Robert left, returning shortly afterwards armed with a two-handed sword, with which he successfully drove off the attackers, killing one of them. This is the Sir Robert Fairley who, during a severe epidemic of the plague in Edinburgh in 1585, gave his three "brew houssis" at Littil Egypt for the production of beer for the "seik fok on the muir" and thus earned the commendation of Edinburgh Town Council. Fairley's gesture as recorded in the city's records provides the first reference to the district of Littil Egypt.

In 1603 Sir Robert's son, John, acquired the late-sixteenth-century Bruntsfield House and was responsible for restoring and extending it. Another son, Alexander, married Martha Knox, daughter of the celebrated reformer. He was given the lands of Over Braid, above the southern slopes of the Hermitage.

In 1610, during Sir Robert Fairley's ownership, the first indication is given of the extent of the Braid estate. Its western boundary was what is now Comiston Road and Pentland Terrace. On the east, the lower slopes of Blackford Hill separated Braid from the lands of Mortonhall. The Braid Hills, along the still extant boundary wall of Mortonhall Golf Club, formed the southern aspect, while the northern frontier was the Jordan Burn. Nether Plewlands (now Greenbank) was included, but this was sold to Patrick Elois, an Edinburgh merchant, in 1610.

By 1631 the Fairleys' ownership of Braid had ended and the lands

Sir William Dick, seventeenth-century owner of the Braid Estate

had passed to a man whose life saw so incredible a change of fortune that his story was told in Edinburgh for generations. This was William Dick, the son of an Orkney merchant, who became extremely wealthy through trading in the Baltic and Mediterranean, and by his steady acquisition of land. Indeed, at one period it was said of him that he could travel from Linlithgow to North Berwick and all the way be within his own lands. At the height of his prosperity his personal estate was estimated to be worth £226,000 Scots; it would make him a multi-millionaire today. In March 1631 he purchased the Grange of St Giles from John Cant, and in August of the same year acquired the Braid estate from Sir Robert Fairley. During his ownership of Braid, he extended its size to four hundred and twelve acres. From 1638 until 1640, William Dick was Provost of Edinburgh. An ardent Royalist and Covenanter, he made substantial loans to the Crown and Parliament, for which he received a Knighthood from Charles I. Sir Walter Scott in *The Heart of Midlothian* describes Dick emptying bags of silver coins from the window of his house in the High Street for the assistance of the army. In 1641 much of the money he had lent to the Scottish Parliament was repaid. It was his lending of money for the Royalist cause in England which led to his downfall. When Cromwell came to power, these loans were not recognised as a liability and, not only was he not repaid, but he was also condemned by Cromwell and fined £64,943. Faced with financial disaster, Sir William set out for London to meet his creditors, one of whom had him seized and confined to the debtors' prison at Westminster, where he died in 1655, with, it was said, not even enough money left "to enable his widow give him a decent burial". Soon after Dick's death, a remarkable pamphlet was published which

"The World and a Friend", famous oak cabinet of Sir William Dick of Braid

By courtesy of Sir George Dick Lauder
Photograph by Mr W. R. Smith

related his misfortunes and set out his petitions to the Crown and Parliament for repayment of the substantial sums due to him. It contains a series of illustrations, including one of Dick's great trading fleet during the days of his prosperity and the tragic scene in prison, where he is shown being visited by his wife and small children. Dick's widow and descendants continued to live in the heavily mortgaged estate of Braid until 1676, as also at the Grange of St Giles and in other properties which Dick had purchased for them in his lifetime.

The ancestry of the Dick-Lauder family, which stemmed from Sir William Dick's descendants, is related in an earlier chapter. Among the many valuable relics of that family, now in the possession of the 15th Baronet of Grange, is a finely carved wooden cabinet which belonged to Sir William Dick. This came to be known as "The World and a Friend", the name recalling Sir William Dick's personal generosity. While Treasurer of Edinburgh Town Council, he kept a certain amount of public money in the lower section of the cabinet, and this he called "the world". Some of his own money he kept in the upper section, which he called "a friend". When people would come to him for financial help, as many did, Sir William would say, tapping the cabinet's lower section: "I have not a shilling in the *world*," then, opening the top part, he would continue, "but I shall see what a *friend* can do."

In 1676 Andrew Brown of Nether Plewlands (Greenbank) purchased Braid from the Dick family, and it remained in the possession of the Brown family for nearly a century. During their ownership, in about 1740, the mansion-house in the Hermitage of Braid was rebuilt. An advertisement in the *Caledonian Mercury* for May 7th, 1743 reveals that the Hermitage of Braid was already known by that name. "The New Mansion House of Braid, commonly called the Hermitage," it was announced, "among enclosures and planting, on the banks of a burn in the neighbourhood of Edinburgh and Goat Whey, consisting of 6 rooms and 4 fine closets, with kitchen, cellars, stable, byre, chaise house, flower garden and park of about 4 acres, are to be let and entered immediately at yearly rent of £18 stg. or less."

In 1772 it was sold to Charles Gordon, Writer to the Signet. A new era then began for the estate, which continues to the present day. Charles was the son of John Gordon, factor to the third Duke of Gordon, and, from 1740, a merchant in Edinburgh. An Aberdonian, he amassed much wealth and acquired several large estates, including Cluny in Aberdeenshire, styling himself "Gordon of Cluny". Charles Gordon duly inherited his father's properties and also those of his elder brother, Cosmo, who, after a distinguished and influential career, died in 1800. Three years after acquiring Braid, Charles Gordon married the daughter of the laird of Mortonhall, his neighbouring landowner. He later exchanged with his father-in-law four acres of the rocky ground forming the dell or valley of the Braid Burn, which had traditionally been considered part of the

Mortonhall estate, for a small area of the Braid Hills. In July 1772 Charles Gordon published *A Plan of the Barony of Braid; with the Hermitage and Policies, the Property of Charles Gordon, Esq.* His surveyor was John Horne. This plan provides much interesting information, denoting the boundaries of the Braid estate and indicating the names by which various areas within the estate were known. The layout of the Hermitage grounds is shown in detail, as is the farm of Egypt and the old roads and paths of the southern part of Morningside.

Soon after his marriage in 1775, Gordon drew up plans for the building of a new mansion-house in the Hermitage, in succession to several previous such dwellings. The architect engaged was Robert Burn, who designed it in the Adam style. Completed in 1785, it was subject to some criticism: one writer referred to its "grotesque style of castellated architecture". It has been suggested that Charles Gordon himself requested the architect to introduce the mock battlements and corner turrets in memory of Braid Castle, the residence of the original twelfth-century owners, the de Brad family. No evidence remains of the appearance of the ancient castle, which probably stood not in the Hermitage dell but high up on the crags, north-west of Gordon's mansion-house. Over the centuries, it may have developed from a simple wooden structure into the grandiose castellated building which Gordon perhaps sought to reproduce.

On the sloping ground above the Braid Burn, north-west of the mansion-house, within the old walled vegetable garden, stands a quaint dovecot. Its air of antiquity has led many visitors to the Hermitage to believe that it might be a relic of the old Castle of Braid, but it is, in fact, no older than the eighteenth century. Restored over the years, the dovecot has two separate chambers, each eighteen feet in diameter on the ground and tapering to an apex. With its 1,965 pigeon-holes, each about ten inches square, it is the second largest dovecot in the Edinburgh area. While providing pigeon pie for the residents of the Hermitage, the dovecot was not popular with local farmers, whose crops suffered from the pigeons' raids.

Another relic of earlier days which Charles Gordon acquired was the old corn-mill which stood on the banks of the Braid Burn about one hundred and fifty yards west of the mansion-house. This is referred to in old charters. Gordon demolished the mill and was later to regret having done so. In 1788 Edinburgh Town Council diverted the course of the Braid Burn within the Hermitage grounds and Gordon claimed compensation on the grounds that his mill had been affected. Witnesses for the Town Council testified that the mill had disappeared ten years previously. Gordon's appeal to the Court of Session and, finally, to the House of Lords was rejected. An old millstone for long lay in the Braid Burn about three hundred yards upstream from the mansion-house, regarded as a relic of the old corn-mill. This belief might have been

Water-mark of the old paper mill in the Hermitage of Braid

By courtesy of the Old Edinburgh Club

perpetuated had it not been for an accidental and quite extraordinary discovery of several old papers in the Edinburgh Register House. These, dated 1700 and 1703, were deeds which bore the watermark "Bred". It was known that early paper-mills had existed on the Water of Leith and the Esk, but not elsewhere in the vicinity of Edinburgh. Then an even earlier deed was discovered, dated 1695, recording a twelve-year lease of the early mansion-house of Braid, then the property of Andrew Brown, to Nicolas Dupyne of London, in which reference is made to the possibility of the corn-mill "being taken down for the building of a peaper-mill". Further, it was granted that, if a man named Dupyne and his partners "should build a peaper milns, ane or mare, upon the same grounds", they should be permitted to dismantle and dispose of "the wheels, axel, ties, mortars, iron plaits, hammers, gripps, fatts, tubs, presses, drying cords and pols, and other instruments of the peaper work" at any time they desired. This evidence of a paper-mill at the Hermitage of Braid was quite unexpected. Careful study of the Hermitage grounds revealed some indications of a mill lade on the south side of the Braid Burn near the entrance lodge and bridge at Braid Road. The Braid paper-mill was apparently short-lived, due to difficulties in obtaining raw materials. It was certainly still in existence in 1703, but may have ceased operation in 1707.

Charles Gordon, soon after the completion of his new mansion-house in 1785, proceeded to give to the Hermitage of Braid the attractive cultivated features it retains today. He levelled the lawns, laid fine avenues and planted beautiful trees. However, if the environment of Gordon's mansion-house became most pleasant, family life within its walls was rather less so. In 1788 Gordon was appointed one of the six principal

Clerks of the Court of Session. He spent long periods in Cluny and his other estates in the north, leaving his wife and family in Braid. When he himself was there, his way of life was strange: he was a miser and kept to his bed as a means of not spending money. His death in Braid House in 1814 was not greeted by much sorrow. His youngest son, Cosmo, had died in the house in 1795. His other sons, John and Alexander, were educated at Harrow. Of his three daughters, Mary, Charlotte and Joanna (known as Jacky), the last had a tragic life. High-spirited, avaricious and vindictive, but of legendary beauty, in 1804 she married John Dalrymple who became the 7th Earl of Stair. Their marriage soon broke up and, although not yet divorced, Dalrymple married Louisa Manners of Grantham Grange. Legal actions followed, Jacky Gordon nevertheless still considering herself the Countess of Stair. She became a recluse at her father's house, subject to violent moods and eventually deteriorating into a state of near insanity. She died in 1847. Charles Gordon's son John, who inherited Braid, also acquired much property in the north, including Benbecula and North and South Uist, Barra and Midmar. After his death in 1878, his lands passed to his widow, his second wife, who married Sir Reginald Cathcart in 1880. She treated her crofter tenants ruthlessly, forcing many to leave for Canada homeless and penniless. In his various

Hermitage House

369

wills, John Gordon, a man of strong likes and dislikes when it came to his relatives, excluded his uncle, aunts and cousins of the Trotter family of Mortonhall from all right of succession to the estate of Braid or any part thereof.

The tomb of the Gordon family of Cluny and Braid is in the burial ground of St Cuthbert's Church in the West End of Edinburgh. By 1868 the family had left the Hermitage and the estate was eventually managed by trustees. In that same year, tenancy of the mansion-house was acquired by one who was to bring to it an air of peaceful seclusion and cultured graciousness it had seldom known in the time of the Gordon family. This was John, later Sir John, Skelton, who with his wife began a new era in the chronicles of the Hermitage. Sir John was an advocate and Chairman of the Local Government Board for Scotland. He was also a distinguished essayist and historian. His *Maitland of Lethington* and *Scotland of Mary Stuart,* important works in defence of Mary, Queen of Scots, are major contributions to the history of Scotland. In other vein, under the *nom de plume* "Shirley", he wrote a series of essays for *Blackwood's Magazine,* later published as books. During his tenancy of the Hermitage, the mansion-house became the mecca of many distinguished writers, notably James Anthony Froude, Robert Browning, Dante Gabriel Rossetti, Thomas Huxley, Thomas Carlyle and Principal Tulloch. Skelton's *Table Talk of Shirley* refers to these guests and others. Further insight into the gracious life of the Skelton family at the Hermitage comes from the letters and autobiographies of the *literati* who were his guests. His dinner parties were especially renowned. On one occasion Thomas Huxley proposed to wear the kilt, "to be as little dressed as possible". On another Froude recalled that Thomas Carlyle gave him his *Reminiscences* to read, and on yet another told him of the letters which his wife Jane was about to have published.

On one occasion — an incident which provides an insight into the development of the district around the Hermitage — the distinguished historian Froude was informed by Skelton, who also made such complaints publicly, that the many pleasant walks he had previously enjoyed near the estate were no longer possible, "the neighbourhood of the poor Hermitage having been badly disfigured of late (*c.* 1890) by the speculative builder." This was the time when the villas of Cluny, Braid Road, Midmar and Corrennie were being built, in streets with names derived from the Gordons' estates in the north. Considering the fine houses being built at that time south of the Hermitage of Braid and the careful avoidance of any encroachment on the seclusion of the Hermitage itself, many letters appeared in the Press suggesting that Sir John Skelton's outbursts were unjustified.

In one of his essays, "Mainly about our Poor Relations", Skelton gives a fascinating account of the Hermitage dell with its wild-life and the changing seasons. One among his wealth of reminiscences concerns an evening walk with his guest Principal Tulloch to Swanston Cottage. Young Robert Louis Stevenson was not at home but his mother showed the two visitors a volume of her son's early contributions to local periodicals. Robert Louis Stevenson was then as yet a largely unknown writer. Skelton and his friend were permitted to take these away with them. He relates that Principal Tulloch read them next morning at breakfast. Later both agreed that "here was a fresh voice with a note delicate and unborrowed as a lark's". "Indeed," Skelton wrote, "I am not sure if Robert Louis Stevenson has ever done anything much better or possibly so good as one or two of the trifles in that cherished volume of scraps."

Sir John Skelton, who was a member of Christ Scottish Episcopal Church at Holy Corner, wrote a short history of this church, the only such account in existence. After living nearly thirty years at the Hermitage of Braid, Sir John died there in 1897. His widow remained in the house until 1922.

The next tenant was Professor C. G. Barkla, who held the Chair of Natural Philosophy at Edinburgh University and was the Nobel Prize winner in physics in 1917. He resided at the Hermitage until 1937. Soon afterwards John McDougal, who lived in Cluny Drive, purchased from the Gordon of Cluny trustees, for £11,000, the 42 acres of the Braid estate, including "the Hermitage, lodge and policies, with dell and valley". In 1938 John McDougal generously presented these properties to the Magistrates of Edinburgh to be used as "a Public Park or Recreation Ground for the benefit of the citizens". At the same time, he presented a sundial, in the form of an astrolabe and ancillary sphere, which stands near the mansion-house.

This charming park with its great trees, some of which are two and a half centuries old, towering above the Braid Burn, is surely unique in Britain. As one writer has commented, "Thanks to Mr McDougal, in these old haunts of medieval knights and churchmen, of seventeenth-century Covenanters, of eighteenth-century horsemen and clandestine lovers, and of such visitors as Froude and Principal Tulloch, the citizens are free to roam by the tall trees which fringe the gurgling brook or burn in the dell that forms part of the Hermitage of Braid." For some years after its acquisition by Edinburgh Corporation, the mansion-house was the residence of one of Edinburgh's best-remembered City Gardeners, the late John T. Jeffrey. In more recent times the mansion has served as a hostel for the Boy Scouts Association and, throughout the years, parties of Scouts and Wolf Cubs from all over the United Kingdom and abroad have spent a night or two within its venerable walls. The Hermitage is a nature-lover's paradise, ideally suited to the outdoor activities of Scouts and school groups. Early in 1974 it was reported that, two centuries after its erection, Charles Gordon's mansion-house was in a serious state of disrepair. One estimate for its restoration was £60,000. Now no longer used by the Scouts, it remains unoccupied. Opinions have been aired in

Braid Farmhouse

372

the Press concerning the mansion's future, but this remains uncertain.

As we re-enter Braid Road from the Hermitage, there may be seen, a short distance south of the bridge over the Braid Burn, at the end of the low boundary wall over which a little tributary of the burn may be seen, winding steps which lead up to Braid Hills Avenue and Braid Farm Road, once a pathway which led to the farm known variously as Upper, Nether or Over Braid. The old byres and steadings have long disappeared and its fertile land is now the site of pleasant villas. The sturdy farmhouse remains, restored and occupied, entered from Braid Hills Drive. It is now named Over Braid. In this farmhouse there died of tuberculosis, on June 15th, 1790, Robert Burns' "Fair Burnet", Elizabeth, or Elsie, Burnet Monboddo, daughter of the learned and eccentric Scottish judge Lord Monboddo, a philosopher and author of high repute, who anticipated Darwin's theory of evolution by seventy years, and earned himself a place in Kay's *Portraits*. She was sent to live at Braid farm as her illness progressed in the hope that its "pure fresh air, good food, including ewe and goat milk, along with rest would bring recovery".

Of rare beauty and fine literary taste, Elizabeth Burnet had spurned many offers of marriage, including one from Professor James Gregory, of "mixture" fame, later of Canaan Lodge, in order to look after her father. Lord Monboddo's family seat was in Kincardineshire, where he was once visited by Dr Samuel Johnson. His Edinburgh house at 13 St John's Street (off the Canongate) was one of the city's most hospitable literary centres and it was here that Burns was introduced to the judge by Sir Henry Erskine, on the basis of their common interest in Freemasonry. Burns was a welcome visitor to this exclusive circle on numerous occasions, and became fascinated by his young hostess, the beautiful Elizabeth Burnet. He alludes to her in his "Address to Edinburgh", written soon after he arrived in the city at the end of 1786:

> Thy daughters bright thy walks adorn,
> Gay as the gilded summer sky,
> Sweet as the dewy, milk-white thorn,
> Dear as the raptur'd thrill of joy!
> Fair Burnet strikes th'adoring eye,
> Heav'ns beauties on my fancy shine:
> I see the sire of love on high,
> And own His work indeed divine.

He also wrote: "There has not been anything nearly like her in all the combinations of beauty, grace and goodness, the great Creator has formed, since Milton's Eve on the first day of her existence." After her death, Burns, in a letter to Alexander Cunningham, wrote: "I have these several months been hammering at an elegy on the amiable and accomplished Miss Burnet. I have got, and can get, no further than the following

Fair Burnet with her father, Lord Monboddo
From Kay's "Portraits"

fragment." In another letter he wrote: "I had the honour of being pretty well acquainted with her, and have seldom felt so much at the loss of an acquaintance as when I heard that so amiable and accomplished a piece of God's work was no more." This was Burns' elegy to Fair Burnet:

> Life ne'er exulted in so rich a prize
> As Burnet, lovely from her native skies;
> Nor envious death so triumphed in a blow,
> As that which laid the accomplish'd Burnet low.

> Thy form and mind, sweet maid, can I forget?
> In richest are the brightest jewel set!
> In thee, high Heaven above was truest shown,
> As by his noblest work the Godhead best is known.

> In vain ye flaunt in summer's pride, ye groves;
> Thou crystal streamlet with thy flowing shore,
> Ye woodland choir that chant your idle loves,
> Ye cease to charm — Eliza is no more! . .

The parent's heart that nestled fond in thee,
That heart how sunk, a prey to grief and care;
So deck'd the woodbine sweet, yon aged tree;
So from it ravished, leaves it bleak and bare.

After his daughter's death Lord Monboddo kept her portrait draped in black until his own death in 1799. Engravings of Elizabeth Burnet are to be found in various collections of the works of Burns, where also appeared an interesting picture of a group of guests in Lord Monboddo's house in St John's Street, in which she and Burns are portrayed.

Another Scottish poem which some writers have associated with Braid farm is the ballad "Jock o' Braidislee", but there is no evidence to confirm this association and the poem may well have been based on a Scottish Border story. Many engravings, paintings and aquatints are still in existence which show Braid farm and its vicinity; several with titles such as "Edinburgh from the South" or "Edinburgh from Braid Hills" give early impressions also of the Hermitage of Braid and its immediate environment.

The "furzy hills of Braid", as Scott graphically described them in *Marmion,* were purchased by Edinburgh Corporation from the Gordon Trustees of the Braid Estate in 1889 at the cost of £11,000. (Many of the interesting features and quaint names of locations in the Braid Hills are indicated in *a Plan of the Barony of Braid* published by Charles Gordon of Cluny in 1772.) Soon afterwards, the mile-long boulevard between Morningside and Liberton, Braid Hills Drive, was constructed, much of it cut from solid rock. At certain points it provides a magnificent panoramic view of Edinburgh and far beyond. The chronicles of Braid Hills go back to very early times, as early, indeed, as the second millennium B.C. Cinerary urns denoting hill-top settlements and burials of that period have been discovered, and cup-and-ring markings of the same era have been noted by archaeologists.

In a much later period, Edward I of England in 1298 launched his campaign against the great Scottish patriot William Wallace, from his camp "apud Braid". After three days' rest at the Braids, Edward, with a large well-equipped army, marched down what is now Braid Road and through the western boundaries of Morningside, *en route* to Falkirk. In August 1298, following Wallace's victory in battle, Edward retreated by way of the old Braid road to his camp on the Braids. In 1335 Edward III made another attempt to subdue the Scots and, meeting with failure, he also retreated by way of the Braid Hills and the Burgh Muir, where his army was defeated by the Earl of Moray, aided by forces from the Earl of Liddesdale. Over two centuries later, the ex-Regent Morton, after his fall in 1580, was conveyed down the old Braid Road as a prisoner *en route* to Dumbarton Rock. An attempt by his friends to rescue him as they concealed themselves among the rocks on the Braid Hills failed.

Nearly a century after this incident, in August 1650, the Braids were occupied by Cromwell and his troops, when detachments moved down Braid Road into Morningside. Cromwell's headquarters were on the Galachlaw, the hill on the Mortonhall estate which rises above the present-day Princess Margaret Rose Hospital.

In more modern times the "furzy hills of Braid" became the scene of more peaceful contests in the royal and ancient game of golf. When, "on May 29th, 1889, the Magistrates and Town Council of Edinburgh assembling at the Royal Exchange in the High Street at 2 o'clock, then drove out to the Braids and formally annexed the new municipal property," the occasion signified the triumph of a strong and persistent campaign by the city's golfers urging Edinburgh Corporation to acquire the site. The story of their purchase of the Braid Hills from the Braid estate began with the growth of the city southwards in the late nineteenth century and its encroachment on the ancient Bruntsfield Links. In 1886 Edinburgh Town Council proposed "to prohibit absolutely or to restrict or otherwise regulate the playing of the game of golf and all or any other games or game on Bruntsfield Links." By this date, two of the original celebrated golfing societies, the Royal Burgess and the Bruntsfield, had already migrated from Bruntsfield Links to their own private courses. Seven clubs, however, remained with the Links as their only home ground, and were represented on its Green Committee. It was this body which launched the campaign to persuade the City Fathers to purchase the Braids. In 1887 the Town Council, influenced by Lord Provost Sir Thomas Clark, who sympathised with the golfers' cause, withdrew their proposal to ban golf on Bruntsfield Links. The campaign had been supported by the Royal Burgess and the Bruntsfield clubs, even tough they were not directly involved, and by other clubs outside Edinburgh, including one in Wimbledon which contributed to the campaign's fighting funds. Although golf was now permitted by Edinburgh Corporation at Bruntsfield, the scope of the course had become restricted by surrounding buildings and golfers who sought a full-scale municipal course now discussed with Edinburgh Corporation the possibility of acquiring the Braids. But the battle was not yet won. Many Town Councillors considered the Braids too remote: there was in 1887 no public transport to this outer fringe of Edinburgh. The suburban railway had, however, been in existence for three years and certain councillors proposed Blackford Hill for the new golf course, as it was accessible from Blackford Hill Station. Alternatively, it was suggested that, if the Braids were acquired, golfers could travel to Blackford Hill Station and then walk to the Braids by the path skirting the west side of Blackford Hill, crossing the rustic bridge over the Braid Burn at the east end of the Hermitage of Braid and climbing the steep pathway to the golf course — an arduous prelude to a round of golf. The walk from Morningside Road Station, though still lengthy, would, other councillors argued, be less tiring.

A scene during the Dispatch Trophy golf contest on the Braid Hills

Old skating pond on Braid Hills, c. 1900

By courtesy of Mr Gilmour Main

On May 26th, 1888, following a visit to the Braids by members of its staff, including the editor, Alexander Riach, who had led the golfers' campaign, the *Evening Dispatch* published a sketch plan illustrating the feasibility of laying out a new eighteen-hole course on the Braids. The plan was widely supported by Edinburgh golfers. A public meeting in Queen Street Hall appointed a deputation to meet the Town Council. The meeting which followed was constructive and, on November 22nd, 1888, the Town Council agreed to purchase Braid Hills. The Council's official visit to the city's new property in May 1889 was a ceremonial formality. The practical lay-out of the course had then not yet commenced, but such was the natural suitability of the Braids that by September 5th, 1889 the new course was ready for play. Its popularity steadily increased. What became known as Braids No. 1 Course was 6,011 yards in length; Braids No. 2, opened later, was 5,244 yards long. Edinburgh's establishment of a municipal golf course set an example for other cities and towns in Scotland which soon did likewise.

The major annual competition held on the Braids is the Dispatch Trophy, commemorating the part played by this former Edinbrugh newspaper in the establishment of the course. Twenty-two golfing societies took part in the inaugural competition in 1890. Fifty years later, ninety-three societies sought entry. Many famous golfers have participated in this long-established tournament, notably James Braid, five times British Open Champion, who designed many municipal and private golf courses in Britain, Tommy Armour, whose achievements are recorded in an earlier chapter and who, with his brother Sandy, played in the Edinburgh Western Club's Dispatch Trophy winning team, and Bobby Cruickshank, another Morningside golfer of world renown. In 1939, according to a Press report, an average of one hundred thousand players were teeing off annually on the two Braids courses. In 1974 only about half this number went round, due probably to the greatly increased membership of private courses. Nevertheless, the Braids is still regarded as one of the most challenging courses in Britain, while the panoramic view from its most prominent greens must surely be unsurpassed.

Golf is not the only sport which has benefited from the excellent natural facilities of the Braid Hills. Many Morningside residents will recall pleasant hours spent on the large skating pond beside the old cart-track round that part of the Braids entered by a gate opposite the top of the Howe of Dean pathway, which ascends steeply from Blackford Glen near the old quarry. The long since dried out bed of this pond may still be clearly seen between the 5th green and the 6th tee on the Braids No. 1 golf course.

The Braid Hills Hotel, a prominent landmark above the sweeping curve of the Braid Road as it passes the Hermitage of Braid, was opened in 1881. As we proceed towards the summit of the road, the pleasant residential district of Riselaw lies on our right, the name of which is

378

derived simply from the fact that the ground rises towards the law or hill of Braid. Just beyond the gateway to the Braids, with its little stile on the left, the boundary wall between the estates of Braid and Mortonhall may be seen, climbing steeply up the shoulder of the hill and continuing faithfully in its task of demarcation over high and low ground almost as far as the boundaries of Liberton.

CHAPTER 5

Buckstane · Mortonhall · Fairmilehead

BUCKSTANE

As the little wall wending its way up the steep slope of the Braid Hills indicates, here on its southern side begins the large, heavily wooded estate of Mortonhall. *En route* to the mansion-houses of Morton and Mortonhall, where the earliest chronicles of this pleasant district begin, a number of features claim attention. The first sign that one has crossed the frontier between the two estates appears just over the summit of Braid Road: it is the board at the entrance to Mortonhall Golf Course. The Mortonhall Club — of which Siegfried Sassoon was a member during his stay at Craiglockhart Military Hospital during the First World War — claims to be the oldest private golf course in the neighbourhood of Edinburgh, having been opened in 1892, the year following the departure of the Honourable Company of Edinburgh Golfers to Muirfield. Other clubs which moved from Bruntsfield Links were at first established at courses outwith Edinburgh's boundaries. Mortonhall course extends eastwards nearly to Liberton, in attractive surroundings, recorded in a fine collection of photographs preserved in the Edinburgh Central Public Library. Each of the course's eighteen holes has a name appropriate to its location. The Khyber is played through a deep gully between the Braid Hills and the high ground of the Mortonhall estate; the Elphin has as one of its hazards the old pond of this name.

A few yards beyond the gateway to the golf course stands the Buckstane, built into the wall at the entrance to the old farmhouse so named. A plaque above this ancient stone summarises its history: "This march stone, a relic of feudal times, stood for over five centuries on a commanding site beside the old Roman Road about two hundred and fifty yards farther north. The name may be derived from its having marked the place where the buck-hounds were unleashed when the Kings of Scotland hunted in this region."

There are many accounts of the Buckstane's origin and these have been most usefully brought together by James S. Bennet, F.R.I.A.S., in his booklet published by the Edinburgh Corporation Libraries and Museums Committee in 1964. The traditional belief that it was at this stone that the King's buck-hounds were unleashed had some confirmation from the historian Maitland in 1753. There is a much earlier reference to the stone in a disposition of the lands of Braid recorded in the "Protocol Book of James Young", an Edinburgh Notary Public, in 1496. The stone, which has probably been reduced in size by its long exposure to the

The Buckstane in Braid Road
Photograph by Mr W. R. Smith

Inscription on the Buckstane
Photograph by Mr W. R. Smith

THE BUCKSTANE
THIS MARCH STONE A RELIC OF FEUDAL
TIMES OCCUPIED A COMMANDING SITE
ON THE OLD ROMAN ROAD ABOUT 250
YARDS NORTH FROM THIS SPOT
BY TRADITION THE NAME WAS
DERIVED FROM THE STONE HAVING
MARKED THE PLACE WHERE THE BUCKHOUNDS
WERE UNLEASHED WHEN THE KING OF
SCOTLAND HUNTED IN THIS REGION

elements on the summit of Braid Road, is a long, rounded piece of tapering freestone, three feet high and one foot broad. It is presumed to have been a march stone, marking the boundary of Crown lands from its prominent position, as originally did the Borestone on the summit of Churchhill. It differs from other march stones, however, in that it has a deep depression or bore-hole in its apex. This has given rise to the belief that the Royal Standard was hoisted in the stone while the King was hunting in the district. As the plaque relates, the stone originally stood on the opposite side of the old Roman Road, now Braid Road, about two hundred and fifty yards to the north, on the highest point of the road. It was eventually built into the wall of the villa named Allermuir and only in recent years, as a result of Mr Bennet's interest, was it transferred to its present site outside the Buckstane farmhouse which for long was his home.

The Buckstane, therefore, would have been used when the King and his nobles rode out to hunt on the fringes of the Pentlands. The Royal Standard would have been hoisted in it for all around to see, indicating the royal presence in the district. The Baron of Penicuik, taking up his stance beside the Buckstane, would have given three blasts of his horn, to signify the King's presence and also as an act of homage. This practice is said to have dated back to a hunting incident in the days of King Robert the Bruce. While hunting on the lower slopes of the Pentlands, near Glencorse, Bruce was constantly baulked by a swift white deer. He challenged his nobles to see whether their dogs might succeed where the royal hounds had failed. Sir William St Clair of Roslin and Penicuik accepted, pledging his life that his two favourite dogs, Help and Hold, would trap the deer. Sir William slipped them, and prayed earnestly to St Katherine for her aid. As he followed the chase on horseback, the deer seemed to be escaping and his fears grew that his own life was in danger. Then Hold drove the deer into a burn while Help leapt in and killed it. The King was delighted. Embracing Sir William, he thereupon granted him in freehold the lands of Loganhouse, a favourite resort of the Scottish Kings, along with Kirton and Earncraig. The Knight of Roslin, in thanksgiving to St Katherine, built a little chapel at the east end of what is now Glencorse Reservoir, dedicated to St Katherine of the Hopes.

A note in the Royal Commission on Ancient and Historical Monuments and Constructions of Scotland Inventory of 1929 for the County of Midlothian places a date on the little chapel's origin which is not at variance with the legend of its foundation. Its description of the remains, when they were visited in July 1915, reads: "St Katherine's Chapel. The foundations of this structure are submerged beneath the waters of Glencorse Reservoir, but were visible on the date of recent visit. A fragment of rubble walling, some 10 feet long and 2 feet 9 inches thick, was seen above the mud and the conformation of the loose debris suggested that the structure, which is orientated, was about 44 feet 9

Ceremony of re-siting the Buckstane, 1964, showing Sir John Clerk of Penicuik (extreme right) with ancient Hunting Horn

By courtesy of "Edinburgh Evening News"

inches long and 20 feet wide internally. These proportions suggest the 13th century as the probable date of its erection . . ." King Robert the Bruce was not crowned until 1306. The note adds: "On 3rd April 1593, the Laird of Rosslynn declared to the Synod of Lothian and Tweeddale that 'he was nane of the parochinaris of Leswaid, but one of the parochinaris of St Katherine of the Hopes, in respect his residence was in Logan House Tower'." The picturesque valley of Loganlea lies to the west of Glencorse Reservoir. The Sir William St Clair who is reputed to have received from Robert the Bruce the lands of Loganhouse was the son of Sir Henry St Clair of Rosslynn and Penicuik, upon whom Bruce also bestowed the lands of Pentland Moor, Morton and Mortonhall. It was thus in homage for the conveyance of such extensive properties that the Lairds of Penicuik were obliged to appear at the Buckstane whenever a Scottish king passed by and to give three blasts of the horn — the origin of the description of this family's lands as being "Free for a blast!" The family crest of the Clerks of Penicuik, who thus came to have superiority over the Buckstane, shows a man blowing a hunting horn. The little hill above Buckstane farmhouse is shown in old maps as Buckstane Snab.

In order to record the chronicles of the Mortonhall estate in chronological sequence, leaving till later the more modern features of the district which would claim attention if we proceeded directly by Fair-milehead, our route, as in early times, is south-eastwards. Just beyond the Buckstane, we pass through old lodge-house gates and skirt the Gallachlaw, crossing its spacious parklands towards the stately Mor-tonhall House, reached today by a driveway on the north side of Frogston Road East, formerly Kaimes Road.

MORTONHALL

Norman Dixon, in *The Place Names of Midlothian,* now regarded as a standard work, cites the first recorded references to Morton as "Mertoun" in 1264 and as "Mortoun" in 1476. The possible derivation of these names he suggests as "mere tun", a farm by a mere or lake, and he notes that there was once much marshy ground in this area. Mortonhall he cites as "Mortone-hall" in 1404 and "Mortoun Hall" in 1492. The earliest owner on record of the lands of Mortonhall is Sir Henry St Clair of Rosslynn and Penicuik, who swore fealty to Edward I of England in June 1292. Sir Henry remained on the side of England during the Wars of Independence and then, in 1317, gave his allegiance to King Robert the Bruce, from whom, in the same year, he was granted the lands of the Moor of Pent-land, Morton and Mortonhall "in free warren for the service of the tenth part of a Knight's fee". A "Knight's fee" was that area of land sufficient to maintain him. Sir Henry St Clair became the Chief Butler of Scotland and was one of the signatories of the Declaration of Arbroath of 1320. It was his son, Sir William, who features in the legend surrounding the origin of the Buckstane. The lands of Morton and Mortonhall, confirmed as the property of the St Clairs of Rosslynn by a charter of James III in 1486, for long remained in their possession.

William Rigg of the Riggs of Carberry next appears on record as owner of Morton in 1630. The lands were subsequently sold by William Rigg's son to the Porterfields of Comiston, though returning to the possession of Peter Rigg, an advocate, for a short time. In 1635 the lands were purchased by John Trotter and, over the centuries following, the name Trotter was to become synonymous with Mortonhall. In an in-teresting detailed account of the *Genealogy of the Trotters of Mortonhall,* it is related that the family originated in Gifford in East Lothian and bore another name now unknown. On a certain occasion, legend has it, a member of the family came quickly on horseback to the rescue of James III who was being molested, or brought the King information of an English force approaching. Since his horse was lame, the King gave to the man who had assisted him the new name of Trotter. The Trotter family coat of arms portrays a man holding a horse's reins and bears the motto, "In promptu".

John Trotter, who became the first Baron of Mortonhall, was the younger son of Robert Trotter of Catchelraw and Charterhall in Ber-

IN PROMPTU.

Coat of arms of the Trotters of Mortonhall

By courtesy of Major A. R. Trotter of Mortonhall

wickshire. He claimed descent from Kings Robert 11 and 111 and was an ardent Royalist. As an Edinburgh merchant he acquired "great wealth and estate", but he was always a man of great charity and generosity. One of his many gifts was the establishment of "two chambers in the College of Edinburgh for two bursars in philosophy". He died in 1641 at the age of eighty-eight and was buried in the family vault on the north wall of Greyfriars churchyard. A Latin inscription on his monument pays tribute to his benevolence. He left 4,000 merks to "the Town of Edinburgh", 2,000 merks to St Paul's Hospital in Leith Wynd, a large sum to Trinity Hospital and 700 merks to the town of Lanark.

John Trotter, first Baron of Mortonhall, was succeeded by his son, also John, who shared his father's Royalist sympathies. He was fined £500 by the parliament of 1645 for allowing the Marquis of Montrose and his troops to camp on his lands. The third Baron, who succeeded to the estate in 1651, was also a generous benefactor of "the College of Edinburgh". He died in Malta in 1665, just twenty-six years old and unmarried. Henry Trotter succeeded to the Berwickshire estates and Mortonhall as 7th Baron in 1763, but in the same year conveyed his title and ownership to his younger brother Thomas. References occur in various

Mortonhall House
By courtesy of Major A. R. Trotter of Mortonhall

books to transactions carried out by Henry Trotter but in fact it was Thomas who was responsible for most of these. Thomas Trotter not only acquired the family estates in the Borders and at Mortonhall but also the lands and barony of Eyemouth, including the harbour and village. Prior to his succession he carried out a successful brewing business in the Cowgate, for some time renting the Tailors Hall, which continued to be associated with brewing until quite recent times. Thomas Trotter was the supplier of beer to Edinburgh Castle. He became a Town Councillor and bailie. In 1765 he pulled down the original fort-like mansion-house of Mortonhall, which had a drawbridge and surrounding moat, and built the present tall Georgian house, completed in 1769. The architect was John Baxter, who designed it in an austere Palladian style. Thomas Trotter died in 1792, and his widow was offered the choice of living in Swanston farmhouse or Blackford House. She chose the latter and lived there for twenty-two years.

Richard Trotter, who became the 10th Baron in 1826, was prominent in the life of Liberton parish and became Convenor of the County of Midlothian. It was he who married the daughter of General Sir John Oswald, G.C.B. of Dunnikier, an event commemorated by Oswald Road on the Trotter lands at Blackford. Richard Trotter's younger brother, Lt.

Thomas Trotter of the Scots Greys, was killed at the Battle of Waterloo in 1815. The proud tradition of military service in the Trotter family has continued.

While much of the estate of Mortonhall is still in the possession of the Trotters, the family seat is now at Charterhall in Berwickshire. The now vacant stately three-storey mansion-house of Mortonhall, with attics and sunken basement, is approached by a driveway on the north side of Frogston Road East, formerly Kaimes Road. The stables and other outhouses are still used as offices by those developing the estate, part of which is being devoted to the laying out of a caravan site. A number of small commercial enterprises including a garden centre have been established on the estate. The many valuable furnishings, including interesting tapestries and a library of two thousand books, once in the mansion-house, have passed into the possession of the present family or been sold. A sale of certain books in 1947, including a copy of John Napier's work on logarithms, realised £8,000. There is a private burial-ground within the precincts of the house. The group of cottages near the house once known as Redcastle have long since gone. Many ancient trees remain beside the mansion-house, including, opposite the main entrance, a sycamore reputedly two hundred years old, while elsewhere a cluster of yew trees is believed to have been planted over three centuries ago. In 1949 the mansion-house was given on a short-term lease to certain staff members of Edinburgh University's Department of Animal Genetics. Here, under the leadership of the late Professor Conrad H. Waddington, twenty-five adults and their families, in the twenty-eight-roomed house, initiated an experiment in communal living, the whole community meeting in council each month.

In the vicinity of Mortonhall House, old maps indicate the site of Kilmorton, which Thomas Whyte in his *History of Liberton Parish* suggests was an ancient Celtic church, though no record of this remains. In more recent years, on that part of the estate between the mansion-house and Frogston Road East, a number of executive-type houses have been built.

Westwards up Frogston Road East, and a short distance south of the point where it becomes Frogston Road West, in the little hamlet of Winton, opposite the Princess Margaret Rose Hospital, is Morton House. Adjacent are the farm buildings of Morton Mains. Morton House was the dower house of the Trotters of Mortonhall. The original east portion of the house is of the Queen Anne period and appears to have been built by Thomas Rigg on the site of an earlier residence. Some writers have ascribed the house to the reign of Charles II. The fine gatehouse pavilions flanking the entrance driveway are contemporary with the original house, although altered in a later period. The main part of the house has two storeys, with attics. The dormer windows bear the date 1702, while in the garden a sundial is dated 1713, and there is a forty-foot-deep well. From

Morton House, Winton
Photograph by Mr W. R. Smith

1630 Morton House, like Mortonhall House, was in the possession of William Rigg, whose family were from Carberry at Musselburgh. He regained ownership after a short period of disposition to the Porterfields of Comiston. In more recent times the house was tenanted by Lord Cunningham, a judge in the Court of Session, and later by the notable Scottish historian, Dr John Hill Burton, who died there in 1881. He had earlier been for many years tenant of Craighouse, and had been most reluctant to leave when the old manor-house was purchased to provide for the extension of the Edinburgh Asylum. Thomas Whyte, in his work on the history of Liberton, written in 1792, comments: "The house of Morton is but undifferent, but the plantations around it are considerable and the prospect most agreeable and extensive. The Belvedere here is mightily well situated." Today, while the Belvedere, contemporary with the original house, is no longer so remote from Edinburgh, it is still "mightily well situated" and is being restored for occupation by the owner of Morton House.

In the woodland surrounding the old dower house there was once a small hamlet named Mounthooley or Holy Mount. The pleasant little community of Winton, clustered around Morton House, was so named in

1936 to commemorate the marriage of Colonel Algernon Trotter of Mortonhall to Lady Edith Mary Montgomerie, younger daughter of the 15th Earl of Eglinton and Winton. A short distance south-east of Morton House was the Barony of Brownhill, the property of the ancestors of Sir John Henderson who owned the little village of Fordel in the Oxgangs district from 1508 until 1660. Bordeaux (Burdiehouse), Straiton and Phantasy were part of the Barony of Brownhill.

While Dixon, in his *Place Names of Midlothian*, suggests that the name Morton was probably derived from *mere-tun*, meaning a farm beside a lake or marsh-land, Alexander Kincaid in the Gazetteer accompanying his *History of Edinburgh* (1787) propounds another origin which many later historians have attempted to support. This was that Morton was the site of a large Roman settlement or town, referred to in Gaelic or the old Celtic language as *More* (great) *ton* (a town or city). There is certainly some evidence that one of the great Roman roads from the south passed over what is now Fairmilehead *en route* to the important Roman base at Cramond. Whether this was a continuation of the famous Watling Street, originating in St Albans, or Dere Street, commencing at

The Belvedere, Morton House, Winton

Photograph by Mr W. R. Smith

Hadrian's Wall and constructed by Agricola, is a subject of controversy. Valuable information regarding an older surface below the present Biggar road at Bowbridge, near Fairmilehead, was discovered a few years ago by the Rev. J. D. Lyford-Pike during the laying of pipes. He observed that a well-laid surface of metalling at a depth of two feet was covered by a nine-inch layer of clay silt. The silt layer represents a long period of abandonment before the present road was made. The Rev. Lyford-Pike's observations seem to support Thomas Whyte in his statement that Sir John Clerk of Penicuik reconstructed the present road at Fairmilehead "on the very line of the old Roman military way", referred to by General Roy in *Military Antiquities*. Early maps also indicate a large Roman settlement north of Fairmilehead and east of the old entrance drive to Comiston House. Sir John Clerk, Baron of the Exchequer and a noted antiquarian, owned many Roman coins found during the construction of the new road between Fairmilehead and Liberton, formerly called Kaimes Road but in recent years renamed Frogston Road East and West. These included a large brass coin or medallion bearing the head of the Emperor Claudius. Another coin bore the inscriptions "Ti. Claudius Caesar Augustus, P.M.T.R.P. IMP," and, on the reverse side, "Nero Claudius Drusus", and the figure of a horseman upon a triumphal arch. One, a well preserved gold medal, had a representation of Antoninus Pius and another the figure of Lucius Septimius Severus, commander of the important Roman station at Cramond. It was possibly struck to mark his achievement of a peace settlement with the Caledonians. During road works in the vicinity of Comiston House two large cairns of stones were removed and below these several stone coffins were found containing human remains and weapons dating from the Roman occupation. The Royal Commission on Ancient Monuments, in its Inventory of Midlothian for 1929, carries an illustration of a bronze scabbard found in the Mortonhall area. This was decorated with a late Celtic design. Whyte in his historical study of Liberton refers to two small tumuli which came to be known as Caer Duff Knowes, near the boundary of Mortonhall with Upper Liberton. *Caer,* Whyte concluded, was the name given to places where the Romans camped and left relics of their workmanship. *Kaims,* the name of the location east of Mortonhall, "in the old language meant", he observed, "a camp or fortification".

West of Mortonhall House and behind the Princess Margaret Rose Hospital is the Gallachlaw, six hundred feet above sea level, described in the records as being "betwixt the Braid Crags and the Pentland Hills" when, in the summer of 1650, Cromwell's army of sixteen thousand men was encamped here prior to the Battle of Dunbar. In Whyte's day, a quadrangular rampart on top of Gallachlaw was still known as "Oliver's Camp". Here, it was said, Cromwell and his officers had camped while the troops occupied tents in the fields below. Certain modern writers have claimed that evidence of Cromwell's camp on the Gallachlaw may still be seen. The name Gallachlaw, according to Whyte, originated with the Romans and meant valour or fortitude. It was here that they held their courts of justice. Other historians have derived the name from "Gallows Law" or "Gallows Hill", the place where Cromwell hanged local rebels and his own soldiers guilty of looting. It is recorded that, when one of his sergeants was condemned for some offence, "there was no tree to hang him on". In later times, the abundance of trees was one of the most pleasant features of the Mortonhall estate. Cromwell's troops also camped on the Braid and Blackford Hills which, with the Gallachlaw, were frequently referred to as the Pentlands. The heights of Wester Craig-lockhart Hill were also occupied.

The small hamlet of Frogston, after which the busy road from Fairmilehead to Captain's Road is named, has long since disappeared. In 1447 Alexander Frog had been granted the right to farm part of the lands extending southwards from this road to Straiton.

The Princess Margaret Rose Hospital is one of the most important orthopaedic hospitals in the United Kingdom. The foundation stone was laid on October 2nd, 1929 by the Duke and Duchess of York (the late George VI and present Queen Mother). The hospital was officially opened on June 10th, 1933, though the first patients had been admitted a year earlier.

FAIRMILEHEAD

The name Fairmilehead is said by some to be derived from the Gaelic *Fair Meall Chuib* meaning "a hill on the cattle fold". Another suggestion is that the summit of the roads which meet here is, in old Scots parlance, "a fair mile" equally from both Hillend and the Braid Hills. Robert Louis Stevenson in his journeys on foot from the city to Swanston Cottage knew Fairmilehead well and had his own inimitable description of it as "A spot where two roads intersect beside a hanging wood." In *Edinburgh: Picturesque Notes,* after referring to the Hanging Stone in Braid Road, he continues: "For about two miles the road climbs upwards, a long hot walk in summer time. You reach the summit at a place where four roads meet, beside the toll of Fairmilehead. The spot is breezy and agreeable both in name and aspect. The hills are close-by across a valley . . . The air comes briskly and sweetly off the hills, pure from the elevation and rustically scented by the upland plants; and even at the toll you may hear the curlew calling on its mate. At certain seasons, when the gulls desert their surfy forelands, the birds of sea and mountain hunt and scream together in the same field by Fairmilehead."

Young Stevenson and his parents were well known to the post-mistress at the old post-office at Fairmilehead which, along with the toll-house, later to become the county roadman's cottage and then the police

Fairmilehead Crossroads, c. 1900

Bowbridge, c. 1887

Pen and ink sketch by Henry Roy Westwood; by courtesy of Edinburgh City Libraries

station, were for long the only buildings at Fairmilehead. It was while writing about the "spot where two roads intersect beside a hanging wood" that Stevenson related the story of the small whisky distillery at Bowbridge, a short distance southwards, over the brink of the hill, where the Swanston Burn becomes the Lothian Burn and passes under the road. Bowbridge later became a dairy farm. The distiller here and the gauger or exciseman were good friends but the latter had the duty of calling regularly to measure his friend's stocks of whisky and to levy tax accordingly. A little arrangement was made between them. While the gauger was about to descend over Fairmilehead, he would play loudly on his flute the old air, "Over the Hills and Far Away". At the sound of the first note, the distiller would hastily load a goodly proportion of his "produce" into a horse and cart and make off to a spot just beyond Hillend on the other side of Caerketton. He would then return to Bowbridge to greet his friend, who would have descended slowly from Fairmilehead to find, on arrival, modest stocks for inspection. A fine meal and a liberal dram round a blazing fire would eventually send the gauger in mellow mood back to Edinburgh, the echoes of "Over the Hills and Far Away" gradually fading as he disappeared over the crest of Fairmilehead.

An established feature of the Fairmilehead landscape is the big water filtration works, the full extent of which is hidden from the passer-by. Now under the administration of the Lothian Regional Council, the establishment has recently been named Comiston Springs to commemorate the source of Edinburgh's first piped water supply from several springs on the nearby Comiston estate. When the filtration works was established in 1908, the original battery of twelve pressure filters was able to treat four million gallons of water per day, supplying the high areas of Fairmilehead and Braid Hills. As the city's demands for water increased, slow sand filter beds were laid. Today, through the operation of the original pressure filters, micro-straining equipment installed in 1953 and other modern techniques, upwards of twenty million gallons of water are filtered daily. This quite incomprehensible volume of water comes primarily from the Talla reservoir, but, if necessary, supplies can also be treated from Glencorse reservoir at Flotterstone. Thirty-three-inch steel pipes bring the water from Talla, while that from Glencorse comes in cast iron pipes twenty-seven inches in diameter. The filters remove all but the minutest particles of organic material and bacteria, and bacterial purification is then effected by chlorination. Unnoticed from ground-level at Fairmilehead, the principal reservoir, constructed from vast amounts of concrete and steel, is 384 feet long and 187 feet wide, its depth being 16 feet 6 inches. When the city's earliest water supply at Comiston proved inadequate, springs at Swanston were tapped. Both these sources, however, were discontinued some years ago, although water from the Fairmilehead filtration plant is supplied to Edinburgh Castle using the Swanston main pipe. Swanston village itself is now supplied from the works at Fairmilehead, where a pump-house boosts the pressure to the cottages. Water is transferred, by the force of gravity, from Fairmilehead to a large tank at Castlehill, near the entrance to the Castle esplanade, and from there, again by gravity, to premises in Princes Street. Edinburgh's other filtration plants are at Alnwickhill and Torduff. The small filter beds beside the old farm of Bowbridge are used to treat the sludge from the Fairmilehead works.

Built into the wall near the entrance to the water filtration unit is an old milestone, now practically illegible, once indicating a distance of three miles from Tollcross. The first of these stones, at the corner of Morningside Place, still stands, but the second, which would have stood on the old Braid Road near the Braid Hills Hotel, has now disappeared.

On the fringes of the waterworks is Fairmilehead Parish Church, opened on April 12th, 1938. The church is built, after the Scottish tradition, in stone, in this case drawn from the quarry at Craigmillar. The dressing stone is from Doddington. The tower is a pleasant landmark at the Fairmilehead crossroads. The architect, Leslie Grahame-Thomson, A.R.S.A., introduced into the interior of the church a new note in Scottish ecclesiastical design by having a plain elliptical vault of rough ivory-toned plaster.

In 1938 the Edinburgh tramways service was extended from the Braids terminus to Fairmilehead. For twelve years prior to this date there had been a special bus service from the Braids. The last tram to Fairmilehead ran on September 11th, 1956, and the last to the Braids on September 16th, 1956.

CHAPTER 6

Comiston · Oxgangs · Hunter's Tryst

COMISTON

The final stages of the journey through the chronicles of South Edinburgh, by way of Comiston, Oxgangs and Hunter's Tryst to Swanston, are made in the footsteps of one resident of earlier days who trod and knew every inch of this then remote countryside — Robert Louis Stevenson. The extensive lands of Comiston are entered most fittingly through the classical stone pillars at the main entrance to Braidburn Valley Park. These once stood at the junction of what is now Camus Avenue and Buckstone Terrace, the beginning of the original driveway to Comiston House. It was from this present entrance to the pleasant park at Greenbank Crescent, then but a narrow gateway, that a path led along the Braid Burn, between well cultivated fields, all the way to Comiston and Swanston, while, along the top of the slope above the auditorium of the open-air theatre, another narrow path led in the same direction. The latter is now entered by a little lane leading off from Greenbank Crescent. Here stood the last thatched cottage of Greenbank. While residing at Swanston Cottage with his parents from 1867 to 1879, Robert Louis Stevenson became a "well-kent" figure to the residents of Morningside as he made his way on foot to and from the University by means of the paths through Comiston. The stooped, pensive figure in a velvet jacket was regarded by the Morningside villagers and the Comiston farmworkers as a little odd — "the gowk" and "no quite a' there". Young Stevenson's recollections of these days are recorded vividly in his *Edinburgh: Picturesque Notes* and *Memories and Portraits*.

The picturesque Braidburn Valley, extending to thirty-one acres, was purchased by Edinburgh Corporation from the Mortonhall estate in 1937 for the nominal sum of £2,000. It was at once laid out as a public park and the open-air theatre was constructed which could hold an audience of two and a half thousand. The stage on the east bank of the burn is enclosed by trees and a little orchestral pit has been carved out on the water's edge. The floral surround to the steep, tiered auditorium, in the form of a crown to mark the Coronation of 1937, was executed by the late John T. Jeffrey, then City Gardener. In 1935, four hundred cherry trees were planted by five thousand Guides, Rangers and Brownies of Edinburgh in honour of the Silver Jubilee of the late King George V. This imaginative project has, now that the trees have reached maturity, provided most pleasant colourful avenues. To mark the completion of the open-air theatre in 1937 a dancing display was given by a thousand school children. The special wooden stage, which was not always used and could be stored in sections

Gate posts at the entrance to Braidburn Valley Park which formerly stood at the entrance to the drive to Comiston House
Photograph by Mr W. R. Smith

The original entrance to Comiston House in Camus Avenue, showing Mr W. E. Evans with hand camera
By courtesy of Mr G. Anderson

was one hundred and fifty feet long. Occasional performances were held in the theatre, even during the Second World War, but it was not until 1945 that there were regular productions, notably of several Shakespearian plays by the Phillip Barrett Company in June of that year, which series of performances attracted a total audience of ten thousand in one week. Another series in the same year played to twenty thousand people. *Rob Roy* was presented by the Scottish Community Drama Association in July 1946. However, due perhaps to the problem of inclement weather, the use of the open-air theatre gradually declined, although sheepdog trials were occasionally arranged there.

The Braid Burn is a modest reminder of the great mass of water which originally carved out the valley in the ancient era of retreating glaciers. The burn is at first so named in the grounds of Dreghorn Castle. Here two small streams which rise on the White Hill, on the west side of Howden Glen, join with the Bonaly Burn to become the Braid Burn. The burn, in a picturesque setting, passes under the bridge beside the former gate-lodge at one of the entrances to Dreghorn Camp at Redford Road. It next flows under Colinton Mains Drive, and, running parallel to Firrhill Drive, skirts the three blocks of high-rise flats named after the peaks of the Pentland Hills which they face, Allermuir, Capelaw and Caerketton. Near the junction of Oxgangs Avenue and Greenbank Crescent a modern bridge has replaced the original wooden footbridge, and from here the Braid Burn flows on through the valley to which it has given its name. Leaving the Braidburn Valley and flowing under Comiston Road, it passes the Mortonhall Tennis Club courts which, in earlier times when the burn flooded, were the site of a curling pond. From the Braid Road, the burn enters the Hermitage of Braid, its most picturesque setting. Leaving under an old rustic bridge, overshadowed by the towering Corbie's Craig on Blackford Hill, it meanders through Blackford Glen to Liberton Dams at the foot of Liberton Brae. At the junction of Craigmillar Park, Nether Liberton and Gilmerton Road it is glimpsed again, in a setting Constable might have painted, under a little bridge before a fine old country villa. Passing through the Craigmillar district, the Braid Burn makes a pleasant appearance in the Inch Park and flows under the Old Dalkeith Road at Greenend near Cameron Toll. South-west of the Edinburgh University Playing Fields at Peffermill it welcomes into its more ample waters its modest travelling companion from Morningside, the Jordan Burn. Morningside's two "rivers", now combined, pass Duddingston Loch to the North, flowing under Duddingston Road West and through Duddingston Golf Course. Just beyond the junction of Milton Road West with Willowbrae Road the Braid Burn loses its identity, being renamed the Figgate Burn. Passing by the western part of Portobello and the artificial waters of the open-air swimming pool, the Figgate Burn, in a concrete channel, emerges swiftly from underneath Portobello promenade, over the beach and at last to the sea.

Braidburn Valley Park

Photograph by Mr W. R. Smith

A performance at the open-air theatre in Braidburn Valley Park

We return to the Braid Burn's native setting at Greenbank. On the south bank beside the sturdy bridge at Oxgangs Avenue, which in 1955 replaced the somewhat precarious wooden footbridge which, in the 1930s, led to a choice of pleasant walks through open countryside in Comiston, Oxgangs and Colinton Mains, a considerable steady stream of water pours into the Braid Burn from the several springs on the estate which provided Edinburh's first piped water supply. In Robert Louis Stevenson's day, and until relatively recent times, a pathway led from the footbridge up the slope of the fields, between pleasant hawthorn hedges, a part of which remain, to Comiston Farm and beyond. This path is still visible and may be joined by branching left beyond the bridge, into the open ground a few yards up Oxgangs Avenue. The little stone house which was once the collecting cistern for the Comiston Springs still stands here.

Further uphill, parallel to Swan Spring Avenue, the sturdy farm-house of Comiston also remains. Its lands, which once extended to 195 acres, were given over primarily to oats, barley, potatoes and turnips. At one time four pairs of Clydesdale horses were employed drawing the ploughs, "grubbers" and binders. Dairy farming was a secondary activity. The pathway by-passes the farmhouse and continues. On the right there once stood the byres and dairy, and, a few yards beyond, rounding the wall on the left, was the fine south-facing walled garden of Comiston House. "A wonderfully productive garden," it was worked by a professional gardener from Morningside until 1946. It is now largely turfed over and the site of modern service flats and lock-ups.

The pathway which we have been following proceeds southwards beyond the garden and emerges into what is now Caiystane Gardens. It used to be known as Cockmylane, after a little clachan which once stood on its route. This may have been the small line of farm cottages which, until about twenty years ago, stood on the present east-west connecting road running between Fox Spring Crescent, Oxgangs Green and Oxgangs Hill. According to Dixon, in his *Place Names of Midlothian,* Cockmylane means "an unfenced cart-track"; he notes that the hamlet of this name was at times referred to as Rosebank. From the path, as it runs to the right of the little wall enclosing the grounds of Comiston House, the rear of this early nineteenth-century mansion-house, now the Pentland Hills Hotel, may be glimpsed through its surrounding trees. We can approach it through the old west gateway, noting the ruined tower beside its stables. This is the most appropriate place to consider the ancient history of Comiston.

Very early references to Comiston have been recorded. According to James Stuart's source book on the district, *Notes Towards a History of Colinton Parish,* in 1292 Edward I of England handed over to John Baliol in Edinburgh Castle documents which included inventories of various lands in the vicinity of Edinburgh. Amongst these was a conveyance, believed to be dated 1286, by William le Graunt in favour of Alexander de

Maynes (Menzies) of half of the manor of Redhall, the name of which was derived from Rubea Aula, the great red-sandstone "hall" or castle of its earliest owners. Redhall was a very ancient estate which became a Barony. Included within its extensive boundaries were the present-day districts of Redhall, Colinton, Bonaly, Woodhall, Dreghorn, Oxgangs, Comiston and Swanston. In 1335 "the high lands of Colmanston" were mentioned in the Rental of the receivers for Edward III as "spoil by the King of England forfeited from the said Alexander de Meignes".

Colmanston was but one early version of the name Comiston. Dixon, in *Place Names of Midlothian,* cites others such as Colmanstone (1336), Cumyngstoun (1494), Comestoun (1531) and Coimistoun (1647), and also gives a reference to "Colman's farm". St Colman, a native of Ireland and a monk of Iona, became the third bishop of Lindisfarne. He died in 670. No historian of the district has, however, been able to discover whether this or any other Colman was associated with early Comiston.

Just within the southern boundary of the estate, in what is now Caiystane View, off Oxgangs Road North, stands the ancient stone known variously as the Caiystane, Camus Stone, Ket Stane, Kel Stane or Cat Stane. Stuart gives the derivation of *Ket* and *Cat* as from a Gaelic-English compound word meaning "Battle Stone". Considering the various battles which took place in this area, certain local historians have suggested that the name Camus was that of a Danish chieftain or commander killed in one of these and that the stone, erected as a memorial, later gave its name, Camus Stone or Comiston, to the district. However, no evidence exists to associate the stone with the name Comiston.

Although early maps indicate the site of a large Roman camp east of Comiston House, near the junction of Braid Road and Pentland Terrace, and other sources have suggested that this camp extended around Fairmilehead, one historian of the district, the Rev. John Walker, submits in his *Essays* that the Camus Stone or Caiystane was not a Roman relic as the Romans never erected memorial stones devoid of sculpture and inscriptions. Similar stones are, in any case, to be found in parts of Scotland which the Romans did not reach.

The stone stands 9' 3" above ground level and, it is believed, an equal depth below. Stuart claims that it is fixed in a bed of tenacious clay of a type which is not local. "A fine monolith of red standstone, roughly rectangular in shape," it faces almost due east and west. On the eastern face is a curved row of six ancient cup marks. The stone is now under the care of the National Trust for Scotland.

From 1335, when Alexander de Meignes is recorded as the owner of "the high lands of Colmanston", the succession of owners is well documented. Meignes was succeeded by William Cunynghame of Kilmaurs, who, in 1531, granted a redeemable right over Comiston to James Foulis, first of the notable family which for generations were to be the "Lairds of Colinton" and its adjoining lands. A few years prior to

The Caiystane in Caiystane View

Photograph by Mr W. R. Smith

The Caiystane in open fields at Comiston, c. 1898

By courtesy of Mr G. Anderson

1531, the name of Philip of Fernele is associated with Comiston, perhaps as tenant, and in 1536 there is a reference to David Farneley of Colmanstoun, this surname thereafter being spelt Fairlie. These were early members of the Fairlie family, for long owners of the Braid estate and later of Bruntsfield House.

In 1608 John Fairlie resigned the lands of Colmanstoun "cum mansionibus, maneribus, pasturagiis", which then became the property of Andrew Creich, merchant and burgess of Edinburgh, and his wife Margaret Dick. It is possible that they enlarged the original mansion-house or castle of Comiston — "the mansionibus" referred to in the disposition by John Fairlie. All that survives of this early residence is a late sixteenth-century angle-tower of rubble incorporated in the south-east corner of the modern stables. These stand a short distance south-west of the relatively modern mansion-house of Comiston, now the Pentland Hills Hotel, and may be reached from the old gate and driveway on the west, entered from the path, Cockmylane. The old ruined tower, which became a dovecote with one hundred and sixty nest holes, is twenty feet high and twelve feet in external diameter, with two oval gun loops for defensive purposes. The old rubble wall which joins the tower to the stables is part of the original castle wall and is four feet thick. On the back wall of the old gate-lodge, once situated beside the large stone-pillared entrance to the original driveway from what is now the junction of Camus Avenue and

The back gate to Comiston House (referred to by R. L. Stevenson), showing the path from Cockmylane

Photograph by Mr. W. R. Smith

Buckstone Terrace, was a sculptured stone, bearing the letters "AC" and "MD" and the date "1610" deeply incised. The stone was ornamented with a rosette beneath and lozenge above. It is presumed that the initials were those of Andrew Creich and his wife Margaret Dick, carved on what was possibly an old dormer stone two years after they obtained the lands of Comiston in 1608, the stone having been fixed later to the more modern gate-lodge. The old west entrance to Comiston House from Cockmylane merited a reference by Robert Louis Stevenson in *Edinburgh: Picturesque Notes*. "The district is dear to the superstitious," he wrote. "Hard by at the back gate of Comiston, a belated carter beheld a lady in white with the most beautiful clear shoes upon her feet, who looked upon him in a very ghostly manner, then vanished. . . "

In the extensive grounds of Comiston House, as elsewhere in this area, are to be seen the effects of glacial action. North-east of the house is a deep gorge, overgrown by trees and shrubs, which for long remained wasteland amidst modern housing development on all sides. Here was once a large sandpit, laid down in prehistoric times from sand carried along by the great sheet of water from melting glaciers. In relatively recent times, the sandpit was for long worked by a Morningside contractor who had stables in Balcarres Street. Some years before the introduction of mechanical diggers, forty men were employed to shovel sand, while a team of sixty horses hauled the sand in carts to the city. The pit ceased to be worked just before 1939. During digging here in 1907 a large section of volcanic rock was discovered measuring 135 to 150 feet long by 4 to 9 feet thick.

Following the ownership of Andrew Creich, recorded in the sculptured stone which had long since disappeared when the gate-lodge was demolished, Comiston House and its lands passed in about 1635 to John Cant of the Grange of St Giles, being inherited by his wife Catherine Creich upon her father's death. Cant was also at one time the owner of Prestonfield House. His daughter Catherine succeeded to Comiston in 1660 and married Walter Porterfield, an advocate, who subsequently acquired Morton House and Hillend. After her husband's death Catherine, known as Lady Colmestone, continued to reside at Comiston. During her ownership began an important chapter in the history of Comiston and, indeed, of Edinburgh itself.

Perhaps the most obvious geographical feature of that area of Comiston to the south of the mansion-house is the extensive marshland with its many springs and little streams. In the mid-seventeenth century, there were an increasing number of references to these in the Edinburgh Town Council Minutes. Eventually, after successful negotiations with Lady Colmestone, the civic authorities were, in 1681, able to draw upon these valuable springs on her land to provide the city's first piped water supply.

The history of Edinburgh's water supply has been recorded by many writers, notably the informative James Colston, an Edinburgh Town Councillor and member of the Edinburgh and District Water Trust whose definitive work on the subject was written in 1890. Colston, beginning with a eulogy of life-sustaining water, stresses how the shortage of water in early Edinburgh prevented the proper control of fire, a frequent occurrence in the old town's narrow closes of timber-fronted houses, and also hygiene during the many epidemics such as the outbreaks of plague. The population within the city walls had to get their water from draw-wells and pumps, located mainly in the Cowgate. In the late sixteenth century, drought was a frequent and serious problem. Water was then brought in barrels and casks from the South Loch (now the Meadows), to which Edinburgh's many brewers were directed for their supplies, from "The Wells O' Wearie" in the King's Park, and from the Pow Burn (later the Jordan Burn). In later times the Nor' Loch was drawn upon. In such primitive conditions disease was rampant.

This situation continued with no sign of improvement until 1621, when, as Maitland wrote, "the inhabitants of Edinburgh having formed a design to bring sweet waters from the country to supply themselves in the city with that precious element, applied to the Scottish Parliament for power to enable them to accomplish so desirable and necessary a work." Such power was readily granted. Edinburgh Town Council were given permission to cast "seuchs and ditches" on the route of their proposed supply from the country but were also bound to pay damages to those whose property might be involved. To finance this undertaking the Town Council proposed a special tax on Edinburgh's citizens. Despite the obvious advantages of an improved water supply, such violent opposition to the new tax was expressed in public meetings that the civic authorities were forced to postpone their scheme. It was not until 1672, more than fifty years after the first Parliamentary approval, that the Town Council were able to proceed.

The source of water from "the country" was proposed to the Edinburgh authorities by a Leith schoolmaster, John Sinclare, previously Professor of Philosophy and Mathematics at Glasgow University and the author of papers and books on hydrostatics. In other vein, he also wrote the remarkable *Satan's Invisible World Discovered*, published in 1683. After his survey of sources he recommended "the sweet waters of Comiston". These springs were some two hundred feet higher than the site of a proposed collecting and distribution reservoir at Castlehill, thus permitting the flow of water between the two points by gravity. For his "attendance and advice in the matter of the water-works", Sinclare was given a fee of £66 13s 4d.

The contract for bringing "the sweet waters of Comiston" to the city was given to a Dutch engineer, Peter Bruschi, at a fee of £2,900. He was awarded a further £50 gratuity "for carrying out the work with diligence and care". His brief was "to bring the water of Tod's Well [the Fox

Water Spring at Comiston

Photograph by Mr W. R. Smith

Spring]at Comiston to Edinburgh in a leaden pipe of a three-inch bore, to be laid one foot deep in the ground". Certain other writers have described Bruschi as German and spelt his name as Breusch or Brauss. He also had other skills, having established a paper mill at Canonmills, the object of a mysterious raid by "enemies who under silence and cloud of night came to the said paper milne, and there most maliciously and invidiously break doune the same and render her altogether useless." The invaders apparently also let the water out of the mill's sluice and threw Bruschi's wife into "the milne dame". Undeterred, he opened another paper mill at Restalrig and, in a different role, was appointed by James VII as printer to the Royal Household in Holyrood, where mob violence again forced him to flee. He is accredited with being one of the first printers in Scotland of playing cards.

Bruschi's work at Comiston was completed in 1681. The "sweet waters" were conveyed to the great tank at Castlehill and from there distributed to five cisterns or wells in the High Street situated at the Weigh House, the head of Forrester's Wynd, the Mercat Cross, the head of Niddry's Wynd and at the foot of the West Bow. Of other such wells

"Waiting at the Well" for piped water from Comiston

three remain, at John Knox's house, the south corner of George IV Bridge and the High Street, and at the foot of the West Bow (Victoria Street) in the Grassmarket. These wells were to provide classical street scenes of old Edinburgh of which many illustrations exist. At first, the water was turned on only at certain times of the day and people queued up long before the appointed hour with their assortment of containers, pitchers, jugs, casks or wooden water-stoups (the latter being a popular wedding present of the time). The receptacles were often left in a long queue beside the wells, often nearly a hundred yards long, the owners appearing only when the water was due to come on. Anyone caught jumping the queue, or expressing impatience over delays through bad language, was subject to a heavy fine. The principal and most colourful characters of this old Edinburgh street scene were the "professionals", the water caddies, who dressed distinctively, the men often in old red army coats and the women in bonnets. They wore official badges and had their own guild or society with mutual benefit schemes. They were given priority in the water queues. Eventually, however, most wells were provided with two taps, one for the exclusive use of the caddies. Their containers filled, they would set off up the high stairs of the tall Old Town closes, selling the "sweet waters" from Comiston at a regulated price per pint.

The first precious water supply from the Tod or Fox Spring was soon increased by drawing upon other springs, the Hare, Swan and Peewit. These were led into the cistern in the little stone building which still stands on the south side of Oxgangs Avenue. Over the end of each pipe pouring its valuable contribution into the cistern was a lead figure of the animal after which the spring was named. Small stone buildings were also erected above the source of each spring to prevent contamination.

The underground route of the pipe from Comiston may still be identified at certain points. The first of these is over the eastern slopes of the Braid Burn Valley, just above the stage of the open-air theatre. Here two small concrete stones marked "5" and "7" indicate, firstly, the diameter of the pipe which replaced the original three-inch one from Comiston in 1704 and, secondly, the diameter of the pipe eventually laid alongside from the Swanston springs. The two pipes then pass underneath the Braidburn Filling Station, above the Mortonhall Tennis Club courts, where they were discovered during the digging of foundations. The next point at which the pipes can be identified is underneath a metal grid within the walls of the Hermitage of Braid in Braid Road. This may be seen by crossing the little bridge over the Braid Burn just inside the Hermitage entrance gates and turning up a little path on the right. Owners of the Braid Estate were paid £1,000 Scots for permission to allow the pipes to go through their lands. The pipes then pass down Braid Road and swing right at Cluny Gardens, passing under the old Suburban

Individual pipes from the Hare, Tod, Swan and Teuchat springs at Comiston, each with a lead figure of the appropriate animal, enter the collecting tank in the water house above Oxgangs Avenue

Photograph by Mr. John Bowman

407

Railway line and the Jordan Burn towards Woodburn Terrace. On the wall of Canaan Lodge two more stones marked "5" and "7" denote the pipes' passage underground. Inside the southern boundary wall of Woodville, north of Canaan Lodge, similar stones are fixed, and on the wall of the modern villa, The Whitehouse, in Whitehouse Loan, they are again to be seen. The pipes then make their way under Thirlestane Road, Spottiswoode Street, the Meadows, the grounds of George Heriot's School and the Grassmarket until, in a channel cut through solid rock below the Castle Esplanade, they enter the reservoir tank at Castlehill.

Despite the benefits of the new water supply, opposition continued through fear of a water levy and the Town Council fixed penalties for anyone caught interfering with or damaging the pipe from Comiston. From the five springs eventually tapped at Comiston, the colume of water collected in winter was eight or nine hundred Scots pints per minute. The amount never exceeded 135,000 gallons per day, and it was often less. In summer it could fall to a quarter of this volume. After the collection of water from the first spring at Comiston, disputes arose between Edinburgh Town Council and the "Laird of Comiston" over the use of other springs in his lands. The civic authorities offered to buy the whole estate but this offer was refused. In 1698 the Town Council persuaded Lady Comiston to grant the use of other springs. Among various payments by Edinburgh's civic authorities over the years to the owners of the Comiston estate, they undertook to provide, for the lady of the mansion-house, "the best silk gown it was in the power of the Corporation to bestow and to pay the proprietor the sum of 7/6d per annum". This latter payment continued into quite recent times.

When the original three-inch pipe was enlarged to five inches in 1704, and other springs were drawn upon, the contracting engineer engaged was the distinguished Frenchman, Dr John Theophilus Desaqulier. His colleague was a German named Covay. The work took several years and on the inaugural day of the increased water supply a great gathering of civic dignitaries assembled at Castlehill. Covay, acting as Master of Ceremonies, opened the valve to release the new supply. No water flowed. Nonplussed, he set out on horseback for Comiston, where he found the valve at the source to be in perfect working order. Covay, who could not face returning to Castlehill, panicked and fled to Berwick. One of his workmen, however, proved more practical and calm. Suspecting an air lock, he drove a nail into the pipe at the source — and, shortly afterwards, water gushed forth at Castlehill. Certain writers have associated this incident with Peter Bruschi, the inaugurator of the first Comiston water supply.

With the steady growth of Edinburgh, the Comiston water supply eventually proved inadequate and the civic authorities directed their eyes further south to another promising source — Swanston. In the reign of George II an Act of Parliament of April 17th, 1758 gave Edinburgh Town

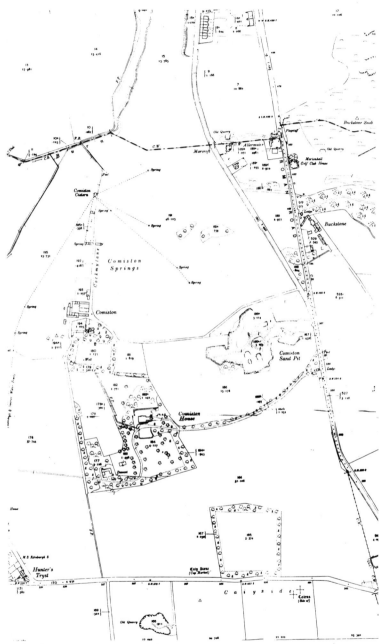

Ordnance Survey map, 1914, showing Comiston and Oxgangs.
By courtesy of the National Library of Scotland.

Edinburgh's first piped water supply from Comiston has, since 1945,
been discharged into the Braid Burn

Photograph by Mr. W. A. Sharp

Council powers to draw upon the several burns and springs at Swanston. Although this new supply never yielded more than sixty cubic feet of water per minute, and in the dry period a fifth of this volume, the city's wells were nevertheless filled and the first private supplies piped to houses in the High Street at a fee of £1 per annum.

As Edinburgh's New Town developed, a further increase in water supplies became necessary and the city authorities looked further south. In 1819 the responsibility of Edinburgh Town Council for ensuring water supplies was conveyed to the Edinburgh Joint Stock Water Company for £30,000. Membership of this body included many prominent citizens. A new era had begun. The original modest trickle of the "sweet waters of Comiston" was soon to be submerged in an increasing torrent from much further south. In 1822 a new supply was brought from Crawley Springs at Glencorse under a scheme devised by the distinguished engineers Thomas Telford and John Rennie, which earned them world renown. In the same year the Glencorse reservoir was constructed. After this an increasing number of houses in Edinburgh received a direct water supply, the cost being 5% per annum upon gross rent. In 1945, with the steady development of surrounding housing estates, the long chapter of Edinburgh's water supply from Comiston and Swanston, which lasted two and a half centuries, came to an end. The dangers of bacterial contamination led to this supply of water being discontinued. The loss of some two hundred gallons per minute into the Braid Burn is negligible in relation to Edinburgh's present consumption of forty-five million gallons per day.

The stone figures of the fox, hare, swan and peewit have long since been removed from the collecting cistern and are now in Huntly House Museum in the Canongate. There, too, may be seen the original tree-trunk pipes from the first Swanston supply. The iron pipes which replaced them are still used to convey water from the Fairmilehead filtration plant to tanks in Edinburgh Castle.

Following its long association with the Porterfield family, Comiston in 1715 passed to James Forrest, a Leith merchant. The estate was to remain in the possession of this family for over one hundred and fifty years. In 1733 Forrest also acquired the neighbouring lands of Dreghorn.

Comiston House, built by James Forrest in 1815

Photograph by Mr W. R. Smith

He was succeeded at Comiston by his son James, also a merchant, who in 1741 purchased the adjoining estate of Oxgangs and the district of Baads. The next of the Forrests to own Comiston, yet another James, inherited the lands in early childhood from his grandfather. It was he who built the present-day mansion-house in 1815. This has been described as "a neat country villa, typical of its time". The house is oblong in shape with a circular bay projecting from its north side and a service wing to the east. The front, which faces south, is pedimented and has various Ionic decorations. A stained-glass window on the left of the vestibule bears the Forrest coat of arms.

Qualifying as an advocate in 1803, James Forrest became prominent in Edinburgh as a supporter and pioneer of many public causes. He was Lord Provost of Edinburgh from 1837 until 1843, and was created a Baronet in 1838. Shortly after his election as Lord Provost he called a public meeting to petition Parliament to introduce voting by ballot and thus prevent intimidation. He was a strong supporter of Dr Thomas Chalmers in his opposition to Patronage within the Church of Scotland and, at the Disruption in 1843, Forrest, while still Lord Provost, along with many Edinburgh Town Councillors, seceded from the established Church of Scotland and joined the Free Church. As the Grand Master Mason of Scotland he laid the foundation stone of the Scott Monument in Princes Street. He was influential in securing legislation which became the Poor Law (Scotland) Act in 1845. The establishment of a Fever Hospital for the city was another of his interests and, with Sir John Stuart Forbes of Greenhill, he led a movement for the abolition of toll fees levied upon those travelling past Wrychtishousis, near Tollcross, the toll being moved southwards from this point to the Briggs o' Braid at the foot of Morningside village in 1861. Forrest Road, a new approach to George IV Bridge, was built during Sir James Forrest's term as Lord Provost and so named in his honour.

Despite so much public service which earned him a high reputation in the city, one episode in his career was to make him the subject of parody in song, and for long a source of amusement to the people of Edinburgh. In 1842, while he was Lord Provost, Queen Victoria paid her first visit to the Capital. On her scheduled day of arrival she disembarked at Granton from the Royal Yacht earlier than had been expected, and found no Lord Provost or bailies there to receive her. Queen Victoria did not wait; she set out for Dalkeith Palace to spend a few days there before entering Edinburgh. The Lord Provost and city dignitaries hastened to Dalkeith and all was soon forgiven, but the *contretemps* gave rise to much public amusement and inspired not a few songs. One of these was a parody on "Hey Johnnie Cope":

> Hey Jamie Forrest are ye waukin' yet?
> Or are your Bailies snorin' yet?

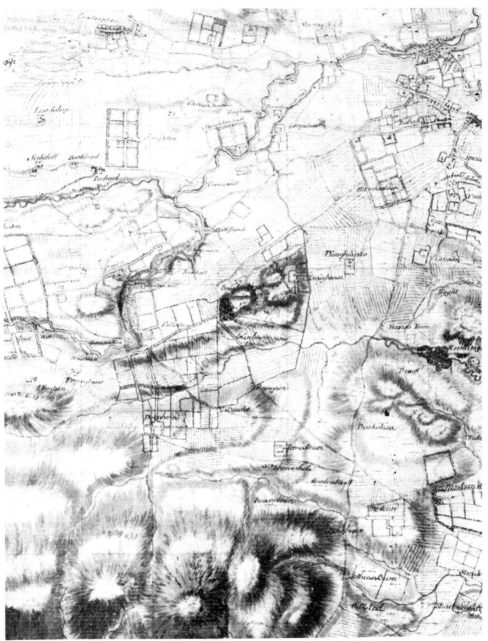

Part of General Roy's Survey of Scotland, 1747

By courtesy of the National Library of Scotland

413

If ye are waukin' I would wit
Ye'd hae a merry, merry mornin'!

The Queen she's come to Granton pier,
Nae Provost and nae Bailies here:
They're in their beds I muckle fear
Sae early in the mornin'!

When Queen Victoria did enter the city, Provost and bailies ensured a specially prompt and fitting welcome.

The Forrest Baronetcy became extinct upon the death of Sir Charles Forrest in 1928, his only son having been killed in the First World War. The family tomb is in Greyfriars churchyard, on the south wall, a short distance east of the Covenanters' Prison.

Among the more notable residents in Comiston House in more recent times was the Dowager Lady Elphinstone, great-aunt of the Queen, who lived there for a few years from 1915. An old lady in her eighties, she drove about the district in a three-wheeled basket chair drawn by a shetland pony. On Monday afternoons she would ride over to Hunter's Tryst for tea. Having been the Pentland Hills Hotel for some years, Comiston House became Caiystane Park Hotel, but is now once again the Pentland Hills Hotel.

OXGANGS

Adjacent to Comiston on the west is the district of Oxgangs. The name is derived from "oxgang" or "oxengait", the extent of land an ox could plough in the course of a year, this being thirteen acres. As Skene expressed it: "Alwaies ane oxengate of land suld conteine threttene acker. . ." The earliest recorded reference to Oxgangs is in 1425, when it is mentioned in relation to the Barony of Redhall. Then the lands of "le Oxgangis" were conveyed by John Whiting to Sir John Forester of Corstorphine. Other early references are to Oxingangis in 1524 and Auchingang in 1635.

In 1539, when Sir William Cunynhame of Redhall disponed to James Foulis of Colinton the lands of Oxgangs, reference is made to Baads, Pilmuir and Fordel. These were locations within Oxgangs. In 1610 Baads appears in the records when its tenant was Andro Plane and it is indicated, along with numerous other place names in the district, in General Roy's *Drawn Military Survey of Scotland* in 1747, spelt Bauds. The origin of the name is either from "bawd", a hare, or, more probably, from the Gaelic "bad" meaning a clump, cluster or hamlet. Until the early 1940s a pathway led from the west side of what is now Oxgangs Road North, past the south boundary wall of Oxgangs farmhouse (now the district police station) and on through a group of cottages, to emerge into Redford Road

The hamlet of Fordel at Oxgangs

By courtesy of Edinburgh City Libraries

nearly opposite Fordel Cottage. These cottages were the last remains of the hamlet of Baads and the ground surrounding them was known as Baads Green. On the east of today's NAAFI stores in Redford Road a lane still leads downhill past the one-time site of Baads to Colinton Mains. On the south side of Redford Road, a short distance west of the NAAFI stores, is Fordel Cottage, still so named on its gate. The hamlet of Fordel, not shown on General Roy's map of 1747 but indicated on John Laurie's Plan of the County of Midlothian, dated 1786, lay a few yards south of the cottage, in the woods. The pathway from Oxgangs farmhouse, which passed through Baads, continued across Redford Road, through Fordel and eventually to the entrance to Howden Glen behind the shooting range. Dixon derives Fordel from "fuar dail", the cold meadow. Another suggestion is that the little hamlet was situated in a dell beside a ford over a small stream which still runs in this vicinity. On the north gable end of Fordel Cottage James Trotter in 1885 set a plaque commemorating General Charles George Gordon ("Chinese" Gordon), with verses praising the British Empire's strength and virtues. This shrine to General Gordon, a footnote indicates, was visited by Sir Charles Wilson in 1886. Other locations within the district of Oxgangs, in certain documents referred to as "rooms", were Little Fordel, Auchingane, Kirkslope and Gallowlee. Oxgangs remained in the possession of the noted Foulis of Colinton family until 1719 when the 8th Laird sold the lands to Alexander

Oxgangs Farmhouse, c. 1898
By courtesy of Mr G. Anderson

The old cedar tree under which R. L. Stevenson wrote some of his early poetry, inside the gateway of the former Oxgangs Farmhouse, now a Police Station
By courtesy of W. A. Sharp

Cleghorn, a merchant in Edinburgh, along with the neighbouring districts of Newmains and Firrhill.

The old farmhouse of Oxgangs which still stands at the west of the junction of Oxgangs Avenue and Oxgangs Road North, became, after renovation about twenty years ago, the local police station. On the left of the entrance courtyard is a very old cedar tree. When the young Robert Louis Stevenson resided at Swanston Cottage with his parents Oxgangs farm was a favourite haunt of his, his father being a close friend of the farmer. Several of the poems in *A Child's Garden of Verses,* not published until many years later, were first scribbled out as he sat on the lower branches of this venerable tree. The old farmhouse was also given a cherished memento. On one occasion young Robert Louis Stevenson marked his height on a wooden door and signed his measurement: "R. L. Stevenson. . . 5' 8¾" — stocking soles". During the renovation of the farmhouse the door was salvaged and now forms part of a Stevensonia collection in Oxgangs Primary School. This also includes a bust of Robert Louis Stevenson, photographs, a map of Treasure Island, a figure of Long John Silver and a model of Stevenson's house, Vailima, in Samoa. The collection has attracted Stevenson devotees from many parts of the world.

Colinton Mains, the district to the north of Oxgangs, was originally the Newmains of Colinton. A large farm was established here by Sir James Foulis, 2nd Baronet and sixth member of this family to own the lands of Colinton. Reputed to be the most distinguished of the powerful Foulis family, Sir James was an ardent Royalist, contributing £6,000 Scots for the establishment of a horse regiment in support of Charles I. When Cromwell invaded Scotland in 1650 he suffered for his generosity. "His whole tenants houses, barns, byres and whole onsets in the town and lands of Craiglockhart and Bowbridge were totally burned by the usurper's army, to his total loss of £77,000. These ravages included destruction of Sir James' byres and farmlands at the Mains of Colinton." In 1719 the Newmains were sold to Alexander Cleghorn. Twenty-six years later "Collington Mains and Firrhill" were again the object of pillage when Bonnie Prince Charlie and his army passed through the district from Slateford and proceeded along the banks of the Braid Burn, through Morningside and on to Holyrood. In 1768 the Newmains of Colinton passed to Thomas Rigg of Morton, and in 1847 they were acquired by Miss Ann Rattray. In 1881 Alexander Rattray sold what had now become known as Colinton Mains farm, and much of its land to the north, to Edinburgh Corporation for the building of the city's first Fever Hospital. Certain of the old farm buildings remained standing and some farming continued in the district until the early 1950s. About this time, when most of the farm buildings were demolished, some were restored to become the Colinton Mains Community Centre which still serves a useful purpose in this now populous residential area. Firrhill High School, opened in 1960, has fourteen hundred pupils. West of the school, concealed in the northern slopes of the hill, are two tanks, which supplement the storage of the Edinburgh water supply filtered at Fairmilehead and also break pressure. They hold one and a half million and four million gallons of water.

The several churches in the Oxgangs-Colinton Mains district are relatively modern. The earliest is Colinton Mains Parish Church, opened in January 1954. The congregation had originally worshipped in a nearby temporary building from 1939. The foundation stone of the church was laid by the late Lord Provost Sir John Falconer, pioneer of the Edinburgh International Festival and a Colinton resident. The architecture of the church is traditionally Scottish and the interior art and furnishings include much of interest.

St John's Church of Scotland further uphill in Oxgangs Road North was opened in 1958 when the surrounding new housing area was rapidly developing. The church had its origins in Old St John's Church at Leith. In the earliest days of St John's at Oxgangs there were no local schools or shops and the church served as the district's first community centre. The minister organised street groups to discuss local needs, thus greatly assisting families to settle into their new environment. The more formalised community service now offered by the Edinburgh Corporation Community Centre, opened a little to the east of St John's in 1967, at a cost of £65,000, was indeed originally stimulated by these church groups. St John's church is modern in design, though the bell in its tower came from Trinity College Church in Jeffrey Street and was originally one of Edinburgh's town bells, rung morning and evening. It was cast in Holland in 1632.

St Hilda's Episcopal Church in Oxgangs Avenue was opened in 1966. Of striking modern design, its origins lie with a small congregation which first met in a cottage in Colinton. A hall adjacent to the present church was opened in 1951. Embedded in the walls of the present church are stones brought from Newbattle Abbey and on the right of the altar is a pinnacle from Roslin Chapel.

Another of the local churches is St Mark's Roman Catholic Church in Oxgangs Avenue, opened by Archbishop, now Cardinal, Gray in 1962. The stone came from the quarry at Nunraw Abbey in East Lothian. The congregation first worshipped in the nearby Hunter's Tryst Primary School. St Mark's is modern, but conservative in design.

HUNTER'S TRYST

Proceeding up Oxgangs Road North to Hunter's Tryst, at the north corner of Redford Road is the Cockit Hat Plantation, laid out to resemble the headgear worn by the gentry in bygone days. Now sparse in trees and less attractive than formerly, the plantation is subject to a preservation order. Immediately beyond, at the south corner of Redford Road, is the

Hunter's Tryst
By courtesy of Mr G. Anderson

East Lodge of the old Dreghorn estate. On the northern chimney stack of this little house is a carving of a small sailing ship and, below, *"ALOHA"*.

When the attractive modern restaurant at Hunter's Tryst was opened in 1969, it restored the long tradition of hospitality associated with this ancient inn which had been closed since 1862. Hunter's Tryst has much historic interest, first appearing in General Roy's survey of 1747, inaccurately positioned. The belief that it was a rendezvous or tryst for early Scottish Kings hunting on the lower slopes of the Pentlands is based more on legend than fact, but from the mid-eighteenth century until 1862 the inn was well patronised. One early account relates: "The ale-house was kept by two respectable old ladies who cooked a capital dinner. In former days it was the custom for citizens of Edinburgh to shut up their places of business early on Saturdays and to go out into the country to dine about four or five o'clock at one of these little inns. The Hunter's Tryst was a favourite resort." The earliest traceable signboard read:

Hostelry: Betty and Katie McCane

Out o'er the hill to Habbie's Howe
Where a' the springs o' summer grow,
Here's corn and hay for horses and asses,
Baps and ale for lads and lassies,

419

And for to try to please the gentry
There's something better in the pantry.

The reference to Habbie's Howe led to some confusion, certain writers suggesting that Allan Ramsay's "Gentle Shepherd" was set in the surroundings of Hunter's Tryst. The scenery described in this rural drama does not, however, match that of Hunter's Tryst and it is more likely that Habbie's Howe inn at Nine Mile Burn near the Carlops was the setting of Ramsay's poem.

In its heyday in the early nineteenth century, Hunter's Tryst was the meeting place of the famous Six Foot High Club of which many of Edinburgh's most distinguished literary figures were honorary members. These included Sir Walter Scott, James Hogg (the Ettrick Shepherd), who was the club's poet laureate, Lockhart (Scott's biographer) and Christopher North. Sir Walter wrote in his Journal for March 5th, 1829: "What a tail of the Alphabet I should draw after me, were I to sign with the indications of the different societies I belong to, beginning with the Presidency of the Royal Society of Edinburgh and ending with the Umpire of the Six Foot High Club." The club was founded in 1826. Membership

Uniform of the Six Foot High Club

By courtesy of Edinburgh City Libraries

was restricted to those over six feet tall, though exceptions were made by bestowing honorary membership on giants of the literary world. The object of the club was to practise the national games of Scotland and gymnastics. The members' town gymnasium was in the club rooms in East Thistle Street and later at Malta Terrace. Field events took place on open ground behind Hunter's Tryst. Reports of the club's contests appeared regularly in the *Edinburgh Courant,* that of May 10th, 1828 reading: "A very fine day with many ladies present. The following performances were turned in: Quoits: putting an iron bullet of 21 pounds — distance: 32 feet. Throwing a large sledge-hammer of 16 pounds 2 ounces — the astonishing distance of 91 feet. The twelve pounds hammer — the no less astonishing distance of 105 feet. The hop, step and leap — 40 feet; and the steeple chase — about 1 mile — 3½ minutes." The last performance would seem to indicate a runner of Olympic standards in the ranks of the Six Foot High Club! Rifle-shooting, golf and curling were also practised. The club dress uniform, of which illustrations remain, was "the finest dark green cloth coat, double-breasted with special buttons and a velvet collar. The vest was of white Kerseymere. Trousers were black. On special occasions, a tile hat was worn." The club was appointed Guard of Honour to the Hereditary Lord High Constable of Scotland in 1828.

Built into the garden wall of a private house opposite Hunter's Tryst inn is an old milestone bearing the weather-beaten inscription: "5 miles from Edinburgh G.P.O. To regulate the post horse duties payable by hackney coaches 1824." The inn was a resting place for stage coaches plying to and from London. In 1824 the journey, including overnight stops at inns *en route,* took from five to eight days and the single fare was £60. When Robert Louis Stevenson wrote *Edinburgh: Picturesque Notes* in 1878 he was twenty-eight years old and living with his parents at Swanston Cottage. The inn had then been closed for sixteen years, though he may possibly have been taken to visit it in earlier days. While at Swanston he eagerly noted the stories related about it by local people. Having described the ghostly lady in white who appeared one night to a carter at the back gate to Comiston House as one sign that "the district is dear to the superstitious", he goes on to relate, in *Picturesque Notes:* "just in front is the Hunter's Tryst, once a roadside inn, and not so long ago, haunted by the devil in person. Satan led the inhabitants a pitiful existence. He shook the four corners of the building with lamentable outcries, beat at the doors and windows, overthrew crockery in the dead hours of the morning, and danced unholy dances on the roof. Every kind of spiritual disinfection was put in requisition; chosen ministers were summoned out of Edinburgh and prayed by the hour; pious neighbours sat up all night making a noise of psalmody; but Satan minded them no more than the wind about the hill-tops; and it was only after years of persecution, that he left the Hunter's Tryst in peace to occupy himself with the remainder of mankind." Stevenson comments: "One cannot help having a good deal of the winter wind in the last story," and adds that indeed the wind has been responsible for making "some of the most fiendish noises in the world" such as terrify country folk.

In an article in the *Dreghorn College Review* or *The Echo* dated May 15th, 1865 and entitled "The Hunter's Tryst Ghost", the writer describes the manifestations of the inn's diabolical visitor, anticipating the explanation suggested by Stevenson thirteen years later. "The ghost took the form of a long moan," says the College Review writer, "especially noisy when there was a west wind present. Rather undramatically the ghost was laid by the discovery that it was loudest at the line of the pipes that conveyed the water from Bonaly Reservoir to Edinburgh. The pipes ran from Bonaly close by the entrance to Howden Glen, linking up with the Swanston supply, and then past Hunter's Tryst to the city. The ghost was noisiest after dry weather. The drought, it seemed, had first caused the ground to parch and crack and had at the same time lowered the water level in the pond (Bonaly) to the level of the supply pipe, which, in these days being made of wood, was liable to rot and give way. The wind thus got into the pipe at the pond and finding vent at some crack or fissure near the Hunter's Tryst caused the unearthly sounds which so alarmed the natives." Such may be the scientific explanation, but the story Stevenson related so colourfully will remain in the treasury of local folklore.

Long after he had left Edinburgh to settle with his wife in Samoa, Stevenson retained vivid memories of Hunter's Tryst which were to feature prominently in one of his last novels, *St Ives*. Like *Weir of Hermiston* it was not completed, though so anxious was he to finish *St Ives* that, despite his steady deterioration in health and his doctor's advice to curtail his writing, he persevered with it, acquiring from his step-daughter a knowledge of the deaf and dumb alphabet and dictating to her the later chapters. The book was, in the end, completed after Stevenson's death by Sir Arthur Quiller-Couch. In Chapter XXVII of *St Ives* Monsieur Saint-Yves, the French prisoner who had escaped from Edinburgh Castle and made his way to Swanston Cottage, where he was concealed by Flora in the hen-house, leaves Swanston and stealthily makes his way by the vicinity of Hunter's Tryst. He relates: "I found a plain rustic cottage by the wayside, of the sort called double, with a signboard over the door; and the lights within streaming forth and somewhat mitigating the darkness of the morning. I was enabled to decipher the description: 'The Hunter's Tryst, by Alexander Henry, Porter, Ales and British Spirits, Beds'." Questioned upon entering the inn, he said he had walked from Peebles. "They jostled me among them into the room where they had been sitting, a plain hedge-row ale-house parlour, with a roaring fire in the chimney and a prodigious number of empty bottles on the floor; and informed me that I was made, by this reception, a temporary member of the Six-Foot-High Club, an athletic society of young men in a good station, who made of the Hunter's Tryst a frequent resort. . ." Though so far from his beloved Swanston and its surroundings in distance and time, Stevenson in *St Ives* recalls his days there most vividly.

After the inn closed in 1862, Hunter's Tryst became an important and prosperous farm. Nothing remains on record of its development during the remainder of the nineteenth century, but a valuable account of the farm and the life of those who worked there has been provided by Mr Rodgers who owned Hunter's Tryst during the 1920s. "The house", he relates, "was lit by oil lamps and cooking was done on a range in the old farm kitchen. The coal supply had to be collected on an old farm cart from the coal pit at Roslin. There was no piped hot water in the house. When each member of the family went to bed they lifted a lighted candle-stick from the dresser. The family rose at 3.30 a.m. every day and soon afterwards milked the cows for the morning delivery." Before beginning the milking, the farmhands were provided for from thirty girdles of scones baked by Mr Rogers' mother. Twenty-five milk cows, three hundred hens and one hundred and eighty pigs were kept. Turnips and potatoes for the livestock were obtained from Comiston and Swanston farms. In the early 1920s, Hunter's Tryst Dairy delivered milk to houses in Colinton Road and Churchhill, then later to Marchmont and Morningside.

At the beginning of the century the children in the Hunter's Tryst district still attended the little school in Swanston, where the teacher was Miss Graham who lived at Juniper Green. Mr Rodgers himself, as a boy, resided at Morton Mains and attended South Morningside School. The district was at one time rich in game, including partridges, pheasants and rabbits. Pheasant was a common dish for the farm folk at Hunter's Tryst. Excess game was taken and sold at the old meat-market in Foun-tainbridge. The game-keeper at Hunter's Tryst used to call at South Morningside School on Fridays to recruit boys to act as beaters on Saturday mornings. The boys were paid five shillings for their assistance between 10 a.m. and 4 p.m., and were given a free lunch. Peacocks strutted in the grounds of Comiston House, and foxes were a problem for local farmers; herons and kingfishers were also commonly seen at the Braid Burn. More dramatically, Mr Rodgers recalled that in 1916, when Redford Barracks had just been completed, a German spy was caught in the vicinity of the Cockit Hat Plantation. He had been drawing plans of the new military barracks at Redford. In later years Hunter's Tryst farm was a rendezvous for those interested in the breeding and riding of pointer horses.

CHAPTER 7

Swanston

A short distance to the east of Hunter's Tryst, along Oxgangs Road North, Swanston Road turns sharply to the right. Here a large framed map enables the visitor to identify places of interest in the magnificent panorama to be enjoyed from this high vantage point. Who other than Robert Louis Stevenson to describe the descent into Swanston, across the valley formed long ago by glacial erosion? In *Edinburgh: Picturesque Notes,* now almost home at the end of his walk from the city, through Morningside, the valley of the Braid Burn, and Comiston, he continues: "The road goes down through another valley and then finally begins to scale the main slope of the Pentlands. A bouquet of old trees stands round a white farmhouse; and from a neighbouring dell you can see smoke rising and leaves rustling in the breeze. Straight above, the hills climb a thousand feet into the air. The neighbourhood about the time of the lambs is clamorous with the bleating of flocks, and you will be wakened in the grey of early summer mornings by the barking of a dog or the voice of a shepherd shouting to the echoes. This, with the hamlet lying behind, unseen, is Swanston." The view which Stevenson so vividly describes remains largely unspoilt. As this was designated a Conservation Area under the Civic Amenities Act of 1967, hopefully his description will serve for some time.

Swanston is usually linked with Stevenson, but its history predates his residence there by many centuries. Dixon, in *Place Names of Midlothian,* notes references to "Swanynystroun" (1214), "Swaynestone" (1336) and "Sveinn's farm" (undated), but these appear to have been isolated entries in ancient records conveying no other information.

Before descending into Swanston it would be appropriate to stop at the top of Swanston Road to consider the early history of the area. The road itself, once a simple cart-track, was the boundary between the lands of Easter and Wester Swanston. The first official reference to Swanston is in a charter from the reign of David II (1329-71). At this period Swanston formed the south-east corner of the Barony of Redhall. In 1462 it was split into three portions, Easter and Wester Swanston and the Temple Lands. Easter Swanston, to the left of Swanston Road as it descends, was, from the mid-fifteenth century, in the possession of a family named Ross. In 1749 it passed to Henry Trotter of Mortonhall. It included the mansion-house of Swanston (now known as the farmhouse) and the farm of Bowbridge on the eastern side of the Biggar Road, beside the Lothian Burn. Wester Swanston was once the property of Sir John Cockburn,

View towards Swanston
By courtesy of W. A. Sharp

Usher to the King in 1462. In 1538 it passed to the Foulis family of Colinton, and in 1670 to the Trotters of Mortonhall. The Temple Lands were small in area and cannot now be exactly located. The name is believed to have originated with the Templars, or Knights of the Temple, an association of men whose vows united those of monks with those of knights, and whose object was to protect pilgrims on visits to the Holy Land. They were introduced into Scotland by David I in about 1153, being established at Temple in Midlothian. Among numerous estates bestowed upon them, Swanston, it is believed, was included, though no precise confirmation of this has been discovered. In a charter by James VI in 1614, which lists all the Templars' possessions in Scotland, a reference is made to "terras templarias de Swainstoun possessas". Certainly a part of Swanston was traditionally known as the Temple Lands. By 1806, when the Trotters of Mortonhall acquired these lands, their ownership of the entire Swanston district was complete.

The village of Swanston, frequently described as a mere hamlet, grew up in the early eighteenth century around the farm. The traditional belief that the farm was once a grange of Whitekirk Abbey in East Lothian, suggested by several writers including Stevenson, cannot be substantiated

425

Plan of the lands of Dreghorn, Oxgangs, Comiston and Swanston

From "Notes Towards a History of Colinton Parish" by James Steuart

from historical records. Certainly the pre-Reformation church at Whitekirk was once within the jurisdiction of the Canons of Holyrood Abbey, and a link between Swanston farm and Whitekirk may have arisen for this reason. The original farmhouse existed in the mid-seventeenth century and was a hospitable refuge for the oft-persecuted Covenanters who frequently held conventicles on the Pentlands above Swanston. Bread, cheese, bannocks and brandy were always available for any fugitive who might arrive under cover of darkness at the farmhouse door. The Covenanters, decimated at the Battle of Rullion Green, near Flotterstone, in 1666, passed through Swanston during their retreat which had brought them hastily from Ayrshire, through West Lothian and by way of Colinton to the Pentlands. The farmhouse, rebuilt in the early eighteenth century, still stands. In recent years it was used as a bothy for seasonal farm-workers; for a period it was a private residence; but today it is deserted and urgently in need of repair.

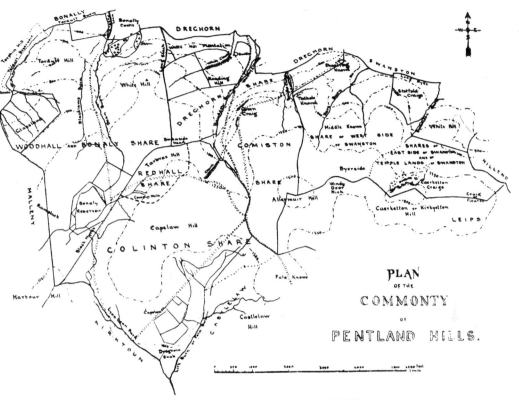

Plan of the Commonty of Pentland Hills
From "Notes Towards a History of Colinton Parish" by James Steuart

Swanston village, about six hundred feet above sea-level, originally consisted of ten thatched cottages, the Hare Burn rising in the lower slopes of Caerketton providing a valuable water supply. Around 1838 its population numbered one hundred and three — forty-nine men and fifty-four women. The life of farm-workers in Swanston and the living conditions in their cottages in early times were in contrast to the romanticised picture conveyed by Stevenson, writing at the close of the nineteenth century. Their primitive way of life was like that of farm-workers in other parts of Scotland, such as has been described in various social commentaries, notably William Somerville's *Autobiography of a Working Man,* published in 1848. The cottages at Swanston each had one main room measuring thirteen feet by twelve feet, a privy and an adjacent midden equal in size to the main room. Some cottages had an additional "closet" which housed the parents' bed. Originally there was no flooring, only the bare earth. Despite such primitive conditions, the interiors of the

427

cottages were, according to Stevenson, "models of neatness, beds with patch-work covers, shelves with willow-pattern plates," and, when floors were installed, these, with the kitchen table, were kept bright with scrubbing and polishing. A brightly polished kettle would sit beside the open fire and the entrance steps would gleam immaculately with pipe-clay.

Swanston farm produced, in rotation, potatoes, turnips, and beans; wheat, barley, hay and oats. Its pastureland extended to 138 acres. The wage of a married ploughman in the mid-nineteenth century was £16 per annum, along with an allowance of sixty-five stones of oatmeal, twelve hundredweight of potatoes, free meat for four weeks during harvest time, a cottage, garden land and coal. Farm labourers received ten shillings per week in summer and nine shillings in winter. Women and boys who worked at hoeing received ninepence per day, but during the harvest their wages were regulated by the labour-hiring market held in Edinburgh every Monday morning. The women of Swanston washed their clothes in the Hare Burn which ran through the village. The family of Finnie was associated with Swanston farm for several generations.

The date of the establishment of the village schoolhouse, now the White House, is not on record. At one time it had twenty-five pupils, but in 1931, the population of Swanston having greatly diminished, the little school was closed. In the early nineteenth century children from Swanston travelled, on foot or by farm-carts, to the old schoolhouse in Morningside. An early teacher at Swanston, Miss Graham, used to walk daily from Colinton to Swanston and back again. After it was closed, the schoolhouse was used for evening classes in dressmaking and woodwork, and as a Women's Rural Institute centre. For some time it also functioned as an important village community centre where dances and social evenings were held. In 1946 Mrs J. Boyd, who was the last teacher in the school, and her husband bought the old schoolhouse, which became their home.

The highlight of the village year was the "Kirn", a lively ceilidh-type celebration to mark "Harvest Home", held in the barn of Swanston farm. The Second World War put an end to this great social occasion. Just after the War many villagers left Swanston and the empty cottages fell into disrepair. Up till this time the village had changed very little in appearance from its early days, but between 1959 and 1962 Edinburgh Corporation undertook restoration of the cottages. The outer rubble walls of the original ten cottages were retained and whitewashed, but they were altered to form seven cottage apartments. The roofs were re-thatched by the late John Brough of Auchtermuchty, one of Scotland's last thatchers, who died in 1972. He used rushes gathered from the banks of the Tay. Rents for the modernised cottages were fixed at between £150 and £200 per annum, tenants being selected by interview. To the north -east of the old village straddling the burn, New Swanston was built about

Swanston Village, showing, in front, John Todd's cottage and beyond, the two-storey village schoolhouse

By courtesy of City of Edinburgh Museums

the turn of the century, its sturdy stone cottages with slated roofs and ornate chimney-pots forming three sides of a square in the style of a typical Scottish farming town.

Above the old village, just within the boundary fence and gate at the path leading to Caerketton, is a commemorative seat presented by his friends in tribute to the distinguished Scottish poet Edwin Muir (1887-1959) who often meditated at this spot. Much of the land of Swanston farm is still under cultivation and most of the principal houses, including the original village cottages, are the subject of a preservation order. The encroachment of new buildings within a specified distance of Swanston is now regulated by statute and in Edinburgh's "Development Plan for the

City", approved by the Secretary of State for Scotland, Swanston is within an area designated as primarily for agricultural purposes. It is within the Green Belt and part of a region recognised as of landscape interest. Perhaps the only "threat" to Swanston's environment is contained in the *Report and Draft Recommendations of the Pentland Hills Technical Group,* published in 1972, which outlines proposals for establishing a Country Park with various recreational facilities on the northern slopes of Caerketton and Allermuir. Past agreements drawn up between Edinburgh Corporation and the Trotter family, the landowners, would, however, make such proposals difficult to implement.

"Straight above" Swanston, wrote Stevenson, "the hills climb a thousand feet into the air" — not an exaggeration as the village itself is just over five hundred feet above sea level while Caerketton rises to 1,568 feet and Allermuir, to the west, to 1,618 feet. The name Caerketton has been rendered in various spellings such as Kirk Yetton and Kerketton. Dixon does not give a derivation of the name but other local historians have suggested "caer", meaning a fort or camp, and "ket", a stone.

There are still the remains of a very large cairn on the ridge of Caerketton, the subject of archaeological study. According to Grant, "Kerketton Craigs are largely composed of clay felspar strongly impregnated with iron oxide. Were the clay not so impregnated it would be a valuable source for pottery, and from its resemblance to the Chinese Petunse or Kaolin, out of which the finest native china is made, it has obtained the name of *Petunse Pentlandica."* At certain times of the year the scree formation of the steep face of Caerketton may clearly be seen to resemble seven ladies in long flowing dresses, traditionally called the Seven Sisters. Flora, Stevenson's heroine in *St Ives,* refers to them when she describes the area to the French officer concealed in Swanston Cottage. The Pentlands, of which Caerketton is perhaps the most celebrated peak, were, it has been suggested by some writers, associated with the Picts, being originally known as Pictland. This is probably based more on legend than historical fact.

Lord Cockburn in his *Circuit Journeys* wrote that four Scottish hills competed as his favourite: Ben Lomond, Goatfell, Demyet and Caerketton — and he was inclined to choose the last.

Allermuir, high above Howden Glen, is noted by Dixon as "Allermore" in 1773, its name meaning "the moor where alders grow". The great landmark between Swanston and the slopes of Caerketton is the T-wood. Resembling a "T" when seen from lower levels, it has the shape of a Maltese cross when viewed from above. It was planted by Henry Trotter of Mortonhall in 1766.

Several burns contribute to the pleasant scenery of Swanston. The Hare Burn, rising on the lower slopes of Caerketton, flows through the old village, dividing one group of cottages from the other, passes the old farmhouse and later absorbs the Hen Burn coming from the west at the lowest part of the valley crossed by Swanston Road. Now called the Swanston Burn it proceeds eastwards, passing under the Biggar Road at Bowbridge. A short distance to the south-east it is joined by the Lothian Burn which runs along the northern boundary wall of Hillend Park. Together, as they flow further eastwards, they become the Burdiehouse Burn, which passes through picturesque Ellen's Glen in the Moredun district. The little burn which originated above Swanston continues to be joined by other waters, changing its name to the Niddrie Burn and, finally, to the Brunstane Burn before it reaches the sea at Musselburgh.

Hillend Park, south of the Lothianburn golf course, was gifted to the city by John White, an Edinburgh builder, and opened by Lord Provost Sir William Sleigh in July 1924. It is now famed far beyond Edinburgh through the construction here in 1965, on the hillside to the east of Caerketton, of the Hillend Ski Centre with its artificial ski slope, now one of the largest of its kind in the world. Administered by the Lothian Regional Council, the centre is open all year round. The main slope is four hundred metres long, with a choice of two runs, and it is served by a ski-tow and chair lift, available also to those *en route* to the summit of Caerketton. Adjacent is the nursery slope for beginners. Many important contests have been staged here, attracting skiers of world renown. The centre is used constantly by schools and youth groups. Beside the gateway to Hillend Park a notice proclaims that here is Edinburgh's southern boundary; the line of this continues westwards along the top ridge of Caerketton.

Today the old village of Swanston is surrounded, happily not to its detriment, by modern property developments, but the chain of events which brought it into an important new era began over two centuries ago, when the civic authorities sought to draw upon Swanston's burns and springs to augment Edinburgh's piped water supply. It is one of those interesting accidents of circumstances such as sometimes influence great artists and writers, that, had it not been necessary to draw upon the area's water, Stevenson would not have come to Swanston and would not have fallen so profoundly and creatively under its spell.

The Act of Parliament which in 1758 empowered Edinburgh Corporation to use the waters of Swanston, as if anticipating difficulties, made provision that "if any proprietors or occupiers of such springs or of the lands. . ." should object or charge too high a price for the water, the city's magistrates were to apply to the Sheriff-Depute of the county concerned. This provision was soon to be tested. In May 1758, a month after the Act was published, Edinburgh Corporation approached Henry Trotter of Mortonhall, owner of the whole of Swanston, for access to the springs. Mr Trotter, who had opposed the Bill on its passage through Parliament, still refused to co-operate, insisting that he required the waters of Swanston for his own uses. He suggested that other sources nearby were suitable and more available, though he believed that, were the

Comiston supply used efficiently, Swanston's would be unnecessary.

The Edinburgh authorities petitioned the Sheriff of Midlothian, who ruled in their favour, provided adequate compensation was paid. Mr Trotter, however, still refused to negotiate. He appealed to the Court of Session but lost his case. In May 1760 he appealed to the House of Lords, but was again unsuccessful. A special tribunal upheld the Lords' decision and stipulated Mr Trotter's compensation, which was to include the payment of £85. Swanston's owner still resisted and statutory powers of access were finally given to the city authorities.

While various reasons have been suggested why Henry Trotter planted the T-wood in 1766 — to commemorate a young member of the family killed in battle, perhaps, or, as it resembles a Maltese cross from above, to mark the ownership of these lands by the Knights of the Temple, whose insignia bore such a cross — it might be that, after his defeat in the legal dispute over the springs, he planted the T-wood as a "T" standing for Trotter, to assert Trotter dominion over these lands. No evidence remains to support or reject such theories.

In 1761 the water from the Hare Burn and other springs was tapped and conveyed in wooden pipes consisting of hollowed tree trunks. The new source was linked with the Comiston supply, travelling alongside it to Castlehill. The Swanston springs produced an average of 300,000 gallons of water per day. In 1790 seven-inch iron pipes replaced the original wooden ones, a small section of which may be seen in Huntly House museum in the Canongate. While the Swanston source is no longer used, the pipe still conveys water from the Fairmilehead filtration plant to a large tank behind the National War Memorial at Edinburgh Castle.

After the introduction of the Swanston water supply, collecting cisterns, filters and other small buildings were erected around Swanston village, all with due regard for the preservation of Henry Trotter's lands. Certain of these installations are still in use. Also in 1761 another building was completed which was to immortalise Swanston in the world of literature. This was Swanston Cottage. Stevenson, in *Picturesque Notes,* now almost at the end of his journey, gazes down on Swanston from the high vantage point just east of Hunter's Tryst and tells us:

> The place in the dell is immediately connected with the city. Long ago, this sheltered field was purchased by the Edinburgh magistrates for the sake of the springs that rise or gather there. After they had built their water-house and laid their pipes, it occurred to them that the place was suitable for junketing. Once entertained, with jovial magistrates and public funds, the idea led speedily to accomplishment; and Edinburgh could soon boast of a municipal Pleasure House. The dell was turned into a garden; and on the knoll that shelters it from the plain and the sea winds, they built a cottage looking to the hills. They brought crockets and

gargoyles from old St Giles, which they were then restoring, and disposed them on the gables and over the door and about the garden; and the quarry which had supplied them with building material, they draped with clematis and carpeted with beds of roses. ...In the process of time, the trees grew higher and gave shade to the cottage and the evergreens sprang up and turned the dell into a thicket. There, purple magistrates relaxed themselves from the pursuit of municipal ambition; cocked hats paraded soberly about the garden and in and out among the hollies; authoritative canes drew ciphering upon the path; and at night, from high up on the hills, a shepherd saw lighted windows through the foliage and heard the voice of city dignitaries raised in song.

In *St Ives* the French prisoner, having escaped from Edinburgh Castle and made his way south, describes his approach to the cottage in similar but more elaborate detail.

Swanston Cottage, almost concealed in the dell, and thus for which the more obvious old farmhouse is often mistaken, is reached a short distance westwards along the little cart road which turns off Swanston Road just before the farm steadings. The original waterman's house is now the entrance lodge. When the cottage was built by the Edinburgh Corporation Water Trust in 1761, it was one-storeyed and thatched, of

The original Swanston Cottage, 1835
By courtesy of City of Edinburgh Museums

Swanston Cottage, 1912

By courtesy of Edinburgh City Libraries; from the drawing by George A. Fothergill

traditional "but and ben" style with a kitchen to the rear. In 1820 the upper storey was built and the thatch replaced by slates. While the records are not clear as regards the architect of the original cottage, it has been suggested that William Burn built the upper storey. The bow windows and other decorative features were added in 1867, shortly after Stevenson's parents had obtained tenancy, and additional accommodation was built to the east. Further alterations were carried out by the distinguished architect Robert S. Lorimer for Lord Guthrie when he became tenant in 1908. At this period a small bungalow was built on the rising ground to the north-west, out of sight of the cottage. This was subsequently demolished. The outside bell above the doorway is also of more recent times. In Fothergill's *Stones and Curiosities of Edinburgh and Neighbourhood* are several sketches illustrating various external features of Swanston Cottage, including Robert Louis Stevenson's bedroom window and the *St Ives* window, slightly to the rear of the house at the east gable.

The garden's many delightful features provide a perfect setting for Swanston Cottage. The Rose Garden, the Queen Anne Garden and the Quarry or Rock Garden remain largely unchanged, though now not perhaps receiving the meticulous care of earlier days. The Hare Burn from the nearby hillside meanders through the garden and under a little bridge. The thickets and holly bushes through which the "purple magistrates" once strode, remain. So, too, decorating the top of a dividing wall, do the quaint weather-beaten gargoyles and crockets brought here about 1830 when William Burn was restoring St Giles. Fothergill has also sketched one of these. Following the Stevenson tenancy of Swanston cottage from 1867 to 1880, it became the residence of an Edinburgh doctor for nearly thirty years. For a few years from 1908 it was the home of Lord Guthrie, one of Stevenson's closest friends of University days and one of his innumerable biographers. In more recent times the cottage was occupied by a number of Edinburgh's chief water engineers. Today, its tenancy is administered by the Edinburgh District Council Housing Department.

So much has already been written about Stevenson that these last pages will be concerned only with two aspects of his life which fit into the context of this book, two major influences on the development of his literary genius. One was that of "Cummy", Alison Cunningham, his beloved nurse from earliest childhood days in Howard Place and Heriot Row, who, long after Stevenson had gone to the South Seas and for nearly twenty years after his death, spent the evening of her life in Morningside, where she died. The other was that of Swanston itself, where Stevenson lived with his parents for twelve years at Swanston Cottage and fell under the spell of the place and the people whom he came to know.

The deep affection which Stevenson had for Cummy and his abiding sense of indebtedness is clearly seen in his many letters to her and to his friends. His feelings were tenderly and movingly expressed when he dedicated to her *A Child's Garden of Verses,* published in 1884, when, after his marriage to Mrs Fanny Osbourne, he was living in Bournemouth. He wrote:

> *To Alison Cunningham from Her Boy*
>
> For the long nights you lay awake
> And watched for my unworthy sake;
> For your most comfortable hand
> That led me through the uneven land:
> For all the story books you read:
> For all the pains you comforted:
> For all you pitied, for all you bore,
> In sad and happy days of yore:—
> My second Mother, my first Wife,
> The angel of my infant life —
> From the sick child now well and old,
> Take, nurse, the little book you hold.

A Child's Garden of Verses, surely unsurpassed as a children's classic, owed much to Cummy's inspiration in childhood days, which Stevenson so vividly recalled. It is still read widely throughout the world, no doubt often by other nurses or parents wishing to while away their children's sleepless nights.

Alison Cunningham was born in the village of Torryburn in Fife on

Alison Cunningham,
R. L. Stevenson's
beloved "Cummy",
in later years

From the painting by Fiddes Watt

May 15th, 1822. Louis, as he was always familiarly known, was eighteen months old, when she, at the age of thirty, was engaged as his nurse in 1852, during the Stevensons' residence at 8 Howard Place, Inverleith. Louis' father, Thomas Stevenson, was a civil engineer who specialised in building lighthouses, a traditional family profession. Their most notable achievements included the Bell Rock off St Andrews, and Skerryvore. His mother, Margaret Balfour, was the daughter of the Rev. Dr Lewis Balfour, minister of Colinton Parish Church, whose names Louis was given at his baptism. In his boyhood, the garden of the manse at Colinton provided him with many happy, adventurous days, later to be recalled in his children's poetry. Mrs Stevenson suffered from indifferent health so that Cummy's task was all the more arduous. Before she joined the Stevenson household, the infant Louis had already had two nurses who had successively proved unsuitable. Cummy was already an experienced nurse, having looked after Walter Biggar Blaikie, later to become famous as an artistic printer with the notable old Edinburgh firm, T. & A. Constable, a leading authority on Bonnie Prince Charlie and the '45

*Robert Louis
Stevenson*

Rebellion, and, in 1894, the year of Stevenson's death, to be involved in publishing the "Edinburgh Edition" of his works in twenty-eight volumes.

Soon after he was born, Stevenson began to be plagued by ill-health, to remain a source of struggle — and conquest — till the end of his life at the early age of forty-four. As a baby he was so small and delicate that, when his father first saw him, he exclaimed that he had never before seen such a small child. "He's just a smout", he said, and "Smout" was the name by which Louis was long to be known. While at Howard Place, there must have been many "long nights" when Cummy lay awake, and when the Stevensons moved to Heriot Row these must have continued. Although by that time Louis was no longer an infant, her nocturnal readings went on. In her latter years she remarked: "You see, he was more than seven years old before he could read. He began to read after a bad attack of gastric fever. They thought he would die. He lay for days unconscious. I was in the next room, when I heard him cry: 'Cummy, I want some bread.' Oh, I was thankful."

Cummy's devotion to Stevenson during the weary, sleepless nights of his childhood was not the only reason for his everlasting indebtedness to her. Lord Guthrie, in his biography, indulges in some interesting reflections on the source of Stevenson's genius, enumerating various intelligent and erudite members of his family from whom he might have inherited his talent. On the paternal side there was a succession of civil engineers, and on the maternal side many distinguished forebears including an uncle who became President of Edinburgh's Royal College of Physicians. However, in the lives of great artists there have frequently been less simple explanations of influences and achievements. Stevenson was no exception. Had it not been for the long sleepless nights and the early years of ill-health which delayed his ability to read, he would probably not have come to write. "They may talk about heredity," wrote Stevenson, "but if I inherited any literary talent, it was from Cummy! It was she who gave me the first feeling for literature."

Cummy was a member of the Free Kirk, established at the Disruption just seven years before Stevenson was born. Although a woman of strict principles, her readings to young Louis were liberal enough. He once wrote that his upbringing was on "The Shorter Catechism, porridge and the Covenanters." But Cummy also introduced him to a wider world. She once remarked with scorn: "People seem to think that I just read the Bible to Lou, even on, — Havers! Early in the morning, before it was light, when he couldna sleep, he would ask for one of his favourite chapters, or it would be Robert Murray McCheyne's song: 'To Yonder Side', or his story: 'A Lily Gathered'. He was very fond of that story and made me read it over and over again. But when it was light, he would say: "We'll take Ballantyne now, Cummy", and then I would read *The Coral Island*." The fund of stories she read to him was almost endless: stories from Bible heroes, Reformers and Covenanters; legends in prose and verse of pirates and smugglers, witches and fairies. She had a strong sense of the weird, and a rich Scottish vocabulary. When Stevenson attributed to her his love for the theatre, she, a devout Free Church member, was shocked. "You know quite well, Cummy," he retorted, "how you acted all these stories as if you had seen them yourself." "And me," she replied, "when I was never in a theatre all my days." Her influence on Stevenson at an early, impressionable age was later expressed in many of his most famous works. Of the poems in *A Child's Garden of Verses* which were first conceived during his early days with Cummy at Heriot Row, perhaps the best loved is "The Lamplighter".

In the spring of 1863 the Stevensons took young Louis, then aged thirteen, on a Grand Tour of Europe. Cummy accompanied them and meticulously recorded her experiences and impressions, published many years later as *Cummy's Diary*. In Lord Guthrie's biography of Stevenson there is a photograph of Alison Cunningham with the Stevenson family at Peebles. She was then forty-four years old and is seen as a still attractive woman. Stevenson in later years often remarked to her that it was strange she had never married, even though at least one man had much attracted her. This she dismissed, with the inference that she was content to devote her life to the Stevenson family. She was with them during their residence at Swanston Cottage from 1867 until 1880. Apart from the daily domestic round there, she enjoyed driving with Mr Stevenson daily to and from his Edinburgh office in a horse and carriage.

In 1880 when the Stevensons left Swanston Cottage and Louis, now married, had gone to Bournemouth, she continued to live with her brother, the waterman, in the gatehouse of Swanston Cottage. An inscription on the lintel above the door, with her initials, denotes the period of her stay. Stevenson often wrote to her there, signing himself "Your Laddie". In 1893 she left Swanston for a flat at 23 Balcarres Street, near Morningside Station, where she lived happily with a succession of dogs, each of which, it has been said, died from over-generous feeding. She was not to enjoy her old age in complete peace or to retire into oblivion, for after Stevenson's death in Samoa in 1894 and the realisation of his genius by literary critics throughout the world, increasing numbers of devotees came to Edinburgh to see his early homes and Swanston Cottage, and many wished to meet Cummy. The most notable of these was the Countess of Sutherland who, in 1908, was in Edinburgh visiting various institutions. Lord Guthrie, at this time residing at Swanston Cottage, arranged for Cummy to be driven there to meet the Duchess. A photograph, taken at the seat in front of the Quarry Garden, recalls their meeting. After much protesting, Cummy had agreed to sit while the Duchess of Sutherland stood beside her. "Look at that," said Cummy later, pointing to the picture, "Fancy me being photographed with a Duchess and me sitting while she's standing."

At Balcarres Street, Cummy's absent-mindedness and deafness worried her neighbours. She would often go out leaving her front door open. Eventually she was persuaded to go to live with her maternal cousin, Mrs Murdoch, at 1 Comiston Place, a short distance up Comiston Road from Morningside Station. She was reluctant at first, saying "Na, na, freends gree best sindrie" — friends agree best apart — but she did eventually accept the kind offer and her last years were spent happily with her cousin.

While at Balcarres Street and Comiston Place, Cummy told to the numerous Stevenson pilgrims who visited her anecdotes which few biographers would know. Two concerned Stevenson's early childhood days. Once, when he had misbehaved, Cummy stood him in a corner. When the specified time was up he chose to remain there. "Why?" she asked. "I am just finishing telling myself a story," he replied.

On another occasion, she placed a piece of bride's cake under her pillow for good luck, explaining this traditional practice to young Louis. By morning the cake had disappeared. "While I was asleep, the little monkey had stolen and eaten it!"

She also used to explain the words "My first Wife" in his dedication of *A Child's Garden of Verses*. "You'll no ken how he cam to call me his wife. . ." She had been with Louis at Waverley Station awaiting his parents' return from London when the minister of the Tron Church, who was a friend, in conversation jocularly remarked: "You'll be thinking of marrying soon, Louis?" The boy replied with a grave face: "I'm married already." "Oh," said the minister, "who is the leddy?" "This is her," replied young Stevenson, pointing to Cummy. The story remained as a family joke.

Two things displeased Cummy. One was the Italian artist Pieri Nerli's well-known portrait of Stevenson, which, she said portrayed him not as he really was but as the author of *Dr Jekyll and Mr Hyde*. The other was the Stevenson memorial in St Giles by Saint Gaudens, which showed him as an invalid lying on a couch with a rug over his knees. She insisted that, although Stevenson had suffered from frequent ill-health, he had never been a victim or slave of his illness: he was its conqueror who should be remembered as cheerful and vivacious.

Cummy regularly received letters from Stevenson when he was in Samoa. One, sent quickly when he had heard she was unwell, teased her about having more important things to do than be ill. Stevenson's wife also wrote frequently and kindly to her, generously supplementing the pension which Louis's parents gave her. Such solicitude continued long after Stevenson's death in 1894, and when, in June 1913, Cummy slipped on the stairs and fractured a leg, Stevenson's widow cabled an offer of every financial assistance towards her care. However, having outlived her beloved Louis by nearly twenty years, Cummy's own time had come. She died on July 21st, 1913, at the age of ninety-one. When she was laid to rest in Morningside Cemetery the Rev. W. B. MacLeod referred to "her long service to one upon whom Thou didst bestow the great gift of genius". A few of Stevenson's closest relatives and friends were at the graveside. On the coffin, beside a wreath from Stevenson's widow, was a simple bunch of roses, honey-suckle and Canterbury bells from the garden of Swanston Cottage. The brief inscription on the headstone reads: "In loving and grateful memory of Alison Cunningham the beloved nurse of Robert Louis Stevenson." Many fine portraits of Cummy remain, notably one by Fiddes Watt. For long treasured in Swanston Cottage, it is now in the Stevenson Museum at Lady Stair's House.

In the shaping of Stevenson, the seeds of inspiration first sown by Cummy were brought to fruition in the fertile environment of Swanston Cottage where, from the age of seventeen, he spent twelve of his happiest years, vitally important and formative years which one biographer has called his "painful and hurrying pilgrimage". The influence of Swanston and its people, a thriving if primitive community, and the beauty and closeness to nature of the place, rekindled the imagination first fired by Cummy. Swanston Cottage was a perfect retreat for a writer in which to distil a ferment of vivid impressions, capturing them in words for all time. This "naturalism" born of Swanston runs through many of Stevenson's essays, poems and songs and brings colour to his novels. The atmosphere of the village, its surroundings and way of life, are immortalised in *Edinburgh: Picturesque Notes* and in "Pastoral" in *Memories and Portraits*. After the style of Fergusson whom he cherished and with whom he shared certain patterns of life, which made him pleased to think of himself as a re-incarnation, Stevenson writes in "Ille Terrarum" of Swanston Cottage:

> Frae nirly, nippin', Eas'lan breeze,
> Frae Norlan' snaw, an' haar o'seas,
> Weel happit in your gairden trees,
>   A bonny bit,
> Atween the muckle Pentland's Knees
>   Secure ye sit.

In the same poem he writes of the peacefulness of Swanston and of its conduciveness to getting things in proportion — even the legendary philosophers:

> Here aft hae I, wi' sober heart,
> For meditation set apairt,
> When orra loves or kittle art
>   Perplexed my mind;
> Here socht a balm for ilka smart
>   O' humankind.

> Here, aft weel neukit by my lane,
> Wi' Horace or perhaps Montaigne,
> The mornin' hours hae come an' gane
>   Abune my heid —
> I wadna gi'en a chucky-stane
>   For a' I'd read!

Yet at Swanston Cottage Stevenson hardly led the life of a recluse. They were full and lively days. In the year of his arrival at Swanston, 1867, he had become a first-year student at Edinburgh University. Probably through his father's pressure and desire for him to continue the family's distinguished tradition of lighthouse construction, he began studying civil engineering which took him to Anstruther and Wick. But his heart wasn't in it. On journeys he made with his father to inspect lighthouses in the Hebrides and Orkney he was less interested in the technicalities of construction than in the stirrings in his mind of the themes of *Kidnapped* and *Catriona*. At twenty he withdrew from the civil engineering course, announcing his intention of becoming a writer. Literature, however, was not considered by his parents a "reliable profession" and, again as the result of paternal pressure, he became a student in the Faculty of Law. During this period he was an active member of the famous Speculative Society which met in the Old College of the University and is still in exis-, tence with an exclusive membership. Stevenson's activities in this and other University societies introduced him to Edinburgh's night-life and his descriptions of the Old Town, if not quite so colourful as those written by Fergusson a century before, have a classic character of their own. He was as alive to life in the congested closes of old Edinburgh as he was to that in its rural fringes.

In July 1875 Stevenson was called to the Bar. He made little effort to establish himself in his profession although his door at 17 Heriot Row did have a brass nameplate proclaiming: "Robert Louis Stevenson — Advocate." Instead he set out for France. This and other visits to Europe resulted in the publication of *An Inland Voyage* and *Travels with a Donkey*, both probably worked on at Swanston Cottage.

At Swanston Stevenson was to become the close friend of one whose powerful personality greatly influenced his literary career. This was John Todd, the Swanston shepherd. Stevenson first encountered Todd soon after his arrival at Swanston Cottage. The first words he heard bellowed by the shepherd were addressed not to himself but to his dog, Coolin, on the hillside below Caerketton: "C'war oot amang the sheep!" For some time Stevenson kept out of Todd's way. "For my own part," he wrote, "he was at first my enemy, and I, in my character of a rambling boy, his natural abhorrence. I skulked in my favourite wilderness like a Cameronian of the Killing Time, and John Todd was my Claverhouse, and his dogs, my questing dragoons." But before long they were on speaking terms, and eventually they became the closest of friends.

John Todd has come to be known as the "Roarin' Shepherd" and this description forms the caption of several photographs. Stevenson wrote: "In the grey of the summer morning, and already from far up the hill, he would wake the 'toun' with the sound of his shoutings. In lambing time his cries were still to be heard late at night. That dread voice of his that shook the hills when he was angry, fell in the ordinary talk very pleasantly upon the ear." The title "Roarin' Shepherd" was not happily received by Todd's family. His son Willie, also a shepherd, explained in later years: "Nae doubt he had a guid pair o' lungs on him, but it was that budy, Patrick, the photographer, that ca'd him the 'Roarin' Shepherd'." John Patrick was an important Edinburgh photographer with premises at Comiston Road in Morningside. He produced many photographs of Swanston, and of Morningside itself. He placed Todd's picture in a showcase outside his shop and the shepherd, in modesty, requested that it be removed.

When Todd set out for the hillside, he would whistle over the wall of Swanston Cottage and Stevenson would climb over to accompany him. Todd became his hero, and an invaluable stimulus to a lively imagination. From him Stevenson acquired an exciting fund of anecdotes and stories,

John Todd, the Swanston Shepherd

Photograph by John Patrick

tales of Todd's experiences as a drover marching flocks into England, sleeping on the hillside, falling victim to robbers, being wrongly jailed in a rustic prison, and of escaping. This was the very stuff of future novels. Sim and Candlish, the drovers in Stevenson's *St Ives,* no doubt owe much to Todd. It was not only the adventures which Todd recounted which captivated the young Stevenson, but also his manner of telling them: "He spoke in the richest dialect of Scotch I ever heard," wrote Stevenson, "the words in themselves were a pleasure and often a surprise to me, so that I often came back from our patrols with new acquisitions; and this vocabulary he would handle like a master, stalking a little before me, beard on shoulder, the plaid hanging loosely about him. . . I might count him with the best talkers, only that talking Scotch and talking English seem incomparable acts. He touched on nothing at least, but he adorned it. When he narrated, the scene was before you; when he spoke (as he did mostly) of his own antique business, the thing took on a colour of romance and curiosity that was surprising."

443

His hillside hours over for another day, Stevenson would return to Swanston Cottage — not always, by any means, to solitude and retreat. There he was frequently visited by many of his close and educated circle of friends, some of whom were already becoming distinguished in their professions and others of whom were to become so — men such as W. E. Henley, Sydney Colvin, Charles Baxter and Charles (later Lord) Guthrie. The cottage had its intellectually stimulating social round, but just as the "simple" Cummy had shaped Stevenson's early days, so the humble Swanston shepherd shaped his latter. Todd's influence was not just a passing pleasure to evaporate into the hillside air.

At times the young Stevenson took to the hills alone, observed by the Swanston folk whose descriptions of him remain: "The lang-haired idle-set laddie in his velveteen jacket. . ."; "He wasna thocht very muckle o'. . ."; "he had a want. . ."; "it wasna jaloosed that he wad ever come to muckle. . ."; "he lay aboot the dyke backs wi' a book. . ." John Todd remarked, in similar vein, to Adam Ritchie, the Swanston ploughman "He's an awfu' laddie for speirin' questions aboot a'thing, an' whenever ye turn your back, awa' he gangs an' writes it a'doon." What Stevenson "wrote doon" and later sculpted into shape at the desk in his bedroom at Swanston Cottage was preciously to enrich the world's literary treasures.

While most of Stevenson's best-known work was published after he married and left Edinburgh, possibly much was drafted in outline, at least mentally, at Swanston Cottage. It was here that he wrote not only *Edinburgh: Picturesque Notes,* in 1877, but also, with W. E. Henley, the play *Deacon Brodie, or the Double Life,* later to inspire his novel *The Strange Case of Dr Jekyll and Mr Hyde.* A wooden cabinet made by Brodie was for long kept in Swanston Cottage, but in recent years it was transferred to the valuable Stevenson collection at Lady Stair's House.

With John Todd, another Swanston "character" with whom Stevenson became friendly, and who earned a chapter in *Memories and Portraits,* was Robert Young, the Swanston gardener, who also was to feature in *St Ives.* The gardener's philosophy was utilitarian: "The very truth was that he scorned all flowers together. They were but garnishings, children's toys, trifling ornaments for ladies' chimney-shelves. It was towards his cauliflowers and peas and cabbages that his heart grew warm . . . cabbages were found invading the flower-pots and an outpost of savoys was once discovered in the centre of the lawn. . ."

Stevenson was married in the United States in May 1880, returning to Edinburgh with his wife and stepson Lloyd Osbourne in August. The somewhat remote possibility of his settling in Edinburgh arose. His father, having failed to influence his son's choice of career, nevertheless attempted to ensure that he should, at least, remain in Edinburgh. In 1881 Stevenson was persuaded to apply for the Chair of Constitutional Law and Constitutional History at Edinburgh University. The father campaigned more actively than did the son, seeking unsuccessfully to enlist the support of his influential friend Sir John Skelton of the Hermitage of Braid. Stevenson was heavily defeated, receiving nine votes against the successful candidate's eighty-two.

While on holiday at Braemar in 1881, Stevenson entertained his stepson with a story serialised in the *Young Folks' Magazine* that year. This was to become his most popular novel, *Treasure Island,* published in book form in 1883. In 1884 Stevenson and his family moved to Bournemouth, to a house gifted by his father and named Skerryvore after the lighthouse. Much of his best-known work was published while he lived there. When his father died in 1887, he visited Edinburgh for the last time. Soon afterwards, with his wife, stepson and mother, he sailed for America. In 1891 they settled in Samoa in a house called Vailima. The family was accepted as a sort of Samoan clan; Stevenson became known to the natives as "Tusitala" — "the teller of tales". His writing continued, even when such effort was forbidden by his doctor, until, on December 3rd, 1894, he collapsed and died. He was buried on the top of Mount Vaea and on his tomb were inscribed his words from "Requiem":

> Home is the sailor, home from the sea,
> And the hunter home from the hill

— an allusion to his days at Swanston.

In his poetry during his last years in Samoa, Stevenson recalled with deep nostalgia vivid memories of Morningside, Swanston and the Pentlands. Brought up as he was on "The Shorter Catechism, porridge and the Covenanters", the monument to those Covenanters' tragic, brave defeat at Rullion Green haunted him. Glencorse and Rullion Green are recalled in the poem which, towards the end of his life, he sent to a friend S. R. Crockett, in gratitude for a dedication written for one of his books. He reminds Crockett of happy days at Glencorse. The atmosphere of Rullion Green, with its Covenanter graves, and of the very essence of the Pentlands, are in the lines:

> Blows the wind today and the sun and the rain are flying,
> Blows the wind on the moors today and now,
> Where about the graves of the martyrs the whaups are crying;
> My heart remembers how.

> Grey recumbent tombs of the dead in desert places,
> Standing stones on the vacant wine-red moor,
> Hills of sheep, and the howes of the silent vanished races,
> And winds, austere and pure

> Be it granted to me to behold you again in dying,
> Hills of home! and to hear again the call;
> Hear about the graves of the martyrs the peewees crying,
> And hear no more at all.

445

Recalling his daily walks through Morningside, to and from Swanston Cottage, he lamented:

> I gang nae mair where aince I gaed,
> By Buckstane, Fairmilehead or Braid,
> But far frae Kirk and Tron.
> Oh, still ayont the muckle sea,
> Still are ye dear, and dear to me,
> Auld Reekie, still and on.

And of Swanston Cottage, in a few essential lines:

> Fair shines the day on the house with open door,
> Birds come, and cry there, and twitter in the chimney,
> But I go for ever, and come again no more.

Finally, recalling his most cherished retreat above Swanston, where, after his many exciting hours of listening to the eloquence of John Todd, he would sit on the hillside to "write it a' doon":

> The tropics vanish, and meseems that I,
> From Halkerside, from topmost Allermuir,
> Or steep Caerketton, dreaming, gaze again.
> Far set in fields and woods, the toun I see
> Springs gallant from the shadows of her smoke,
> Cragged, spired and turreted, her virgin fort
> Beflagged. About on seaward drooping hills,
> New folds of city glitter. Last, the Forth
> Wheels, ample water set with sacred isles,
> And populous Fife smokes with a score of towns.
>
> The voice of generations dead
> Summons me, sitting distant, to arise,
> My numerous footsteps nimbly to retrace,
> And, all mutation over, stretch me down
> In that denoted city of the dead.

CHAPTER 8

The Living Past

Any study of local history would be incomplete were it based solely on ancient archives and printed sources. History is about people and is shaped by people. In this final chapter an attempt will be made to link past and present through personal recollections, gathered either first-hand or from the families of earlier residents.

How much could still be remembered about South Edinburgh's ancient lands and mansion-houses, its notable families, its distinguished writers, artists and medical men, its important institutions? — all the things which built up a rich history before the area grew into a populous expanse of Edinburgh suburbia. Were all now museum pieces neatly labelled and catalogued, merely meriting reference in printed records? Or did living links exist with modern consciousness?

The search for evidence of a living past was pursued through each area that has been covered in previous chapters. A beginning was made in Causewayside, from earliest times one of Edinburgh's principal highways to the south. Extending from the west end of Preston Street to Duncan Street and the beginning of Ratcliffe Terrace, Causewayside is still one of the city's busiest thoroughfares. Its name derives from days when the highway was little more than a cart-track paved with large stones known as "causies". No part of Edinburgh has undergone greater trans-formation than this area. Long gone are the early mansion-houses and villas which once straddled this ancient route. Gone, too, the old toll-house at its junction with Grange Loan, the ancient highway from Morningside through the Burgh Muir and the lands of the Grange of St Giles. Of the two-storey cottages with their outside stairs, once a feature of Causewayside, little remains. The premises of several of the firms, notably printers, confectionery and biscuit manufacturers, which at the turn of the century brought employment to Causewayside, remain, some with their original names still visible above modern frontages, but the relentless work of the demolition hammer and bulldozer has transformed Causewayside.

The contrast between past and present emerges vividly from the graphic account of old Causewayside in James Goodfellow's *The Print of His Shoe,* and also from the records of Newington Parish Church. Goodfellow, a lay missionary appointed at the turn of the century by the Duncan Street United Presbyterian Church to work in the district, describes much earlier days, when Causewayside offered a bustling village scene with picturesque and "spotlessly clean" cottages housing a thriving community of hand-loom weavers, which included several skilled

447

bleachers from Haarlem in Holland. They produced, among other things, the famous Edinburgh shawls. Four linen manufacturers had premises in Causewayside, and beside the weavers' cottages stood the large mansion-houses and villas of earlier times.

By the 1850s a slump in trade brought drastic social changes. At this time, Dr Alison, the Minister of Newington Parish Church, also responsible for the pastoral care of Causewayside, was to describe a part of it as "the worst bit of Edinburgh". The thriving weaving industry had long since gone, and, with it, prosperity. Many venerable villas, notably Wormwood Hall, had been subdivided and the picturesque weavers' cottages were occupied by poor families from other parts of the city who lived in grossly overcrowded conditions. High, depressing brick tenements were built, which were also soon overcrowded. One of these, known as "the Brickie", contained eighty one-room flats, many housing large families. This was Dr Alison's "worst bit" — of which Goodfellow wrote in detail, describing the infectious diseases, including typhus, which were rife, and the prevalence of drunkenness. Parents neglected their children; adolescents ran riot to such an extent that wooden barricades were erected between Causewayside and Minto Street at Salisbury Place and Duncan Street to prevent the "Causewayside Keelies", as they were called, invading the "respectable" residential district of Newington to the east.

With the sad deterioration of Causewayside in mind, I set out to collect comments and recollections of old inhabitants. However, although I was referred from one person to another, reputed to "know all about the early days", I met with scant success, though I did have interesting discussions with the former Minister of Newington Parish Church (later Newington and St Leonards), the Rev. Edwin S. Towill, who had served his congregation for sixteen years before retiring in 1956. He kindly let me search through early issues of *The Review,* the monthly church magazine, and drew my attention to articles which threw light on life in Causewayside and on the efforts of his church to improve social conditions. Notable was "The Social Union Experiment" carried out in the Brickie. Newington Parish Church had obtained two small flats here, which were combined to create a mission hall and church centre providing advice and assistance. Eventually, when the whole property was put up for sale, it was purchased by the Newington Social Union Limited, a company established by church members with a nominal capital of £3,000. Improvements to the premises were made: many one-roomed flats were combined to provide larger accommodation, while interior walls were stripped and disinfected. A resident caretaker was appointed and a set of rules for tenants was drawn up: those who would not co-operate were forced to leave. Classes were organised to educate people in such domestic subjects as economy and a Penny Savings Bank was established. The quality of life in the Brickie improved steadily until the Newington Social Union Experiment ended in 1941 and the tenement and adjacent

The soup kitchen in Buccleuch Terrace sponsored by Newington-St Leonard's Church

By courtesy of Rev. Edwin Towill

properties were demolished soon afterwards. Today an exploration of the area around 183 Causewayside reveals only a few fragments recalling the era of the Brickie.

The Rev. Edwin Towill also described to me another social service which his church rendered to the South Side in the days of unemployment and widespread poverty. A soup kitchen, transferred from Simon Square, was opened on the north corner of Buccleuch Street and Buccleuch Terrace (premises still in existence now as a shop), providing coal and other basic domestic necessities to the unemployed of Causewayside, Sciennes and the Meadows.

The Rev. Towill recalled many interesting anecdotes not only of Causewayside but also of other South Side areas. At the time of our conversations, in the spring of 1977, Newington St Leonards Church in South Clerk Street, of which he had been minister, but which had been closed for several years, was about to begin a new era. The fine one-hundred-and-fifty-year-old, neo-classical building, with the clock-tower which is a South Side landmark, had just been purchased by the Scottish Philharmonic Society, which planned to convert it into a much-needed Edinburgh International Festival concert hall at the projected cost of

£300,000. Little adaptation of the already suitable interior would be required to assure a useful future for this fine old church.

The Rev. Towill wrote several of the articles in *The South Side Story,* as well as two scholarly contributions for the Old Edinburgh Club on the history of the Merchant Maiden and Trades Maiden Hospitals, and told me that, when the Merchant Maiden Hospital moved in 1854 from Chambers Street to Rillbank House in the Sciennes district, the girls were taken on Sundays to Newington St Leonards Church, where they sat in the gallery. Opposite them sat boys from a private school in Newington, whose religious devotion was not infrequently distracted by glances across the gallery to the girls opposite. During his ministry, renovations to the church were carried out and, when the gallery pews were being repainted, various carved declarations of the boys' interest in the girls were uncovered. One read: "Elle est partie." The girl who had attracted this boy's interest, alas, had gone.

Another story concerned Newington Session School, a quaint little building which still stands in Dalkeith Road, facing Holyrood Park Road. When its long period as a school ended it became a canteen for the staff of Nelson's printing works, formerly opposite, and, in more recent years, the Map Sales department of the Ordnance Survey. Originally, when it was a

Replicas of figures from Newington Session School

By courtesy of Mrs Marjorie Langdon; photograph by Mr W. R. Smith

The chimney of Bryson's Brewery in Summerhall felled about 1914 to make way for the new Royal (Dick) Veterinary College

By courtesy of the Royal (Dick) School of Veterinary Studies.

school, a lead figure of a small boy had stood on one side of the little tower above the entrance. This, the Rev. Towill had discovered, was not unique: identical figures stood above the entrances to at least two London schools. When the school in Dalkeith Road was closed, he acquired the figure and a replica and installed them in his church; when this too was closed, they were acquired by a lady living in the district who presented them to St Peter's Episcopal Church in Lutton Place, where they remain, to the left of the entrance to the centre aisle.

One historic part of the Causewayside district which remains is the tastefully restored Grange Court, entered through a pend on the west side of the thoroughfare between Sciennes House Place and Grange Road. Here lived many of the hand-loom weavers, while later a slaughter-house was established. By the 1950s, the quaint three-storey houses, with outside stairs and balconies, had become seriously dilapidated, but in the following decade the original houses on the north side of the court were extensively restored, and new houses of a more contemporary design, but in keeping with the original ones, were erected on the south side. Grange Court, with its picturesque red tiled roofs, has been admirably preserved. In view of the transformation of Causewayside during the last century, I

The construction of the Royal (Dick) Veterinary College, 1914

By courtesy of the Royal (Dick) School of Veterinary Studies

was interested to explore the history of the Court, and talked to a number of its elderly residents. None had lived in the district for any great time, however. In fact no-one residing in Grange Court could claim links with its past.

Returning to the districts of Hope Park, Summerhall and Causewayside, recollections of the early 1900s were provided by my father, a "Southsider" who had witnessed half a century of changes in this area. He recalled, while residing in Summerhall Square, the building of the Royal (Dick) Veterinary College on the site of Bryson's brewery. Those living in Summerhall Square had been informed that the brewery's tall chimney would be most carefully felled, but they were requested to keep windows closed against dust and grit. In the event, the chimney was demolished quite unexpectedly a few days earlier than had been announced, and, my father recalled, "for many days afterwards a massive clean-up operation was necessary."

William Dick, the originator of Edinburgh's world-famous veterinary college, known familiarly as "the Dick-Vet", was born in 1793 in Whitehouse Close in the Canongate, of Aberdeenshire parents. He is commemorated by a plaque at the entrance to the close. His father was a blacksmith and for some time young William was his apprentice. Having heard of the London Veterinary School, founded in 1791, Dick, at the age of twenty-four, went there as a student. When he returned to Edinburgh he gave occasional lectures between 1819 and 1823, and in 1827 the Highland and Agricultural Society provided financial support for his inauguration of Edinburgh's first course in Veterinary Medicine. This was a most successful venture. The city's first veterinary college was opened, at William Dick's own expense, in Clyde Street in 1837. Following the formation of the Royal College of Veterinary Surgeons in 1844, the original college established by Dick, by then Professor William Dick, was affiliated to the College. Whereas, in the London Veterinary College, teaching centred almost exclusively on the horse, Dick's lectures in Edinburgh ranged more widely and attracted large numbers of students. After his death in 1866, Edinburgh Town Council took over "Dick's College" and eventually, with the legacy which he had left, Edinburgh's Royal (Dick) Veterinary College, was, by Act of Parliament, established in 1906. In 1911 Edinburgh University instituted the degree of Bachelor of Science in Veterinary Studies. Three years later, Dick's Clyde Street premises, for long inadequate, were closed and the present college in Summerhall was built.

In the early 1900s many thriving firms began to provide employment for South Side residents. My father was for many years a clerk with Messrs W. & B. Cowan, gas meter manufacturers of Buccleuch Street, until they moved to Manchester in 1928. On the site of Cowan's eventually arose the New Victoria Cinema, renamed the Odeon. The working week of men employed by Cowan's used to be fifty-one hours, each day starting at 6 a.m., with a break for breakfast at 9. Next to the factory gates was Campbell's bar, and here were lined up ready the morning breakfast "nips" of whisky for the workers, at a cost of threepence.

Some of my father's most vivid early recollections of Causewayside were of colourful and lively General Election campaigns. For many years the area was represented by Charlie Price of the well-known biscuit manufacturing family, who, as a pioneer member of the Congregationalist Church at Holy Corner, laid its foundation stone. Mr Price was a Liberal, but his personality and dedication to the welfare of all his constituents made him popular with everyone. Election campaigns in the early 1900s were lively affairs. Children paraded with pictures of the candidates, singing jingles in their support and finding it all great fun; voters were given every encouragement to turn out and vote. Messrs Millar & Richard, the type-founders in Nicolson Street, had an excellent brass band, and a few hours before the polling booths closed it would set off towards the Bristo Street polling station, and then to the St Leonards School booth, voters joining in behind the band as it passed along South Side streets. Charlie Price was eventually succeeded in Parliament by another well-known South-Side M.P., Willie Graham.

Another of my father's vivid recollections was of the populous Buccleuch Street district in the early 1900s. Here much service was given by the congregation of the Mayfield United Free Church, now Mayfield

Church. The mission hall, opened in 1890 at 52 Buccleuch Street, was the social centre of the district. Its meetings were so well attended that the premises soon became inadequate, and the much larger Mayfield Guild Hall in Gifford Park was opened in 1909. This was especially appreciated by the 3rd (Mayfield) Company of the Boys' Brigade whose membership had reached two hundred. Many of the boys had backgrounds of poverty and social hardship, and the activities and influence of the B.B. under their memorable Captain John MacLaren was a vital influence in their lives. Even today reunions of the Company's Old Boys are attended by men who joined the organisation in Buccleuch Street in the early years of the century. My father himself has been associated with the Company for seventy-three years. While the Boys' Brigade still meets in the Mayfield Guild Hall, it is a sign of the times that, with the movement of the population to the outskirts of the city, its membership has steadily fallen and the future of the hall is now in the balance.

Still standing at the east corner of the junction of Causewayside with Grange Road and Salisbury Place are the substantial premises of the former well-known biscuit manufacturers, Messrs Middlemass, long since closed. In 1974 the building was acquired by the National Library of Scotland and now houses its map collection. Opposite the west side of the old biscuit factory there once stood Causewayside school, also long since gone. There is now no trace of various locations which existed in James Goodfellow's day such as Wright's Buildings, Stewart's Close, Burnett's Buildings and Amos Land, though on the east side, just beyond the old biscuit factory, is a pend, above the entrance to which is inscribed, "Wright's Close, West Newington".

In the chronicles of St Catherine's-in-Grange Church, at the corner of Chalmers Crescent and Grange Road, reference is made to its pioneers meeting, in 1862, in Clare Hall Academy, Causewayside, which was also entered from Findhorn Place. No trace of this building remains, and indeed maps of the period do not indicate the academy, although they do show "Claret Hall" on the appropriate site, which may be a mis-spelling. However, there is an account of Mayfield Church which refers to its establishment having been discussed at a public meeting held in Clare Hall at 18 Minto Street, now the Minto Hotel. I was unable, in discussion with local residents, to solve this confusion over the location of the elusive Clare Hall.

While the many firms established in Causewayside in the early 1900s or before have disappeared, in Duncan Street, leading east from Causewayside, one long-established business remains, which now enjoys worldwide renown. This is Bartholomews, the cartographers. During my early researches I was indebted to Mr John C. Bartholomew, great-great-grandson of the founder, for providing information about his forbears. In preparing this chapter, I found that there was no need for a lengthy interview with him concerning the history of the firm of which he is Cartographer Director, for he kindly presented me with a copy of their sesquicentennial history, *Bartholomew 150 Years* by Leslie Gardener. This splendid publication presents the impressive story of Edinburgh's only cartographers, and of the family which, over five generations, created its great reputation. The famous firm was founded a century and a half ago by John Bartholomew, an engraver whose father had been trained in the same craft by Daniel Lizars, one of Edinburgh's earliest and most notable artists in this field. After also serving an apprenticeship with Lizars, John Bartholomew, from June 1826, worked freelance, becoming the first Edinburgh engraver to specialise in maps. After a struggle to establish himself in a succession of small premises, he set up at 4 North Bridge, opposite the *Scotsman* offices, in "two large rooms and a closet at £12 per annum". His firm grew steadily, producing, during its first fifty years, maps of all sorts — school maps, maps of the British Empire, maps of new territories in Africa, of the Polar ice-caps, of changing national frontiers — Edinburgh and Leith Post Office Directory plans, diagrams for new railway routes, and for new world shipping routes. At Robert Louis Stevenson's request, John Bartholomew drew the map of Treasure Island for the first edition of the book. He also lithographed the official "artist's impression" of the Forth Railway Bridge, a copy of which is today treasured in Duncan Street.

John Bartholomew, junior, who in 1859 succeeded his father, moved the business to the site in Chambers Street now occupied by the Dental College and Hospital. His son John George in turn moved to Parkside Works in what was then Gibbet Loan, a continuation of the present-day East Preston Street, crossing Dalkeith Road. John George Bartholomew quickly changed the street's morbid name: in his next issue of the Edinburgh Town Plan it appeared as Park Road. In recent years it has become Holyrood Park Road.

Bartholomews' final move to their present premises in Duncan Street removes them from Causewayside to the annals of Morningside. John Bartholomew himself relinquished control of his rapidly expanding and world famous business in 1859, as a result of failing health. He retired to Grangebank Cottage, the large manor-house which was the nucleus of the tiny village of Boroughmuirhead, situated between present-day Colinton Road, Churchhill and Albert Terrace. Here he died in 1861. This sombre house, all that remains of the little village, still stands. Having undergone considerable renovation, it is now the Masonic Lodge Abbotsford.

John George Bartholomew, who was responsible for the move to Duncan Street in 1911, had innumerable honours bestowed upon him. He was appointed Geographer and Cartographer Royal in 1910, while, the previous year, he had, along with J. M. Barrie, been made an Honorary Doctor of Laws by Edinburgh University. He founded the Royal Scottish Geographical Society in 1884 and sought the establishment of a Chair of

Geography at the University. Though this was not achieved in his lifetime, he personally financed the first lectureship to be established. In 1898 he purchased Falcon Hall in Morningside, and lived there for nine years. When vacating the mansion he had its pillared facade dismantled and re-erected as the frontage of the new Duncan Street premises of Bartholomew's, known in those days as the Edinburgh Geographical Institute.

Adjacent to Causewayside, with its chequered history of development and deterioration, are the pleasant residential districts of Newington and Mayfield. I was interested to learn what recollections people had of changes in the area since the first classical villas of Minto Street — "the new road" to the south — were built, and, later, the fine terraces of Mayfield. Looking through *Mayfield 100,* a useful booklet published in 1975 to mark the centenary of Mayfield Church, I saw that several elderly members of the congregation, who had been able to recall early days in this part of South Edinburgh, were mentioned. Unfortunately I found, upon investigation, that a number of the people named had since died or left the district. I was lucky, however, in being able to meet Mr Alexander Hunter, for long a resident of the district, who, with the late Mr J. A. Symon, had researched the history of the area for the Mayfield Church booklet and earlier publications. Mr Hunter, who has also written several newspaper articles on the history of South Edinburgh, suggested that his recollections might be prefaced by these lines from Scott's *Marmion:* "And oe'r the landscape as I look, Nought do I see unchanged remain." Recalling his South-Side boyhood days in the early 1900s, Mr Hunter pointed out that, before radio or television, children had to make their own entertainment. In the days of so much less traffic, side-streets were quiet playgrounds for games such as "kick the can" and marbles (the latter unhygienically rolled along the gutters). Boys played with coloured "peeries", kept spinning by a whip or skilful kicking, and girls played diabolo with a piece of wood shaped like an egg-timer, which was cast high into the air and caught on a string held by two wooden handles. "Peevers" was another popular pavement game, as was the strangely named "Hos-p-y". These were the days of street or back-green singers hoping for pennies thrown down from tenement windows wrapped in newspaper. Children would gather round barrel organs which regularly serenaded residents, and often had chained monkeys perched on top. And there were dancing bears, frequently very large animals, shuffling pathetically round their masters to a musical accompaniment. A special feature were the German bands, small groups of three or four musicians playing a variety of instruments who drew crowds as they moved from street to street. After the outbreak of the First World War, many people, Mr Hunter said, suspected them of having been spies. As darkness fell, the "leerie", immortalised in Robert Louis Stevenson's poem, began his rounds, carrying a long pole with a flaming torch to light the gas lamps in the streets. In those days street names were carried on the cross beams of lamp-posts.

Mr Hunter recalled horse-drawn trams from the city to Newington and people's consternation when the horses, frightened by a sudden noise, bolted, or slipped and fell on icy roads in winter. There were many smiddies in the Causewayside area to service these trace horses. Mr Hunter also had vivid memories of horse-drawn fire-engines making their way through Newington from the tiny fire-station in Braid Place (now Sciennes House Place). On Saturday evenings many people would walk from Newington down the Pleasance to St Mary's Street, where shops and street stalls stayed open till ten at night. All kinds of things could be bought, including coconuts, ad cockles and mussels from the Newhaven fishwives. The lively street scene was lit by naphtha flares.

A new era began in Newington in 1884, with the opening of Newington Station on the Suburban Railway, the results of which were evident in Mr Hunter's boyhood days. Alongside the passenger station was built the Newington Goods and Mineral Station, at which arrived a constant stream of wagons bringing roofing slates from Wales and the Western Isles, stone from the various Edinburgh quarries and timber from Granton docks. Unloaded into bays rented by local tradesmen, these materials helped to build the rapidly expanding Newington district at the turn of the century. They were transferred from the railway trucks into two-wheeled carts drawn by Clydesdale horses, to be taken to various building sites. Mr Hunter recalled the carters, attired in moleskin trousers, with "nicky tams", sitting sideways on folded sacking on the shafts of their carts.

Two years after its opening, Newington Station was to serve an important purpose. When the International Exhibition of Industry, Science and Art was held in the Meadows in 1886, Newington was the nearest goods siding, so that most exhibits and supplies were unloaded there. On display at the Exhibition was the North British Railway Company's latest locomotive engine, with tender and first-class carriage, manufactured at Cowlairs in Glasgow. These too were brought into Newington siding. Transporting them to the Meadows seemed an impossible task. However, after certain alterations to the station, the engine and carriage were dragged on trolleys drawn by teams of horses up Findhorn Place, an undertaking which took two days.

On September 18th 1906, the last Review of the Scottish Volunteers was held at Holyrood Park — in perfect weather, unlike the famous Wet Review — and many troops from all over Scotland arrived by train at Newington Station Goods and Mineral Siding in the early hours of that morning. Mr Hunter described how sleeping quarters and breakfast were provided for them in local halls and schools. Later the Volunteers mustered in Mayfield Road, then marched through the King's Park to Holyrood, where seventy thousand men paraded before King Edward VII to the accompaniment of gun salutes, rousing martial music and the loud cheers of spectators seated on the grassy slopes above Holyrood. One unfortunate accident marred the spectacular occasion. Sir Thomas Lipton, Honorary Colonel of the 6th Battalion of the Highland Light Infantry, was thrown from his horse and seriously injured. The Volunteers were superseded by the Territorial Army after this last Review, the occasion of which was also Edward VII's last visit to Scotland.

Among Mr Hunter's many recollections were some about the changing seasons: these seemed to be more clearly defined in years past. he said. Winter was normally severe, with snow and ice for long periods. Skating was a regular sport. The first of Edinburgh's ponds to be "bearing" was always the large one on the Braid Hills, on account of its altitude and exposed situation; next came Blackford Pond and Duddingston Loch. (Sir William Russell Flint, R.A., the distinguished artist, recalled in his autobiography, *In Pursuit,* that the apprentices — of whom he was one — at Banks & Co., the Causewayside printers, were allowed a skating half-holiday in the '90s.) Enthusiastic skating scenes would be floodlit after dark by naphtha flares. However, the severe winters brought more than pleasant hours on frozen ponds: they took their toll on the elderly; the death rate was high, especially from pneumonia. This was before the discovery of antibiotics and other therapeutic drugs. Mr Hunter recalled the many funeral processions

The village of Powburn
From "The Print of His Shoe" by James Goodfellow

which ended in Newington Cemetery during these severe winters. Hearses drawn by stately black horses with nodding head-plumes of purple feathers were followed by mourners in tail-coats and tile hats, walking solemnly behind the cortege, often for a considerable distance. Many a man, remarked Mr Hunter, must have hastened his own death by attending on foot, in snow and bitter weather, the funeral of a friend. A feature of such occasions was the appearance of a man, solemnly attired, who regularly took his place behind the official mourners although he had never known the deceased. This may have been "Funeral Tam", one of Edinburgh's "characters" of the turn of the century.

Just west of Newington Station, across Mayfield Road at its junction with West Savile Terrace, was the little village of Powburn. Its focal point was a substantial mansion-house, and it had a number of tanneries. In a field there, which cannot now be located on old maps, one of Edinburgh's renowned football clubs, the Heart of Midlothian, played its earliest matches. "The Hearts", who recently celebrated their centenary, first played at the Meadows before taking part in matches organised by the Edinburgh Rifle Volunteers at their own ground on Powburn. The Volunteers were the originators of competitive football in Edinburgh.

We turn now to the district of Sciennes, where we have noted that nothing remains of the sixteenth-century Convent of St Catherine of Sienna except a small collection of stones in the front garden of 16 St Catherine's Place. In the mid-nineteenth century part of the original site of the convent had been acquired by the Rev. James McLachlan, formerly incumbent of Old St Paul's Episcopal Church in Carrubber's Close, off the High Street, who proposed to build a small chapel to commemorate the convent. A plan was drawn up by the architect John Biggar in 1863, which included sketches of the remains of the convent which have been reproduced in a number of engravings, but the chapel was never built. Some years prior to the Rev. McLachlan's proposal, another had been made by the late Mrs Colonel Hutchison, sister of Lord Cunninghame, for the building of a convent on the site of the ancient one, but this likewise did not materialise.

Instead, in 1860, a convent was built at Lauriston Gardens dedicated to St Catherine of Sienna, which was regarded as the re-establishment of the original convent. The nuns who came to Lauriston were not, as their predecessors, of the Dominican Order but were sisters of Mercy, whose vocation was to work among the poor and establish schools. The latter were a boarding school for girls, long since closed, and the surviving establishment of St Thomas of Aquin. I talked to the Mother Superior of the new Convent of St Catherine of Sienna, Sister Annunciata, about the relationship of her religious house to the sixteenth-century foundation. She observed that, while there was no direct link, they were conscious of the perpetuation of the name, and she drew my attention to a hawthorn tree in the grounds at Lauriston known as St Catherine's Thorn. Sister

Annunciata kindly lent me a rare book from the convent's archives: an account of the foundation of the Convent at Sciennes, giving much detail not in other sources, which contained several illustrations of the last remains of the old building. Entitled *The Convent of Saint Catherine of Sienna, near Edinburgh,* it was a paper read by George Seton, advocate, before the Architectural Institute of Scotland on April 11th, 1867 and published for private circulation in 1871. It was George Seton who built, and for long resided in, St Bennet's at 42 Greenhill Gardens, which eventually became the residence of the Roman Catholic archbishops of St Andrews and Edinburgh. This booklet contains one point of particular interest, which solved the mystery of who had erected the tablet in the garden of 16 St Catherine's Place: a footnote reveals that it was George Seton himself who had placed it there. He relates that, by the time of writing, in 1871, the mere fragment of the convent which had remained "was razed to the ground and its site is now occupied by a semi-detached villa erected by his congregation for a Wesleyan Methodist minister. With that gentleman's permission," he added, "I propose to fix a cast-iron tablet on the corner of the villa with a short inscription indicative of the site of the convent and the lines from *Marmion* above quoted." (Details of this inscription were given in my chapter on Sciennes in Volume I.)

Turning now to Grange Loan, we must try to recapture the scene where the old toll-house stood, though this is not easy. There are a few old tiled cottages, now shops, on the east side of Ratcliffe Terrace, but the high tenements at the entrance to Grange Loan and the terraced villas beyond are more recent additions. When the old toll-house stood at the corner of Grange Loan there were several quaint two-storey cottages with steep outside stairs in its vicinity. For centuries Cant's Loan, as it was originally called, was little more than a rough pathway over the Burgh Muir, leading from the "wester hiegait" (which skirted the Muir at Morningside), by way of what are now West and East Mayfield (formerly Mayfield Loaning) to the "easter hiegait" (now Dalkeith Road). Fortunately many interesting illustrations remain of the old Grange Toll and its immediate vicinity.

For anyone proceeding by Grange Loan in the late twelfth century, and for long afterwards, the only habitation *en route,* acting as a landmark and refuge, was the simple keep of the Grange of St Giles, surrounded by the great trees and rough undergrowth of the Burgh Muir. By the early nineteenth century, Grange Loan had become a pleasant avenue from east to west, and towering high above the toll-house and its adjacent cottages on the west, was the elegant mansion, Grange House, the creation of Sir Thomas Dick-Lauder.

Strangely, while I could find no living link with the more recent past of Grange House, I did find one with the Grange of six centuries ago. It was a fascinating experience to talk to Sir George Dick-Lauder, 12th Baronet of Fountainhall and Grange, and to be permitted to see and photograph heirlooms of the Grange and of the Lauder, Dick and Dick-Lauder families who had owned the lands from earliest times. We looked at a series of illustrations of Grange House which revealed its gradual development from the original primitive tower to its transformation by W. H. Playfair in 1827. I showed Sir George a number of photographs in the press-cuttings collection of the Edinburgh Central Public Library dramatically illustrating in stages the demolition of the mansion-house in 1936. Contrasting Playfair's work with the final mass of rubble, Sir George recalled how tragic had been the disappearance of a house visited by so many distinguished literary and artistic men, and one which had been such a treasured landmark. However, by the early 1930s the house had remained unoccupied for many years and the cost of restoration would have been in the region of £20,000 — a high price at that time. The upkeep of a house of that size might well have been beyond the means of a private owner, and its spaciousness unnecessary, while the cost of purchase and restoration was forbidding even to institutions or charities.

However, if Grange House itself has gone, much remains to perpetuate it. The two Lauder griffins on stone pillars, marking the east and west extremities of the house in Grange Loan, were mentioned in an earlier chapter, as was the large sword of Sir Robert de Lawdre, staunch right-hand man of Sir William Wallace. Also mentioned was the "World and his Friend", a finely carved two-tiered cabinet, the top portion Dutch, the lower Jacobean, in which Sir William Dick, Lord Provost of Edinburgh from 1638 to 1640, kept part of the city's treasure and a portion of his own vast wealth, which was the "friend" often put at the disposal of the needy.

The close support of the Dick and Seton branches of the family for the Stuart cause is recalled by several fine Mary, Queen of Scots tablecloths in Sir George's possession. There are photographs of the drawing-room and dining-room of Grange House in Sir Thomas Dick-Lauder's day, the latter showing, it would seem, these very tablecloths. Many stimulating after-dinner conversations must have taken place in that room. Another relic, of which Sir George has only a photograph, is a finely carved "Memento Mori" watch in the shape of a skull — a reminder of the fleeting passage of time and inevitable death. Though traditionally believed to have been presented to Mary, Queen of Scots by a member of the Dick-Lauder family when she visited Grange House, according to an expert at the National Museum of Antiquities of Scotland, to whom I spoke, the watch dates from some years after Mary's reign. Nevertheless, it is of great interest and value both on account of its age and its fine workmanship in silver. After being on loan to the Museum of Antiquities, the watch was sold in London in the 1930s to King Farouk of Egypt, who in turn sold it to a private collector.

In the vast collection of letters and papers, inherited by Sir George, which are now in the process of being catalogued, is an interesting volume of notes and correspondence relating to Queen Victoria's tour of Scotland in 1842. To mention one final family treasure, in a special place of honour above the fireplace in Sir George's drawing-room is the original portrait entitled "Sir Thomas Dick-Lauder and his Lady" by W. Nicholson, R.S.A., one of a large number of family portraits.

The Grange has always been one of Edinburgh's most pleasant residential areas; many fine villas arose around the mansion-house, some of considerable grandeur and many of them the homes of well known men. Some of the families of the original owners of these houses have continued, for generations, to reside in the Grange, although a number of the larger houses have been converted, and others demolished. It was interesting to talk to a number of elderly residents about their recollections of the district and Grange House, and also about the life-style of their younger days.

I spoke to Miss Margaret Buchanan at her home in Lauder Road and she told me that her father had joined Duncan, Flockhart & Company, the famous Edinburgh pharmaceutical chemists, as an apprentice in 1846, at the age of seventeen. Their original shop was at 52 North Bridge, but, on the same day that her father began his apprenticeship, a new branch was opened at 139 Princes Street, now the premises of a travel agency. James Buchanan was the first apprentice to be indentured. In these days there were no classes to attend or degree to be obtained: qualification was achieved by daily experience. In the days before proprietary medicines and antibiotics, Duncan, Flockhart & Company had their own "physic garden" at Warriston, producing ingredients for herbal and other medicines. A knowledge of botany was fundamental for a chemist and James Buchanan became so proficient in the subject that he was appointed an examiner of medical students and became renowned in pharmaceutical circles for his training of apprentices.

James Buchanan was eventually to become a senior partner in Duncan Flockhart's with a record of over fifty years service, and was responsible for the busy Princes Street shop, but the most memorable day of his career was during his first year of apprenticeship. On November 8th, 1847, when he was the shop message-boy, he was sent on an errand with a precious package to be delivered to a doctor's house at 52 Queen Street, the residence of Dr James Y. Simpson. The package contained a bottle of purified chloroform, to be used that evening in Simpson's famous experiment with a number of student friends to study its anaesthetic effect. The historic scene of the unconscious students, one just recovering, which was to have such important consequences for mankind, has been represented in a number of illustrations. Simpson had followed with keen interest the early development of anaesthetics. Nitrous oxide had been introduced in 1800 and he himself had used sulphuric ether. But he was searching for a better "drowsy-syrup" and had been promised "perchloride of formyle" by a Linlithgowshire surgeon and chemist.

462

The bottle of chloroform taken to Professor James Simpson for his famous experiment on November 8th, 1847

From the "History of Duncan Flockhart & Co.", 1946

When this failed to materialise he turned to the resources of Duncan, Flockhart & Company. The outcome was the production of the historic bottle of chloroform which young James Buchanan delivered. Two days later Simpson read a paper describing his experiment and chloroform was soon in great demand by Edinburgh surgeons, including Dr William Beilby, then President of the Edinburgh Royal College of Physicians, who is referred to later in connection with Morningside. A whole new department of Duncan Flockhart's was set up to produce chloroform and the firm's fame spread worldwide. In 1854, with the outbreak of the Crimean War, the increased need for anaesthetics was soon being supplied by the Duncan Flockhart team.

As a welcome retreat from heavy daily responsibilities, James Buchanan, in 1876, built a house for his family in the then secluded Oswald Road. This was a spacious villa known as Oswald House, with a fine view of nearby Blackford Hill. Here he was able to devote his precious leisure hours to a different and more relaxing study of his special subject, botany. A splendid collection of orchids was the particular feature of his large greenhouses, which also contained vines and a wide variety of other plants.

This was an era, Miss Buchanan recalled, when domestic staff, chamber- and table-maids, and gardeners, were considered part of the family. There was a stability and regularity in life: the menu followed a weekly pattern to simplify the servants' duties, and there were fixed days for washing and household chores. Some of the staff were "characters", like a maid who over many years had been in and out of the family's employ. Years after she had finally left her post she returned to visit Oswald House. Times had changed. There were fewer servants and technology had arrived in the shape of a Hoover vacuum cleaner. The former servant, who had never been averse to "speaking up" to Miss Buchanan's mother, looked at the Hoover for a few silent moments, and then remarked in characteristic manner: "Well, at least that'll no' speak back to ye!"

I asked Miss Buchanan what profession she had taken up after leaving school and she reminded me that in families such as hers at the turn of the century it was not customary for girls to take employment. The father of the house was the provider, and daughters assisted their mothers or helped in the garden. Some studied music — an asset in family social gatherings — or perhaps followed courses at the University or Art College. Father paid the fees and there was no anxiety about passing examinations or failing to have renewed Education Department grants.

James Buchanan retired from Duncan, Flockhart & Company in 1904, after nearly sixty years, and died five years later. Soon afterwards the family moved to Lauder Road. Oswald House was sold and demolished to make way for modern flats. Miss Buchanan claims one living link with Grange House and its association with Bonnie Prince Charlie: in her front garden in Lauder Road is a vigorous bush of delicate white roses grown from a cutting obtained from the parent plant which grew in the garden of the great mansion-house of Grange, and from which Bonnie Prince Charlie's rose was plucked (see Volume 1).

Before leaving Grange I talked to another resident, Dr John Martin, of the family of well known Edinburgh bakers. Our conversation overlapped into Morningside, for in 1947 there had been established the Martin Foundation which provided accommodation and board for twenty ladies, originally old employees of Martin the Baker's, in Newbattle House, Newbattle Terrace. In 1966 the Martin Foundation was incorporated in a scheme inaugurated by the Edinburgh Merchant Company which led to the combination of Newbattle House with the rebuilt Pitsligo House in Pitsligo Road. In the early 1930s Martin's purchased Canaan Grove, the stately red sandstone villa at 82 Newbattle Terrace, as a recreational centre, with a bowling green and tennis courts, for its employees. This property was eventually sold to the Edinburgh Corporation in 1960 and converted for public use.

Leaving Grange for the adjacent lands of Whitehouse, we see that all that remains of the original sixteenth-century mansion of Whitehouse is now incorporated in that part of St Margaret's Convent which stands on the east side of Whitehouse Loan, just south of the entrance to the convent and facing St Margaret's Place. While the convent retains many relics of its foundation and development, for reasons of security one of its most

Sanctus Bell, part of the altar plate of James VIII now in the Scottish National Museum of Antiquities

From the "Antiquaries Journal", 1968

valuable and interesting treasures was placed in the custody of the National Museum of Antiquities of Scotland in Queen Street. This is part of the collection of silver altar plate which James II and VII had made for the Chapel Royal of Holyroodhousee in 1686.

On February 6th, 1685, James had succeeded his elder brother Charles II, though his reign was to last for only four years. Before his accession, he had returned to the Catholic Church of his Stuart forefathers: this resulted in the provision of Chapels Royal at Whitehall, Windsor, Dublin and Edinburgh where he could worship according to the rites of the Roman Catholic Church. Each of these was furnished with suitable altar plate, but while that provided for the English and Irish chapels has disappeared, the silver plate made for Holyrood has survived. These are candlesticks and vessels of superb craftsmanship and quality which arrived on the King's yacht at Leith on November 23rd, 1686. They were inscribed only with his Scottish title, James VII.

In May 1687 the people of the Canongate, who had used the Abbey at Holyrood as their Protestant parish church, were transferred to Lady Yester's Church and the Abbey was furnished as the Chapel Royal and the Chapel of the Knights of the Thistle, which Order James intended to restore. The best wood-carvers of Europe and expert London silversmiths were engaged. It was in this magnificently restored chapel that the altar plate was installed.

On his accession, James was no stranger to Edinburgh for on three occasions he had visited the city as High Commissioner to represent his brother. In December 1688, however, after the landing of the Prince of

Orange at Torbay, James returned to France. Soon after his departure, a mob invaded the Holyrood Chapel Royal. The contents were thrown out of the windows; its woodwork was hacked to pieces and burned in the Abbey Close; the Abbey library was destroyed. There was a mock procession round the town carrying statues from the chapel which were later burned at the Mercat Cross in the High Street. But the altar's silver plate was saved. One of the chapel's priests, Father David Burnet, anticipating the invasion, had hastily gathered the sacred vessels and, under cover of darkness, had set off with them on horseback for Leith. In the early hours of the morning he crossed the Forth; he was pursued, but, on arriving in Fife, he took to the open fields. At dawn he set out north, again followed. He shook off his pursuers and reached Enzie in Banffshire, between Keith and the Moray Firth. This was a Catholic area. For some time he and another priest lived in a remote hut on the hill of Altmore while the Holyrood plate came to rest with a sympathetic farmer at Preshome. It was not discovered during the '45 Rebellion, and in about 1880 was taken to Blairs College, the Catholic Junior Seminary near Aberdeen. Eventually some of the vessels were brought to St Mary's Catholic Cathedral in York Place, Edinburgh. After the foundation of St Margaret's Convent in Whitehouse Loan in 1834 certain items were entrusted to the nuns, and were in regular use until 1967, when the Scottish Catholic Hierarchy and the nuns of St Margaret's agreed to deposit their valuable treasure in the National Museum of Antiquities in Edinburgh.

A short distance from St Margaret's is Bruntsfield Hospital, built in 1911, which faces an uncertain future. It has been proposed that its traditional function as a hospital for women and children should be discontinued and the hospital put to more general purposes, though petitions have been presented to the health authorities urging that it remain unchanged.

I discussed the history of the hospital with its Matron, Miss Elspeth Baxter, who edits its informative magazine in which historical notes are regularly published. The only relic of its famous foundress Dr Sophia Jex-Blake, which the hospital possessed was, I learned, a portrait, and this, when I called at the hospital, was not in its normal place but on loan to an exhibition in the Royal Scottish Museum in Chambers Street, commemorating the 250th Anniversary of Edinburgh's Medical School.

The hospital's archives, however, contain many of Dr Jex-Blake's letters, written on a wide variety of subjects. These were frequently headed "Bruntsfield Lodge". In the first Edinburgh Ordnance Survey map of 1852, Bruntsfield Lodge is shown as a large villa just north-west of the present-day Bruntsfield Hotel, while, on the site of what is now Bruntsfield Hospital, Greenhill Cottage is shown, which, in 1834, was the residence of Bishop Gillis, founder of St Margaret's Convent. Reference to Edinburgh Post Office Directory maps of the period showed that the family house in Whitehouse Loan, in which Dr Jex-Blake came to live in

1898, was also eventually renamed Bruntsfield Lodge, having earlier been called Greenhill Cottage. The original Bruntsfield Lodge of the 1852 Ordnance Survey map was probably on the same site as the later Glengyle Lodge, a fine villa which remains today, entered from a lane just north of Bruntsfield Hospital in Bruntsfield Place. When the original Bruntsfield Lodge had disappeared, Dr Sophia Jex-Blake's family had perpetuated its name by changing that of their house from Greenhill Cottage to Bruntsfield Lodge.

As I looked around the hospital with Miss Baxter, we discussed the wards which had been named after colleagues of Dr Jex-Blake or other benefactors. The Beilby Ward recalled the generous financial support given to Dr Jex-Blake's efforts by Lady Emma Beilby, daughter-in-law of Dr Thomas Beilby who was Morningside's village doctor from 1840 to 1895, and whose family history I shall discuss in connection with Morningside.

The James Gillespie's High School magazine, which carries contributions of a very high literary standard, also publishes occasional articles reminding pupils and parents of the history of the school and its origins in Gillespie's Hospital. Dr Patricia Thomas, the Head Teacher, assured me that, despite the school's change of function, pupils were very much aware of its proud traditions. One of the school's houses is, appropriately, named Spylaw, after the place where Gillespie's snuff mill stood, and another Warrender after the family whose name is synonymous with Bruntsfield House.

In June 1977 the school magazine published news of a happy link with its living past. Linda Urquhart, then school captain, and Sheila Prestage had recently visited Mrs Margaret Ashton, aged 102, who had been a pupil at the original James Gillespie's School in the "hospital" building in Gillespie Crescent. Mrs Ashton, who lives in Thetford in Norfolk, is believed to be the school's oldest former pupil. She had interesting memories of her schooldays and residence in Marchmont. Born in February 1875, Margaret Carruthers was one of eleven children. Her parents owned a dairy at 5 Gillespie Place (later for many years a shoe repair shop), and lived in Marchmont Street. Her education began at the Normal School beside Edinburgh Castle, and was continued at James Gillespie's. Classes were held in a large hall partitioned by curtains. The desks were in tiers, girls sitting on one side and the boys on the other: they never mixed. If they spoke in class they were punished with the tawse. Staff called pupils by their surnames. Female teachers taught the children until the age of nine, then men took over. The school day was long, with only one short break at lunchtime. Mrs Ashton remembered seeing Queen Victoria open the International Exhibition of Industry, Science and Art in the Meadows in 1886. To her young visitors Mrs Ashton described a bygone way of life vastly different from their own experiences.

Stone plaque in Glengyle Terrace, showing the arms of the builders, W. and D. McGregor

Photograph by Mr W. R. Smith

High up on the wall of the flats at 1 Warrender Park Crescent is a carved stone slab bearing a coat-of-arms. It is too high for the details to be clearly noted, but its main features are evidently a lion's head bearing a crown. After referring to a few books on heraldry I decided that the crest might be that of a branch of the McGregor family. I submitted a rough sketch of the coat-of-arms to the ultimate authority, the Lord Lyon King of Arms at Register House, and it was confirmed that they appeared to be those of a branch of the McGregor family: the carving on the stone could probably be described as "a lion's head erased, crowned with an antique crown", while the motto might be "Een do and spare nought". A closer study from the street revealed that the crest matched the Lord Lyon's description. Further information, however, solved the mystery. This was offered by Mr David Walker, principal historic buildings investigator of the Scottish Development Department, who, from his records, was able to confirm that Warrender Park Crescent had been built by W. and D. McGregor who had also constructed nearby Glengyle Terrace, where, at the east end, a similar plaque may be seen. It was quite common, Mr Walker informed me, for architects and builders to place either their initials and a date or more elaborate carvings and crests on their work.

Certainly there are many other parts of the Marchmont district where such markings may be seen, as also in Bruntsfield Place, between Forbes Road and Bruntsfield Gardens.

"Ye Olde Golf Tavern", as its sign proclaims, remains after centuries the hub of golfing activity on Bruntsfield Links. Opposite is the first tee beside the old cabbie's shelter from which unfailingly, in summer and winter, enthusiastic devotees of all ages drive off. For almost half a century "Mine host" at the "Gowf", as the tavern is familiarly known, has been Mr Michael Shaw. I spoke to him about the early golfing relics which adorn his walls in the public bar. These include a pair of ancient golf "cliques", the exact origins of which are not known, a framed plan of the links, Wrychtishousis and district, as they appeared in the days of the Edinburgh Burgess Golfing Society, and an extensive collection of golfing cartoons, originally printed as illustrations for the annual calendar issued by the manufacturers of Perrier mineral water.

In view of the Golf Tavern's claim to antiquity, and to having been for centuries the Links' "19th green", I mentioned the reference in several publications to another Bruntsfield golfers' tavern called Lucky Maggy Johnston's, the precise location of which I had been unable to trace. Mr Shaw suggested that in fact the celebrated Maggy Johnston may for some time have been the proprietrix of the Golf Tavern, which during her tenure therefore came to be known familiarly as "Maggy Johnston's". The term "Lucky" as in "Lucky Maggy Johnston's" was commonly used to describe a middle-aged and rather prim hostelry proprietrix: there was also "Lucky Jenny Ha's" tavern in the Canongate.

On the evening I met Mr Shaw, the Golf Tavern was displaying a poster inviting short-hole golfing enthusiasts to enter the annual "Tappit Hen" competition, known also as the "Tavern Trophy". Application was to be made to Mr Norman Inglis, Secretary of the Bruntsfield Links Short-Hole Club. Having formed a vague impression that most devotees of the Royal and Ancient game at Bruntsfield were elderly gentlemen whiling away their retirement in a healthy way, I was surprised to learn from a youthful Mr Inglis that most of his members were young players.

The Bruntsfield Links Short-Hole Club was founded in 1895. The Links course of eighteen holes in winter and thirty-six in summer is maintained by the Edinburgh District Council's Recreation and Leisure Department; the scratch score for thirty-six holes is 104. Club membership costs fifty pence per annum but play on the course is free: according to a writer in *Golf World,* Bruntsfield is probably the only free golf course in the world, since membership of the Short-Hole Club is not obligatory for its users.

The Tappit Hen or Tavern Trophy, an old pewter ale-measure, is the club's principal prize, and was donated by Mr Michael Shaw in 1950. "Gang bring her ben, the Tappit Hen," is the invitation printed on the competition entry forms — which, translated into standard English, means: "After victory, fill her up at my place!"

Another annual competition which attracts many participants is between club members and the Edinburgh Corporation Golf Club. Others are for the Inches Trophy, donated by Lord Provost Robert Inches in 1904, and the Bob Burnett Trophy, formerly the championship trophy of the now defunct Pentland Club.

The Bruntsfield Short-Hole Club has produced several young players who have gone on to achieve distinction in the wider golfing world. Notable have been Jack Burnside, the former Scottish Internationalist, and Roddy Gray, one-time Scottish and British Youth Internationalist, who reached the final of the British Boys Championship in 1964. While a student at Edinburgh University he reached the final of the British Universities Championship.

A very lively link with Bruntsfield's golfing past is the Veterans Club, founded in 1906, the membership of which is confined to players of over sixty-five. Their club-house is a hut near the bowling green in Melville Drive, purchased from Edinburgh Corporation for £200. Doyen of the club is eighty-seven-year-old Andrew Baptie, who told me that he first began playing over the world-famous St Andrews course when he was eight years of age. His father was a local golf-club maker with Forgan's. Since his retirement as a baker in Edinburgh, Mr Baptie has spent most of his spare time, summer and winter, playing with his "elderly young friends" over the Bruntsfield course. He has also found time to be a member of the Merchants of Edinburgh club at Craiglockhart for thirty-three years. He achieved his first "hole in one" at Bruntsfield when he was seventy-six. Mr Baptie acts as a referee in the Tappit Hen and Inches Trophy competitions. The highlight of the Veterans Club year is the game played at the Links on alternate years with the Royal Burgess Golfing Society and the Bruntsfield Links Golfing Society, both of which originated at Bruntsfield but now have private courses at Barnton and Davidson's Mains respectively. After these events players adjourn to enjoy the hospitality of Mr Michael Shaw in the traditional 19th green.

While in the earliest days of golf on Bruntsfield Links it was Alexander McKellar who emerged as the most immortal "character" — he was undisputed "Cock o' the Green" — in the nineteenth century the most notable eccentric was "Caddie Willie". He was William Gunn, who came to Edinburgh from the Highlands in about 1800. While distributing religious tracts in the city, he came to Bruntsfield where he would stop and watch the golfers. Certain players, including Douglas McEwan, one-time golf-club manufacturer at Bruntsfield, recorded his tall figure and several layers of clothes. Eventually he was invited to carry the players' clubs, which he was willing enough to do for a shilling an hour. The job appealed to him, and he found himself a garret room, rented from a gardener employed on the nearby Leven Lodge and Valleyfield lands. After earning enough money to pay his fare, Caddie Willie would return to the Highlands from time to time. In about 1820 he told Mr McEwan that he had earned enough to save him from his one fear — a pauper's burial. He set off for the Highlands for the last time and, to the concern of golfers, never returned. What happened to him after that was never discovered.

From the Golf Tavern it is but a stone's throw to a much smaller hostelry, the Auld Toll Bar in Leven Street, under the towering steeple of the Barclay Church. The toll commemorated stood here from about 1800 until, as mentioned earlier, it was removed further south to the foot of Morningside Road. Although the Wrychtishousis toll-house is traditionally believed to have stood on the very site of the bar, the latter has no pictures or other relics associated with its predecessor. The adjacent row of two-storeyed tiled cottages with outside stone stairs at the rear clearly points to earlier times.

South Edinburgh is a rapidly changing scene and Gillespie Crescent is a notable example of this development. In 1975 the main building of the Royal Blind Asylum workshops, the original Gillespie's Hospital built in 1802, was demolished to make way for flats and it has left even fewer traces than the ancient mansion-house of Wrychtishousis which earlier occupied its site. Of this unique fourteenth-century building certain associations can still be traced, as described in Volume I. The stones salvaged from the old mansion and built into the east boundary wall of Gillespie's Hospital were eventually removed to the temporary keeping of the Curator of the Huntly House Museum. In February 1978 I talked to one of the architects responsible for the block of flats on the Wrychtishousis site and was informed that his firm was very conscious of historical associations: while part of this area was to retain the name Gillespie Crescent, the section within the new complex was to be named Wrights Houses. They were also anxious to replace the ancient stones of Wrychtishousis somewhere in the complex. If, because of the problems of weathering and other factors, this were not feasible, it might be possible for synthetic simulations of them to be installed in a suitable setting.

Other ancient sculpted stones taken from Wrychtishousis after its demolition are still to be seen in places outwith Edinburgh. Some, including a particularly fine sundial, were removed to adorn the former stately mansion of Woodhouselee in the Pentland Hills near Flotterstone, associated with the famous Scottish historians Dr John Hill Burton (whose wife Katherine was the daughter of Professor Cosmo Innes) and Patrick Fraser-Tytler. Several writers relating the history of Craighouse have referred to Woodhouselee. I was interested to discover whether any links existed between the ancient mansion-houses of Wrychtishousis and Craighouse, and the Tytlers of Woodhouselee. I was fortunate to obtain some information from Lady Fraser-Tytler, whose late husband, the former British Minister to Afghanistan, was a descendant of William Tytler, who had originally purchased Woodhouselee in 1748. William

Tytler had pulled down most of the old fortalice of Fulford which stood on the site of Woodhouselee and his son, Alexander, Lord Woodhouselee, built the mansion-house. This was demolished in 1964, but some of the Wrychtishousis stones have been built into an arch near its site. In *A Memoir of Patrick Fraser-Tytler* by the Rev. John W. Burgon, author of *History of Scotland,* there is a detailed account of the Tytler family and their associations with Woodhouselee. It does not, however, refer to the historian's residence at Craighouse.

Descendants of the Fraser-Tytlers have a collection of Tytler family portraits, one of which is a drawing of William Tytler by Allan Ramsay, done when artist and subject were both about seventeen. Other family treasures include a roundel of stained glass bearing the arms of James VI and Anne of Denmark, dated 1600. This is on loan to the Museum of Antiquities of Scotland in Queen Street. Perhaps the most valuable of the relics, now no longer in the possession of the Tytler family, were a watch and solitaire belonging to Mary, Queen of Scots: the watch is believed to have been a wedding gift to Mary from the Dauphin of France. An early member of the Tytler family had been in the Queen's retinue when she came to Scotland. After the Tytlers sold Woodlouselee the Wrychtishousis heraldic panels, the coat of arms and pediments were in part dispersed. A sundial made from some of the stones is now in the grounds of Holy Trinity Church, Haddington, and another in the Huntly House Museum.

As one proceeds from Gillespie Crescent up Bruntsfield Place, the tall flats give way to a row of four fine villas. According to Andrew Patterson in an article in Volume XXXII of the *Book of the Old Edinburgh Club* (1966), these, and a fifth villa demolished to make way for the Bruntsfield Hotel, were once known "The Doctors' Row", each being at one time a doctor's residence. The first of the villas, No. 46, now owned by a dental surgeon, Dr G. Macgregor Rose, bears the name Firenze. Mr Patterson, while curious, did not discover the reason for this name. According to its present owner the wife of an early occupant was named Florence, and her husband gave the house the Italian version of her name. Dr Rose told me that in early days there had been a home farm in the vicinity.

Still residing and practising in Doctors' Row, at 53 Bruntsfield Place, is Dr George Brewster, who was kind enough to talk to me about his half a century of medical practice in Bruntsfield. As a newly qualified doctor at the City Fever Hospital in Greenbank Drive, he worked under the famous "fevers" specialist Dr Claude Kerr. Before systematic immunisation, diphtheria was endemic and frequently fatal: the treatment of children by tracheotomy was a harrowing experience. In the late 1920s, as the country moved towards economic depression, Dr Brewster recalled that, when the father of a family was laid off sick, it was a serious financial problem, for, while he may have received benefit from "the Panel", as it was known, his wife and children received nothing. Frequently men could simply not afford to stay off work.

Dr Brewster commented on the modern phenomenon and problem of widespread longevity. In his days as a young doctor it was unknown for large numbers of elderly people to survive into advanced old age. In the 1920s many old people would contract pneumonia in winter and, in the absence of antibiotics, would die. Modern medical care had created a whole new problem.

While the doctor of today has a sophisticated schedule of drugs and other forms of therapy to prescribe to his patients, Dr Brewster recalled that, in his day, the general practitioner's "black bag" contained three basic remedies: castor oil for stomach conditions, iodine for wounds and digitalis for ailments of the heart.

Dr Brewster could recall some of the eccentric medical men who at one time lived in Doctors' Row. One, who was here in about 1900, perhaps in the villa named Linkview, sold his house on condition that the purchaser would look after his donkey until it died, and then have it buried in the back garden.

Immediately south of the fourth house in Doctors' Row, a narrow lane leads to Glengyle Lodge, the substantial villa hidden within the triangle formed by Bruntsfield Place and Gillespie Crescent which was mentioned before. It was built by Duncan McGregor who, with W. McGregor was responsible for the building of Warrender Park Crescent and Glengyle Terrace. As stated earlier, at the east end of Glengyle Terrace there is a stone plaque, similar to, though smaller than, the one at Warrender Park Crescent which I have described. It bears the date 1869. Glengyle was the name of the Macgregor lands in the north of Scotland, which is why Glengyle Lodge and Terrace were so named. The lands of Leven Lodge and Valleyfield were also acquired by W. and D. McGregor.

Glengyle Lodge was built in 1867. I pointed out to the present owner that the Ordnance Survey Map of 1852 showed a villa named Bruntsfield Lodge which, it would appear, occupied the same site. Resident for some years in Glengyle Lodge was Lord Alness, a Senator of the College of Justice, who broke with tradition by choosing to live in South Edinburgh rather than join his colleagues in the New Town.

Today one can cross the Links from Bruntsfield Place and enter Greenhill Gardens, but such access was not always possible. Prior to 1852 the boundary wall of the lands of Greenhill ran from Bruntsfield Place along what is now Bruntsfield Terrace to Greenhill Cottage, around which Bruntsfield Hospital was built.

In response to my appeal in the Press for interesting recollections of old South Edinburgh, I heard from a lady, Miss Alexandra E. Beveridge of Greenhill Gardens, who had spent her childhood in Morningside at the turn of the century. She also showed me a fascinating little book of notes

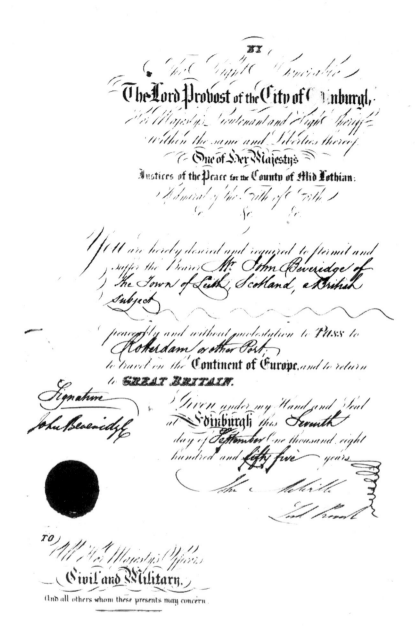

Passport issued to Alexander and John Beveridge

By courtesy of Mr H. W. Beveridge; photograph by Mr W. Weir

on the history of various parts of Edinburgh which she had compiled during her schooldays.

Some of Miss Beveridge's reminiscences wer similar to others I had heard from ladies brought up in the "villadom" of Grange and Morningside: reminiscences of a large house with servants treated as members of the family, set weekly menus, a regular washing day and fixed days for other household tasks, and the maid's weekly evening off, when she would perhaps attend a social evening specially provided in one of the local churches in Morningside. Afternoon tea in Torrance's first-floor tearooms at the corner of Comiston Road and Belhaven Terrace was recalled as a pleasant excursion.

Miss Beveridge's interesting family history soon took us beyond Morningside and the city and into European history. In the mid-nineteenth century there was a great butter shortage throughout Europe and prices soared. Manufacturers began to experiment with substitutes. In 1855 Miss Beveridge's grandfather, John Beveridge of the Leith firm of Alexander & John Beveridge, made special application for a passport from the Lord Provost of Edinburgh, John Melville. Duly received, it stated that it "permits and suffers the bearer peacefully and without molestation to pass to Rotterdam or other parts to travel on the Continent of Europe". John Beveridge and his brother Alexander were manufacturers of animal fats, and the object of John's visit to Holland was to explore the possibilities of manufacturing a butter substitute.

In Rotterdam he met the Jurgens family who were pioneering the manufacture of such a substitute in Europe. In 1862 Anton Johannes Jurgens came to Leith and visited the Beveridge family. Miss Beveridge told me that her grandmother, Margaret Beveridge, prepared various concoctions of animal fats and other oils, suggested by her husband and Anton Jurgens, in the kitchen of her home in Leith. Eventually a satisfactory compound was mixed. In the course of its preparation it had produced lots of "pearly bubbles" and they thought first to name it "Pearline" or "Butterine". Jurgens, however, proposed that, since Margaret Beveridge had been kind enough to carry out the experiments, the product should be named after her: thus the name "Margarine" was given to the first butter substitute.

Having made a business deal with Jurgens, the firm of Alexander & John Beveridge, which moved from Leith to a factory at Hawkhill, was soon extremely busy. Their part in the new deal was to produce the basic ingredients of margarine known as "premier jus" and "olio". This they did on a large scale, and ships then plied regularly between Leith and Holland carrying their valuable cargo. It was on account of the unpleasant odours resulting from the manufacturing process that the Beveridge factory moved to Hawkhill, then a district of open fields.

The famous firm of A. & J. Beveridge remained a family business until 1964. The company which then took over retained the original name and now produces a wide range of cleaning materials, as well as distributing chemicals and providing many products required in the North Sea oil industry.

The Beveridge archives remain with Mr William Beveridge, a cousin of Miss Beveridge of Greenhill. He was the last member of the family to be associated with the long-established Leith company. At his home in the ancient village of Inveresk, I was able to see and photograph the original passport issued to John Beveridge, a simple parchment document, partly printed and partly handwritten, and the firm's patent, in the form of a large embossed and inscribed plaster medallion in a copper case, granted by Queen Victoria in 1872. The inscription on the medallion reads: "To John Beveridge, Merchant of Leith in the County of North Britain, who has indicated to us that he is in possession of an invention for improving and clearing animal fats, of great public utility, communicated to him by Anton Jurgens."

Talking to Mr William Beveridge led me even farther from Morningside. His wife's family was connected with the civil engineering firm of Blyth & Blyth, who had a distinguished record extending over 125 years. He showed me an illustrated book which listed their achievements, including construction of Edinburgh's Waverley, Caledonian and Leith Central Stations, Glasgow Central Station and the Broomielaw Bridge over the Clyde, Grangemouth and Methil docks, Edinburgh's new North Bridge, the Rugby Union stadium at Murrayfield and a number of new towns and hydro-electric projects.

Miss Beveridge's father, perhaps on account of the long association with Leith of the family business, and of shipping to Holland, retained a deep interest in the small paddle steamers which at one time plied between Granton, Aberdour and other "ports" in Fife. Some years ago, Miss Beveridge presented to Trinity House in Leith one of her family treasures: the bell obtained by her father from the Forth paddle steamer of 1866 to 1900, the *Lord Aberdour,* when this ship was broken up.

Entering the Merchiston district, a permanent and visible link with the past is the admirably restored Merchiston Tower in the Napier College of Commerce and Technology in Colinton Road. Nearby is Napier Road where, as mentioned earlier, Sir James Gowans built the "astonishing" Rockville in 1858. Between Gowans' departure from the extraordinary house in 1887 and its demolition, described as "vandalism", in 1966, it was successively occupied by Morningside College (for a brief period), John Harrison, the City Treasurer and his family (for over half a century) and then by Dr Isaac Newton and his family. I was fortunate enough to meet members of both these families and to talk to them about their residence in Rockville.

When I talked to Miss Agnes Harrison at her home in Tipperlinn Road, she was in her ninety-fifth year; sadly she died a year later, in December 1977. She spoke of her family's long record of distinguished public service, recalling her grandfather, Sir George Harrison, who, in addition to other involvements in Edinburgh life, had been Lord Provost of the city and a Member of Parliament until his death in 1888. He is commemorated not only by the "Harrison Arch", as it is known, at the entrance to Observatory Road, leading to Blackford Hill, but also by the pleasant amenities of Blackford Hill itself, one of Edinburgh's "green spaces" which offers relaxation and enjoyment. Harrison Park on the north bank of the Union Canal and several adjacent streets also commemorate Lord Provost Harrison.

Miss Harrison recalled how Blackford Hill came to be acquired by the city. Her grandfather, when residing with his family in Blackford Road, had attempted to gain access to Blackford Hill for a pleasant walk. He was turned back at one of the gates by a worker on the Mortonhall estate, for Blackford then was still part of the extensive lands of the Trotters of Mortonhall. This experience convinced George Harrison that the city should acquire Blackford Hill as a public park. As a result of his efforts, which were not without opposition, Edinburgh Town Council were persuaded to purchase Blackford from the Trotter family in 1884 for the sum of £8,000.

Miss Harrison herself had maintained her family's proud tradition of municipal service, having been a bailie for many years. A woman of dynamic energy and purpose, she served with the Red Cross at Calais in the First World War and was a co-foundress of Avenol, now a School of Mothercraft and Home for Babies in Colinton Road, concerned with adoption and fostering under the auspices of the Church of Scotland.

I discovered that Dr Isaac Newton, the Harrisons' successor at Rockville, was indeed connected with his immortal namesake, the seventeenth-century physicist and mathematician who enunciated the principle of gravity. I talked to Mrs Newton, whose great-grandfather was Lord Provost Cowan of Edinburgh and whose husband was at one time Director of Medical and Sanitary Services for Hong Kong. While he was serving in the Far East, Mrs Newton brought up her large family in Rockville and had many recollections of Gowans' remarkable villa. She was able to cast some light on a query submitted by a reader to John Oddie's "Here's Your Answer" column in the *Edinburgh Evening News*. It concerned the statue of a crowned woman placing wreaths on the heads of two small children, which now stands near the park ranger's house in West Princes Street Gardens, not far from the Royal Scots Memorial. The columnist had replied that the statue, sculpted in 1862 by W. Brodie, R.S.A., probably represented "The Genius of Architecture rewarding the science and the practice of the arts". It had been exhibited at an international exhibition in London. It was also suggested that it had once stood in the grounds of Rockville as a symbolic representation of motherhood. Mrs Newton clearly recalled the statue at Rockville, hidden among some tall rhododendrons, and was inclined to support the view of a niece of Sir

The statue in West Princes Street Gardens which once stood in the grounds of Rockville

By courtesy of "Edinburgh Evening News"

James Gowans, who was the son-in-law of the sculptor Brodie, that it did in fact represent the "Genius of Architecture".

At 16 Colinton Road is Merchiston Cottage, built in 1846 for the Bursar of Merchiston Castle School, upon the site of which Napier College was built. Here I talked to Mrs E. S. Phillipps who had long memories of Morningside and of one of its best known architects. This was John Henderson, Mrs Phillipps' grandfather, who was born in Brechin in 1804 and died in Edinburgh in 1862. When he first came to Edinburgh he was apprenticed to Thomas Hamilton who built the new High School at Regent Road in 1862. In his relatively short life, John Henderson could claim a prodigious record of architectural achievements, including the Parish Church at the corner of Newbattle Terrace, opened in 1838, of which his original drawing is still extant. Within a short distance of the Parish Church, he built a villa for Dr Thomas Chalmers at No. 1 Churchhill, as well as St Bennet's, originally for George Seton, though in 1890 it became the residence of the Roman Catholic Archbishops of St Andrews and Edinburgh.

Several fine villas from Henderson's drawing board are to be found in Greenhill Park. He built 7 Greenhill Park for himself, and the adjacent No. 9 for his brother-in-law. Two villas in Greenhill Gardens were also to his design.

On a larger scale, his work included the Longmore Hospital in Salisbury Place, Granton Harbour and, above the harbour, Granton Hotel, in which Queen Victoria stayed on one of her visits to Edinburgh, and which many years ago was taken over by the Royal Navy. Henderson also built Glenalmond School and twenty-seven Scottish Episcopalian churches, including Holy Trinity Church at the Dean Bridge, and, St Baldred's at North Berwick. The Mariner's Church at Leith, which was also his work, originally had spires representing the masts of a ship. Newhaven Parish Church — "the fishwives' church" — was yet another of Henderson's creations.

A close friend of Sir John Steell, the famous sculptor who resided in Greenhill Gardens, used John Henderson as his model for a statue of Alexander Henderson, the Reformation preacher of the church at Fordel Castle in Fife, commissioned for the Church of the Holy Rude in Stirling. Mrs Phillipps told me that her father, also an architect of distinction, had been of the belief that Alexander Henderson of Fordel and his own family were related. John Henderson, from a deep sense of humility, would never allow himself to be photographed, so the only portrait of him is the Stirling statue, which is now too weathered to convey a true likeness. Mrs Phillipps, however, does treasure many of her grandfather's architectural drawings and plans, many of which have been copied for preservation by the Royal Commission on Ancient and Historical Monuments of Scotland.

Mrs Phillipps' father, George Henderson, trained in the Edinburgh City Architect's Department, after which he was engaged with William Hay (a business partnership of Hay & Henderson was established) in the third restoration of St Giles' Cathedral; the restored West Door of St Giles' was George Henderson's work. He subsequently left Edinburgh for Canada, and, afterwards, Australia, and in the latter built Geelong College in Victoria.

Mrs Phillipps had many recollections of Morningside at the turn of the century. Her early home had been in Hermitage Gardens. She recalled being taken along Braid Crescent to Comiston Road to watch the great state procession, led by the Horse Guards, when Edward VII and Queen Alexandra, watched by great crowds, rode up to open the City Fever Hospital in May 1903. She also remembered the old horse-trams well, and the changing of trace horses at Braidburn Crescent after the terminus had been moved southwards from Morningside Station. Falcon Hall she remembered glimpsing through the wide gates in Morningside Road. Of Tipperlinn, close to her house in Colinton Road, she recalled the traditional belief that in very early times there used to be an inn behind Viewfield House in Tipperlinn Road, near the ancient draw-well which supplied water to the eighteenth-century weavers. Here, it was said, pilgrims making their way westwards across the morass of the Burgh Muir to the pre-Reformation parish church of St John the Baptist in Corstorphine, would shelter. In modern times, Mrs Phillipps recalled a meeting at her house in 1965, at which representatives of various Edinburgh societies made a final plea to the authorities to stay the demolition of nearby Rockville — but, alas, to no avail.

At Churchhill two links with the past merit brief reference. On Dr Thomas Chalmers' villa at No. 1 Churchhill, still a pleasant private residence, a metal plaque reminds the passer-by of its first owner. However, the famous leader of the Disruption would probably regret that his most treasured memorial now faces an uncertain future. This is the former Chalmers Territorial Church on the south side of the historic West Port, leading into the Grassmarket, which was built shortly before his death in 1847. Closed many years ago, the church premises have, in latter days, served as a furniture warehouse and, most recently, a cafeteria for Edinburgh College of Art students. Much of the north side of the West Port was demolished several years ago to make way for the building of the multi-storey Argyle House. When I spoke to a member of staff in the Conservation Section of Edinburgh District Council's Planning Department, I was informed that the future of the south side of the West Port had not yet been decided. The possibility of restoring former residential property was being considered. It was believed that the College of Art had plans for expansion downhill from Lauriston Place which might include finding a use for the Chalmers Territorial Church, but plans had not been finalised. Today, few passers-by are aware of the origins of the Church, although, until a few years ago a small wooden noticeboard still bore its name, and details of church services could just be deciphered. Fortunately an interesting lithograph of the church in its heyday remains, signed by Dr Thomas Chalmers, who presented it to Mr William Cowan, whose family became closely associated with Edinburgh Public Libraries.

East Morningside House in Clinton Road has become something of a mecca for Susan Ferrier admirers — and there do seem to be signs of a revived interest in her work. Through the kind hospitality of the present owners, Dr and Mrs Michael Oliver, members of further education classes have been able to visit the house and see the oak-panelled study in which Susan Ferrier did much of her writing. On certain occasions Mrs Oliver, attired in appropriate costume, plays the part of Susan Ferrier and gives a brief description of the history of the house, enacting scenes from the novelist's life and reading excerpts from her writings.

There was one link with Susan Ferrier which led me, surprisingly, to the Rockefeller Institute in the United States and to Funchal, the capital of Madeira. An Edinburgh doctor told me that, while her husband was studying medicine at the Rockefeller Institute, he came across a modern edition of Susan Ferrier's first highly successful novel *Marriage;* early editions of the novels are extremely rare. Fascinated by the theme and style of the work, he became a devotee of the author. Later his wife came to share his enthusiasm. Some years ago, while holidaying in Funchal, they heard of the "English Rooms", once a popular club for the large British community of former days. It had had a large library with a lending section and a department of old and rare books, eventually transferred to the English church in Funchal. An expert from London was called upon to evaluate the rarer books, and these were duly sold, the remainder being disposed of in an open sale which was to prove a stroke of good fortune for the two Edinburgh doctors. Searching carefully through the books on sale, they found two of the three volumes of the first edition of *Marriage* at a modest price.

In Morningside I was able to talk to many residents of long standing whose reminiscences enabled me to construct an impression of the development of Morningside from a quiet village out in the country into a large, bustling suburb. Of the district at the turn of the century, I learned much from Mr John Grant of Falcon Gardens, one of the early pioneers for the establishment of the tall-steepled Baptist Church near Holy Corner. He recalled that, when the not inconsiderable interior expanse of this church was painted in 1895, the total cost was £29! Mr Grant kindly let me have a number of booklets and papers from which the history of Morningside Free Church could be traced.

Recalling the old horse-trams, whose original route was from Salisbury Place, via Grange Road, Whitehouse Loan and Clinton Road, into Churchhill, Mr Grant told me of the generous Morningside baker, David Kay, whose shop was at Churchhill, who every Christmas gave a parcel of shortbread, currant loaf and cake to each tramway driver and conductor who passed his shop. Mr Kay eventually gave up his prosperous business to devote himself to voluntary work in Edinburgh Royal Infirmary and Carrubber's Close Mission in the High Street.

Mr Grant told me that the second milestone between Tollcross and Morningside had been situated at Braid Road, just outside the Braid Hills Hotel. I checked the distance between the hotel and Tollcross on a car mileage recorder and found the distance to be correct, though I could not trace the present whereabouts of this milestone. A baker's shop once situated between what are now a plumber's premises and the south boundary wall of Bank House at Churchhill, Mr Grant recalled, for many years had a flourishing vine over the bakehouse, but this had long since disappeared. The Co-op supermarket at the corner of Morningside Road and Morningside Park today attracts shoppers from far beyond Morningside. Mr Grant recalled that, when the original small St Cuthbert's Co-op shop was opened at what is now 241 Morningside Road, there was a petition of protest from local shopkeepers. Mr Grant was one of the first pupils at South Morningside School soon after it opened in 1892, and he showed me a photograph of his woodwork class in about 1900. He became a joiner and carpenter, and one of his first jobs as an apprentice was to build wooden frames for the construction of the stone steps opposite South Morningside School, leading up from Comiston Road to Braid Crescent. Mr Grant was still teaching woodwork when in his eighties.

Assembling facts for a reliable local history means recourse not only to published sources but also to private papers such as title deeds in the possession of local residents. Problems arise when people have long since moved from the district, taking with them information of importance. The discovery of useful material is often a matter of chance, as was my discovery of a unique collection of photographs which threw new light on the history of Morningside. After lecturing to a large audience here, I happened later to meet a lady who had been present at my talk, and learned that some years ago her husband had acquired an album of old photographs of Morningside and its neighbouring districts. Some of the most important of these have been reproduced in this work.

I was fortunate to meet Mr George Anderson of Morningside Park, who had acquired this most valuable collection of photographs from his neighbour, the late Miss Charlotte Ethel Evans, whose brother, the late Mr W. E. Evans, had taken most of the pictures. They were the great-grandchildren of David Deuchar — he and his sons were for long the "lords of the manor", owners of the extensive Morningside estate; Morningside Place was originally known as Deuchar Street, commemorating their ownership. The carefully annotated photographs were neatly mounted in a small album. Most had been taken around the turn of the century. Of special interest was one hitherto unpublished, showing the stone-pillared gates at the entrance to Comiston House. They stood at what is now the entrance to Camus Avenue, but were removed in 1937 to Braidburn Valley Park at the corner of Greenbank Crescent. Another photograph was of Falcon Hall, viewed from its main gateway in Morningside Road and showing more of the driveway than was seen in other published illustrations. There was also a close-up of the gates themselves. Another picture of special interest was of Paradise Cottages which once stood between Canaan Lane and Jordan Lane.

However, the photograph of most importance is probably that which shows the hitherto uncertain sites of some old buildings in Morningside Village. This is the picture which William Mair reproduced in *Historic Morningside*. Taken in about 1865 by Miss Evans's uncle, David Deuchar, the fourth son of the first David Deuchar of Morningside, it indicates Morningside House, with, immediately to the right, the very small "Joiner's shop — Robertson the wright", the Free Church School and, just visible on the extreme right, Denholm's smiddy. Mair's caption did not indicate the joiner's shop, and described as the smiddy what was in fact the Free Church School. The photograph indicates the appearance and proper location of the school, which had not been clear from maps or printed sources. Mair also stated incorrectly that Morningside Public Library was built on the site of Morningside House. It was in fact built on the site of Denholm's Smiddy.

Miss Evans of Morningside Park merits further mention on two other counts. As a great-grand-daughter of the artist and engraver David Deuchar, she inherited a collection of his etchings, and also several seal engravings and cameos, many of them heraldic designs cut from garnets and other gem stones. In 1943 a magnificent two-volume folio edition of Deuchar's etchings was bequeathed to the Edinburgh Public Library by the late Mr Kenneth Sanderson, W.S. In 1947 an exhibition on the history of Morningside was mounted in the Parish Church Hall in Newbattle Terrace, William Mair having contributed some of the interesting relics on view. These included a linen damask tablecloth made by the weavers of Tipperlinn, and loaned by Miss Charlotte Ethel Evans. I asked Mr George Anderson, who had known Miss Evans, if its whereabouts were now known. He was uncertain but wondered if, when Miss Evans's estate was being wound-up and her house cleared and sold, the tablecloth might not have been discarded by someone not knowing its historical value. It would seem that now no remaining example of the once famed work of the Tipperlinn weavers is known to exist.

In Mr George Anderson's home I met his father, Mr James Anderson, then in his ninety-first year. In 1891 he had been one of the last pupils to enrol at the Old Schoolhouse in Morningside Road: a year later the little village school was closed and he was transferred to South Morningside Primary School in Comiston Road. Mr Anderson could recall the village school "maister", Mr Andrew ("Cocky") Cockburn who was also transferred to South Morningside School. After serving in various men's outfitting shops in Edinburgh, Mr Anderson left for the United States and took up animal husbandry and dairy farming. At the outbreak of the First World War he decided to return to Edinburgh to join the Lovat Scouts and, later, the Machine Gun Corps. After the war he set up as a market gardener at the top of Morningside Park, on land next to No. 52, once named Harlaw House, which was built by one of the Deuchar family and later became the Parish Church manse. Subsequently he transferred to a site at 39 Morningside Park, at the north corner of Morningside Terrace. Many Morningside residents will recall that, in the heyday of this market garden, there was a hut at the front wall of the garden where produce was on sale. The charming little house here, which Mr Anderson later acquired, was once known as Glencorse Cottage. Now called simply The Cottage, it is the home of Mr Anderson's son and his family. His healthy life as a gardener has stood Mr Anderson in good stead: just nine years off his century, he still plays golf regularly over Lothianburn course and was for three years captain of the "Over 65" Club.

In seeking to link Morningside's past and present, I was indebted to Mr Gilmour Main, not only for his own detailed recollections and the valuable old photographs he kindly gave me, but also for mentioning other interesting people I would not otherwise have met. Mr Main's fishmonger's shop in Morningside Road is one of the longest established family businesses in the district. His grandmother had been a fishwife: attired in traditional colourful dress, with heavy creel on her back, she had first come to Morningside in about 1800. Very early in the morning she would travel by horse-lorry from Fisherrow to the Newhaven fish-market, and then make her way on foot and by horse-tram to Morningside, where she would call upon regular customers in "the big houses". Mr Main's mother, a fishwife as well, also came to Morningside, but she would probably have been able to travel on the Suburban Railway opened in 1884. The family shop was opened in 1901, in premises shared with the St Cuthbert's Co-operative Society butcher, whose main premises were then on the west side of Morningside Road, between what are now the Trustee Savings Bank and the modern Co-op.

One of Mr Main's earliest recollections was of sitting in the front window of his parents' shop and watching the Horse Guards leading the State Procession of Edward VII to open the City Fever Hospital. Wooden grandstands were erected at various points along the route of the procession from the city. Another early memory was of the building or Morningside Public Library on the site of Denholm's smiddy in 1904.

In its early days, the fishmonger's employed message boys who, starting at 8 a.m., would cycle to the villas of Cluny, Midmar and Hermitage with daily price lists, taking orders which were duly delivered before lunch-time. Mr Main had detailed recollections of many of the other family businesses which had been a feature of Morningside before the advent of chain stores and supermarkets. He provided an interesting commentary on the change in life-style which had gradually taken place. On both sides of Morningside Road and Comiston Road, between Churchhill and Comiston Drive, he could remember almost every shop by name. He recalled the large number of dairies which had once existed throughout Edinburgh, and which have now almost entirely disappeared. They sold only milk, butter, eggs, scones and oatcakes. The milk was kept on the counter in large earthenware containers, often blue-striped, and poured into metal pitchers with a special hand-filler. Bottles came only later, and were filled from large containers with another type of filler with a spout. A cardboard disc was then pressed by hand into the neck of the bottle. The dairies in Morningside received early morning bulk deliveries of milk from such farms as House o' Muir near Flotterstone, Bowbridge at Lothianburn, Hunter's Tryst, Buckstane, Comiston and Braid. There were also "dry" dairies — Paterson's in Jordan Lane and another in Balcarres Street. In these, the cows were not put out to graze but were kept, summer and winter, in byres.

Mr Main spoke of the delivery services provided by the family businesses of Morningside, almost all of which had a horse-drawn cart or van, or at least hand barrows, standing outside their shops ready to set off on their rounds. In addition, there were numerous message boys who, normally before or after school, made deliveries, often on carrier-bicycles made with special frames on the front handlebars to hold large baskets. Prior to the First World War, many shops remained open late in the

Delivery carts ready to set out from a grocer's shop, Blanche & Company of 155-7 Bruntsfield Place

evening, some until 11.30, especially on Saturdays. Many of the family businesses would give their customers a cake or tin of biscuits when the monthly account was paid. There was a close personal relationship between shopkeeper and customer, so different from the present era of impersonal supermarkets.

Mr Main could remember the opening of the original St Cuthbert's Co-operative Society shop in what is now the fish-and-chip shop at 241 Morningside Road. Later it moved to larger premises at the north corner of Falcon Road West (to become Campbell's bicycle shop), then to the corner of Morninside Road and Springvalley Gardens, and finally to the corner of Morningside Park, on the site of the front garden of Morningside House.

He also recalled the heyday of the Suburban Railway's Goods Yard at the end of Maxwell Street. A familiar sight in the 1930s were the flocks of Shetland sheep arriving by goods train and being driven by their shepherd, Mr Crosbie of Morningside Road, across the busy main streets — to the dislocation of the traffic — into the fields at the east end of Hermitage Drive, below Blackford Hill.

Turning to Morningside's sporting history, Mr Main recalled two once thriving football teams, Morningside Primrose and the Southern Hearts. There was also the Cluny Rugby Club, playing in the early 1900s, and Salmond's Sons, another early Rugby team which took its name from the Rev. Charles Salmond, first minister of South Morningside Free Church in Braid Road.

One of the many photographs of old Morningside which Mr Main kindly gave me was of particular interest. This was of the short row of cottages which once stood on the east side of Morningside Road, immediately north of the entrance gates to Falcon Hall, between what are now Falcon Road West and Falcon Avenue. These were probably the houses of workers on the Falcon Hall estate. I had obtained from another Morningside resident a phtotgraph of the once popular skating pond at Braid Hills, the existence of which I had previously been unaware. Mr Main had known this pond and took me to its site. Though long since drained and now part of the Braids Golf Course, its appearance obviously indicated that it had at one time been a large pond. Near it had been a big house known as Winchester's which sold sweets and soft drinks.

I asked Mr Main about Morningside "characters" of early days and he recalled one whom several other residents I had spoken to had vaguely remembered, and who is referred to by Mr Andrew Patterson in his article in Volume XXXII the *Book of the Old Edinburgh Club*. This was Theodore Napier, who lived in Merchiston. Although an Australian, he habitually wore the full regalia of an eighteenth-century Highland chieftain and was an ardent Jacobite, being a strong upholder of a German prince who claimed descent from the House of Stuart and, therefore, the British throne. At dinners, Mr Napier would give the Jacobite toast, raising his glass across a bowl of water to signify his loyalty to "the King across the water".

Lastly we talked of old street-sellers and their cries, a familiar and tuneful feature of Morningside in times before the present-day roar of traffic. One dealer with a horse and cart — and powerful lungs — proclaimed that he was selling: "Jeely rhubarb... jeely rhubarb!.. three ha' pence a bunch!" Another, seated on his horse-drawn cart, announced: "Briquettes!... Eglinton briquettes!... a shillin' a dozen." Then there was the rag and bone man, who would arrive with a sack slung over his shoulder and place a large wicker basket on the pavement. He would tunefully announce himself in each street with a few blasts from a bugle. Children seeing his basketful of balloons, cheap toys and imitation canaries on sticks would hurry up their tenement stairs and beg their mothers to look out old woollen rags to exchange for these glittering offerings. On Saturdays an old Italian woman with a pony-drawn barrel-organ would visit Morningside; a little monkey performing tricks on top of the organ would be rewarded with titbits from passers-by. The "Ingin Johnnies" from Brittany were also regular visitors who brought an international dimension to the scene; attired in black berets they had strings of onions draped over their bicycle wheels. The back-green singers were also recalled, and their rendering of songs, often sad, such as "The Old Rugged Cross". Their begging eyes would look up to the kitchen windows at the back of the tenements, some of whose residents, either in appreciation or to encourage the singer to move on, would throw down a

486

penny wrapped in newspaper, which was gratefully acknowledged by a glance up to the window and a touch of the singer's hat.

Just before the middle of last century, when Morningside retained much of its rural atmosphere, the village doctor was Dr George Beilby of Falcon Cottage, the most northerly and largest of the cottages on the east side of Morningside Road, between what are now Falcon Road West and Falcon Avenue. Long since demolished, it latterly became 161 Morningside Road. Hoping to learn more of Morningside's long-serving and much respected G.P., I attempted to trace his descendants, and in the process discovered that his was a distinguished family with several claims to fame.

I succeeded in contacting several members of the Beilby family, a number of whom were doctors, and was particularly indebted to Mr Michael Beilby of West Garleton in East Lothian, a great-nephew of the Morningside doctor. We discussed his ancestors, who are on record from the thirteenth century, and he kindly lent me relevant family papers, including an interesting family tree and a rare pamphlet entitled *The Genealogy of the Children of William Beilby, M.D., and Maria Catherine Moller.*

Although the Beilby family has, through several generations, been associated with the medical profession, certain of its early members became distinguished in another sphere, which led one author to entitle his study of them "The Ingenious Beilbys". This referred to the artistic skill of William Beilby who, working in Newcastle-upon-Tyne in the late eighteenth century, became the foremost enameller on glass in England.

The first recorded member of the Beilby family was Hugo di Boelbi, High Sheriff of Yorkshire during the reign of Richard I, at the close of the thirteenth century. For generations the Beilbys were associated with Yorkshire and Northumberland. Dr George Thomas Beilby, M.D. (1811-95), the Morningside family doctor, was the son of a distinguished Edinburgh medical man, Dr William Beilby, M.D., President of the Royal College of Physicians of Edinburgh. It was he who delivered the Address at the opening of their new hall in Queen Street in November 1846. This was a scholarly historical account of medical practice in Scotland, and Edinburgh in particular, and of the origins of the Royal College of Physicians. Among Dr William Beilby's contemporaries were many famous doctors who at that period earned for Edinburgh's Medical School a world-wide reputation. He married Maria Catherine Moller, whose family were also of ancient lineage, being descended from Frederick I of Denmark (1471-1533) and related to "Dietricus, one-time Senator of the Germanic Roman Empire", whose family can be traced back to the thirteenth century. Mr Michael Beilby of West Garleton kindly allowed me to copy miniatures of Dr William Beilby and his wife.

Dr George Thomas Beilby of Morningside was the third son in a family of nine. He was educated at Edinburgh Academy and obtained his

Doctor of Medicine degree at Edinburgh in 1834. In those days this was the primary qualification in Medicine; it became a post-graduate degree only in 1861. His thesis, like many others submitted before the degree was upgraded, has unfortunately not been preserved in the Edinburgh University Library. It would probably have been no longer than an essay, and written in Latin. Dr Beilby's medical studies were possibly continued at Trinity College, Dublin, and he is thought to have had an appointment with the Dublin authorities before settling in Morningside in about 1840. He was still residing in Morningside Road until a year before his death in 1895.

Dr Beilby's son, born in Morningside in 1850, was also named George Thomas. He gained a doctorate in science and was a pioneer in physical and industrial chemistry, being elected a Fellow of the Royal Society and awarded a Knighthood in 1916. For some time associated with Imperial Chemical Industries, he invented various pieces of scientific equipment including the "Beilby retort". The Beilby family were commemorated by a ward in Bruntsfield Hospital where the second Dr George T. Beilby found time to serve for a period as a trustee. Even after he and his wife moved to Glasgow in 1901, the Bruntsfield Hospital records indicate a succession of anonymous gifts such as microscopes and other expensive pieces of equipment. When she lived in Colinton Road, Mrs Beilby, later Lady Beilby, was a close friend of Dr Isabel Venters, who was a colleague of the

A Beilby wine glass in the Royal Scottish Museum.

Reproduced from "The Ingenious Beilbys" by James Rush

hospital's foundress Dr Sophia Jex-Blake, and Mrs Beilby was invited by Dr Jex-Blake to serve on the management committee of the original Grove Street "hospital" (which had only five beds) and, later on, that of Bruntsfield Hospital itself. On her death in 1936, Lady Beilby left a legacy of £5,000 to the hospital, having, during her lifetime, donated around £15,000 to Bruntsfield Hospital and its sister hospital founded by Dr Elsie Inglis at Abbeyhill. Beds were endowed in the two hospitals and both Sir George and Lady Beilby's service and generosity are commemorated by Bruntsfield's Beilby Ward. The family's medical traditions have continued in recent years. Several other members of the family are doctors, some bearing the name Julius, which, as the family tree indicates, was given to many Beilby sons through the generations.

The name of Beilby is also known, as already mentioned, to collectors of valuable antique glass. Most standard books on fine glass devote some space to the work of the Beilbys, but it is James Rush who, in his comprehensive and beautifully illustrated work *The Ingenious Beilbys,* presents the most fascinating account. The work of William Beilby, the famous enameller on glass, who worked in Newcastle-upon-Tyne, assisted by his young sister Mary, between 1762 and 1778, is on display in museums throughout Britain: there are several pieces in the Royal Scottish Museum in Chambers Street. These include a tall wine glass with a twisted stem, its opaque surface painted with exotic birds, and an ale glass made about 1770.

One of the largest and oldest institutions in Morningside is the Royal Edinburgh Hospital founded over one hundred and sixty years ago as "an Asylum for the cure and relief of mental derangement". In his office off one of the busy main corridors, I talked to Dr J. W. Affleck, the Physician Superintendent. The office is that once occupied by Dr Thomas Clouston, one of the Royal Edinburgh's most distinguished past Medical Superintendents, whose personal wash-hand basin still occupies a corner of the room. The hospital originated, as we saw earlier, through Dr Andrew Duncan's shocked reaction to the appalling conditions in which Scotland's young poet of genius, Robert Fergusson, died in 1774. I discussed with Dr Affleck the short note which appeared in a biography of Fergusson, published in 1952 and edited by Sydney Goodsir Smith, in which Dr Chalmers Watson presented a retrospective medical history of the poet. This suggested that Fergusson was a manic depressive and that, had modern treatments been available to him, he would probably have recovered. Dr Affleck felt that, despite the lack of precise case notes available to Dr Chalmers Watson, his observations were probably valid.

We also discussed the passage in Sir Thomas Dick-Lauder's *Scottish Rivers* in which he quotes the Edinburgh Asylum's report for 1846, which set out "the principal causes of the insanity of those admitted for treatment". (These are quoted in detail in Volume I.) Dr Affleck expressed the view that, although in the years which followed Sir Thomas

Dick-Lauder's time of writing, psychiatrists placed more emphasis on genetic concepts and other factors, modern psychiatry nevertheless to some extent recognised this list of "causes". They may be regarded as possible precipitants of mental illness to be studied in conjunction with individual personality and the way in which it reacts to stresses.

Commenting on modern methods of treatment in comparison with those of the earliest days of the hospital, Dr Affleck pointed out that treatment of the custodial type had been largely replaced by out-patients methods, which had transformed the institution and extended its use-fulness to a wider and less embarrassed clientele. Dr Affleck contrasted primitive early conditions and treatment with the situation today, when, as a result of the advancement of drug therapy, the prognosis of patients was so much more hopeful. However, psychiatry now had a much wider area of concern, dealing also with the problems of depression, drug addiction, violence and alcoholism.

When I commented that it was incredible that Dr Andrew Duncan had had to campaign for over thirty years to establish the original asylum, Dr Affleck drew attention to present-day situations in which obviously urgent projects to improve hospital conditions could still be delayed for many years, not only through the lack of financial support but also through having to await the decisions of innumerable committees.

In a little bay off the main corridor outside Dr Affleck's office are three treasured reminders of the hospital's origins: the foundation stone of the original building, the East House, laid on June 8th, 1809, a portion of a newspaper of the time, which had been deposited below the foun-dation stone, and a portrait of Sir John Sinclair of Ulbster, M.P., Chairman of the Select Committee of Parliament on Forfeited Estates, which in 1806 awarded a grant of £2,000 from forfeited Jacobite estates to endow "an asylum for the cure and relief of mental derangement".

One continuing link with the young poet Robert Fergusson, whose untimely death in the city Bedlam in 1774 led to the establishment of Edinburgh's "proper asylum", is the Cape Club. It was of this club, which then met in Johnny Dowie's tavern in Libberton's Wynd, that Fergusson was "Poet Laureate". Mr Donald Macleod, a Morningside resident of long standing, informed me that the club still meets regularly.

Turning my attention to the "Land of Canaan", I found a number of links between past and present, and some features of the changing scene which merit comment. The small area behind the Volunteer Arms between Canaan Lane and Jordan Lane, was in early times known as "Paradise". Little information about this area was to be found in booklets or on old maps, but the photograph of the cottages at Paradise in 1865, taken by W. E. Evans and loaned to me by Mr George Anderson, threw valuable new light on this little district and is the only known illustration. The cottages had their own small vegetable gardens known as the

The cottages of "Paradise", c. 1895

Photograph by W. E. Evans; by courtesy of Mr George Anderson

"Kailyards of Paradise" and their owners were known locally as the "Paradisers".

On the right just after entering Canaan Lane, and immediately beyond the entrance to the old police station, is a row of old cottages, the first of which for long had a metal plate at the corner of its west gable-end bearing the name "Goshen". It is regrettable that this disappeared mysteriously as it had been the only visible reminder to passers-by in Canaan Lane that the tiny district of this name had once existed just east of Paradise. Soon some of the last cottages of Goshen will also disappear, making way for a small block of flats.

Immediately beyond these cottages, and just before the tenement on the right, a lane leads up to the tall, austere villa, shown on early maps as Goshen Bank or Goshen House, which presided over the humbler cottages of Goshen. In this house, for a short period from 1868, resided Henry Kingsley, brother of the celebrated Charles, when editor of the *Edinburgh Daily Review*. My nearby neighbour, Mr Wilfred Taylor, the *Scotsman* columnist and an author, received a telephone call, a few years ago, from Professor Stanton Mellick of the Department of Literature at the University of Queensland in Australia, who was writing a biography of

Henry Kingsley. When visiting Edinburgh he wished to see and photograph Goshen Bank. Mr Taylor contacted me and I duly met Professor Mellick, to whom I was able to confirm Henry Kingsley's occupation of the house. Together we studied its exterior, deciding that the best place from which to take a photograph would be one of the rear windows of the tenements on the north side of Jordan Lane. This meant disturbing residents at a relatively early hour, but they were most interested and cooperative. Eventually a suitable window was selected. Thus a living link with Henry Kingsley and Morningside's old Biblical district of Goshen had interestingly arisen from a quite unexpected quarter.

Morningside, and in particular Canaan, has from early times attracted resident artists. Miss Norah Black, a Morningside lady now in her eighty-ninth year, knew many of them. Her father, William Small Black, was himself a designer and portrait painter of some distinction. While employed by Messrs Brook & Son, goldsmiths, of George Street, he designed the Lord Provost of Edinburgh's Chain of Office, still used today and first worn by Sir Mitchell Thomson, on July 6th, 1899, when the freedom of Edinburgh was bestowed upon the Prince of Wales, later King Edward VII.

Miss Black's parents first came to Maxwell Street, Morningside, in 1879, moving later to 30 Canaan Lane, a villa named Zion Mount (in the tradition of Biblical names in Canaan) but later renamed Blair Mount. Her father at that time taught design in the Edinburgh College of Art, then at the foot of the Mound. He was a close friend of many Morningside artists of his day, including Sam Bough, R.S.A. and Miss Hannah C. Prestoun Macgoun, R.S.W., who lived in Banner Villa next to Morningside Parish Church and who illustrated Dr John Brown's *Rab and His Friends* and *Pet Marjorie*. Other artists of Morningside who were friends of Miss Black's father were Robert Alexander, R.S.A., a fine painter of animal subjects who lived for some time in Greenbank farmhouse, and Robert McGregor, R.S.A., who resided in Bloomfield, a villa on the corner of Canaan Lane and Newbattle Terrace. Miss Black's father was also a close friend of Sir James Alexander Russell, a distinguished Edinburgh doctor who was Lord Provost from 1891-4 and who resided in Woodville, the beautifully secluded villa opposite Norwood, near the junction of Canaan Lane and Newbattle Terrace.

Another resident in Canaan whom Miss Black recalled was Walter White of Stonefield, a villa almost opposite her house at 30 Canaan Lane, who was the author of *My Ducats and My Daughter*. Miss Black's mother was a close friend of Mrs Mark, probably the same lady who had lived in the old toll-house at the Briggs o' Braid. After the toll-house was removed she opened a little dairy to the left of the entrance to Canaan Lane, where strict rules were enforced: she would not sell sweets on a Sunday.

Miss Black attended a small private school at 18 Nile Grove, conducted by Miss Hunter, and her two brothers attended another run by Miss Cummings in a large house at the corner of Morningside Drive and Ethel Terrace. She had many early recollections of Morningside and in particular Denholm's smiddy and the building of Morningside Public Library on its site, where she recalled city dignitaries performing the opening ceremony in 1904. One of her most vivid early recollections was of the colourful procession of Horse Guards leading the carriage of King Edward VII and Queen Alexandra down Morningside Road *en route* to the opening of the City Fever Hospital in May 1903. Local schools, then mainly private, were given two days holiday to celebrate the occasion. She was also able to confirm, from her recollections of local gossip, an incident at the opening ceremony referred to in Andrew Patterson's article in Volume XXXII of the *Book of the Old Edinburgh Club.* Lord Provost James Steel presented Edward VII with a golden key with which, ceremonially, to open the door of the administrative block, which duty the King duly performed. There was a pause, then, when no-one seemed to know what to do next. Edward asked the Lord Provost, "Shall I go in?", whereupon the latter replied in broad Scots, "Hoots aye! We'll a' gae in thegither!"

After leaving school, Miss Black devoted her time to various charitable causes. She enjoyed attending musical recitals and concerts in a hall in Springvalley Gardens which later became the Springvalley Cinema, long since closed. She could remember John Reid's byres, between what later became Springvalley Gardens and Terrace, and told me that one hundred and twenty-five cows were led out each morning to graze in the field at the east end of Hermitage Drive, below Blackford Hill. Milk from Reid's dairy was delivered around Morningside by milk-maids in colourful dress. I told Miss Black that Mr George Anderson had given me an interesting photograph of the curling pond which once existed on the site of the Braidburn Tennis Club's courts, between Greenbank Parish Church and the low wall in Braid Road to the right of the entrance to the Hermitage of Braid. She remembered watching curling matches there in winter and recalled the common cry: "Gie'im mair broom!" — an ardent instruction from spectators to the players who were sweeping the ice in front of the curling stone in order to accelerate its progress towards the target!

Pausing at the corner of Canaan Lane and Woodburn Terrace and looking towards the junction of Nile Grove and Braid Avenue, it may be recalled that here stood Egypt farm. The name "Littil Egypt" first appeared in the city records in 1585, as discussed in Volume I; it seems that a gypsy colony once existed here. During a visit to Kirk Yetholm in the Borders, from early times the gipsies' "capital" in Scotland, where there is still a house known as the Gipsy Palace, I obtained some interesting information about Scottish gipsies of more recent days. I met Mr Gordon Townsend, Squadron Leader, R.A.F. (retired), proprietor of the Border

Charles Faa Blyth, the Gipsy King, crowned at Kirk Yetholm in 1898

Hotel, who directed me to a local joiner's shop where the owner was in the process of re-framing two old photographs for the hotel. One was of Charles Faa Blyth, the Gipsy King, taken at his coronation in Kirk Yetholm in 1898; the other showed the coronation of the Gipsy Queen. The present King of the Scottish Gipsies is Mr Charles Douglas, who lives with his family in a large caravan at Larkhall in Lanarkshire. A few years ago he was awarded the M.B.E. for his services "to the Gipsy Groups in Scotland", now known as "the travelling people". There is, incidentally, a small Border village known as Egypt, though its name is not connected with the gipsies. It is believed to be associated with Lord Kitchener, Commander-in-Chief of the Egyptian Army in 1892.

Just beyond Woodburn Terrace is the entrance to Woodburn House. This elegant villa built in 1806, for long the residence of Mr George Ross (who, from its establishment in 1823, helped administer the Old Schoolhouse in Morningside), recently suffered damage by fire. Fortunately it has been completely restored.

The history of the Astley Ainslie Hospital was given in Volume 1. It has recently been announced that the stately villa in the hospital grounds, Canaan Park, once a private school for girls but for some time used to accommodate patients, is to be renovated and, along with the villa to the east named St Roque, to retain its function within the hospital complex.

During a discussion with Mr Robert Copeland, the hospital's administrator, I noticed a picture of the ancient chapel of St Roque. Hitherto the only illustration of the chapel I had come across was the engraving made by Hooper in 1889, and that in Mr Copeland's office presented a quite different aspect. Entitled "The Kirk of St Roque" and engraved by Beugo, it appeared in only certain editions of the book *Poems on Various Subjects* by James Macaulay, published in Edinburgh in 1888, three years before the final demolition of the chapel and a year before the date shown on Hooper's illustration, published in Grose's *Antiquities*. In Macaulay's book, it illustrated a long romantic poem centred on the chapel of St Roque. In the background a tall mansion-house is shown, which may have been the Grange of St Giles in Grange Loan, and, beyond this, Arthur's Seat.

After I had given a lecture at the Edinburgh University Medical School, in which I related the history of the little chapel as the focal point around which, from the sixteenth century, rough wooden huts were built as rudimentary isolation wards for plague victims, a specialist in infectious diseases raised with me the question of whether, in fact, the successive epidemics had not been of cholera rather than plague. However, according to Dr Haldane Tait in his book *A Doctor and Two Policemen*, an historical study of infectious disease in Edinburgh, the Black Death was a frequent visitor to Edinburgh, and other authoritative books on the Burgh Muir also refer to people quarantined there as having been victims of plague.

On the left, at the top of Canaan Lane, just before it joins Newbattle Terrace, is the drive leading to Woodville, a most pleasant secluded villa built in 1804, a typical early nineteenth-century country residence such as many wealthy Edinburgh citizens built in rural Canaan. One writer described those early residents of the "Biblical" land of Canaan as being "ensconced in snug boxes" probably a play on the words from the Book of Amos, "Woe to those ensconced so snugly in Zion". A distinguished recent owner of Woodville was the late Rt. Hon. Lord Strachan, a former Scottish judge, in whose day the house became a port of call for adult education summer-term walks around South Edinburgh. Lord Strachan would kindly welcome such groups, talking to them about the history of the house and its notable residents, and taking them on a conducted tour of his large garden.

Round the corner, at 9 Whitehouse Terrace, is the large mansion-house purchased in 1905 by André Raffalovitch, the friend of Canon John Gray, parish priest of St Peter's Roman Catholic Church in Falcon Avenue. Here Raffalovitch held his celebrated lunch and dinner parties for many great authors of his day. Father Brocard Sewell, the biographer of Raffalovitch and Canon Gray, telephoned me some time ago to say that, although his books had contained detailed references to 9 Whitehouse Terrace and St Peter's Church, he had not seen either. I had the pleasure of taking him to visit them. At St Peter's we were hospitably received by Canon Gray's present-day successor, the Rev. Walter Glancy, who talked to us in what had been Canon Gray's study, which retains much of his extensive library. Father Sewell was then shown the foundation stone of the church, built in 1907, on which was a sculpted portrait of Canon Gray. At 9 Whitehouse Terrace we were kindly welcomed by the present owners, Mr and Mrs Massie, who are greatly interested in the period when Raffalovitch resided in their house. We talked of the literary lunches and dinners in the dining-room in which they had taken place and enjoyed a glass of wine made from the still flourishing vine Raffalovitch planted in the greenhouse. Mr Massie, an advocate, was for some time Solicitor-General of Malaysia.

In the Falcon district I was pleased to meet a lady from Falcon Gardens who had interesting reminiscences of Morningside. Mrs William Burnett's late husband had been a prominent singer in Edinburgh musical circles, and his brother Robert a distinguished professional baritone. Mr William Burnett, an Inland Revenue Inspector, was a native of Dalkeith, who had for a time worked in North Shields, becoming interested in the English reaction to Scottish humour. This prompted him in 1955 to compile his book *Scotland Laughing* (published by the Albyn Press in Edinburgh) which became something of a best-seller; having gone through several editions it is still much in demand not only in the United Kingdom but also in the United States of America, Canada and Australia. In more serious vein, William Burnett and his wife Isobel published *Give us ... the Quiet Mind* (Mitre Press, London), an anthology of daily readings on many aspects of life, the title of which was a line from Robert Louis Stevenson.

Mrs Burnett's early recollections of Morningside included seeing Lady Skelton, wife of Sir John Skelton of the Hermitage of Braid, riding through Morningside in a horse and trap in the early 1900s. During her childhood in Bruntsfield she recalled playing singing games with her young friends on that part of Bruntsfield Links near the foot of Melville Drive. Some of these traditional songs have appeared in books such as James T. R. Ritchie's *Golden City* and *The Singing Street*. The rear windows of Mrs Burnett's flat in Falcon Gardens overlook the quaint district of Eden, and just beyond is the red sandstone villa, Canaan Grove, at 82 Newbattle Terrace, now the club-house for the bowling green and tennis courts of the Recreation Department of Edinburgh District Council. Mrs Burnett told me of a family called Morrison who once lived in Canaan Grove. One of the sons, William "Shakespeare" Morrison, who was a close school friend of Mrs Burnett's husband at George Watson's College, became a distinguished Speaker of the House of Commons. He died in Canberra in 1961.

Through the kind interest of a Morningside lady, I was given a unique photograph of the laying of the foundation stone of Braid Church in 1886, which has subsequently been used by the church authorities to illustrate a fund-raising appeal. The Rev. Dr Roderick Smith, who retired as Minister of Braid Church in 1976, kindly allowed me to photograph the original water-colour by E. Michie, A.R.S.A., of the little iron church on the site of what is now the junction of Braid Road and Comiston Road. Built in January 1883, this was the place of worship for the Braid congregation before the opening of the present church in Nile Grove in 1887. Following an illustrated public lecture which I gave in Braid Church in February 1978, during which a slide of Michie's painting was shown, a number of people expressed confusion over the sites of the three "iron kirks" which once existed in Morningside. St Matthew's Parish Church, opened in 1890, which in 1974 united with South Morningside Church in Braid Road to become Cluny Parish Church, also had its origins in a little iron church built in November 1883 as a "mission station" of Morningside Parish Church at Churchhill. It is illustrated in Gowans' booklet on the history of Morningside Parish Church, published in 1912. It was indicated by Gowans, and also suggested to me by some Morningside residents, that this little church stood adjacent to the original Braid iron kirk at the corner of Braid Road and Comiston Road. However, according to William Mair, the author of *Historic Morningside* and official historian of Morningside Parish, which he researched in great detail, and to Henry J. Finlay, who wrote a history of South Morningside Church, the St Matthew's iron kirk was built on the site of 2 Cluny Avenue. The two iron kirks of Braid and St Matthew's would, therefore, have faced each other across what became, shortly after their erection, the suburban railway line. The third iron or "tin kirk" was that built by the congregation of Christ Scottish Episcopalian Church at Holy Corner in 1896 at the corner of Braid Road and Comiston Terrace, a site now occupied by a garage. Named St Fillan's, and removed in 1906, it was the forerunner of the church of the same name opened in Buckstane Drive in 1937.

After St Matthew's Parish Church, at the corner of Cluny Gardens, united in 1974 to form Cluny Parish Church, the fine old red sandstone South Morningside Church was closed. After a successful public appeal for funds, it was converted into the Cluny Church Centre, consisting of a spacious hall and ancillary offices. Thus after eighty-six years, this beautifully conceived building (opened in 1892 as South Morningside Free Church, re-uniting in 1929 with the established Church of Scotland and amalgamating in 1974 with St Matthew's) today lives on. That is a fortunate thing, as its fine high steeple has become a part of the skyline of Morningside.

Among many other old photographs, mostly dating from around the turn of the century, kindly given to me by local residents, are several of Morningside's focal point, the busy six-road junction beside the former suburban railway station, which, since 1910, has been presided over by the station clock on the central island which is today the pedestrian's refuge.

The photographs provide a striking contrast between past and present, revealing a more leisurely scene of horse-cars, their trace horses being rested and fed by the boys who took charge of them. One photograph shows a group of telegraph boys in the middle of the then quiet road near the clock, awaiting the shrill cry from one of the two ladies who owned Plewlands post office, at the beginning of Comiston Road, which would send them running with an urgent message to one of the "big houses" in the Cluny, Midmar, Hermitage or Morningside Drive districts. A Morningside resident of long standing who knew this scene well was the late Mr Robert McDougall, whom I met at his home in Balcarres Street shortly before his death. For many years he had been a "cabbie" who operated a horse and cab service from the stance beside Morningside Station. He had also driven a "brake and pair" and "four-in-hand" coaches. His working day was from 8.45 a.m. until late evening, and until 10 p.m. on Saturdays. The cabbies obtained their fares from the many people arriving at Morningside Station by the Suburban railway or leaving from there on the short journey to Waverley Station, and from there on, perhaps, to London or the north.

Mr McDougall gave me much information on Morningside which I had not found in scattered published sources. Apparently, it had originally been intended that Hermitage Terrace, running parallel to the last section of Morningside Road, on the east side of "the plantation", should have joined Braid Road by means of a bridge across the suburban railway line. This bridge would have been built a little to the east, and instead of, the present one. However, the construction of villas on the north side of Cluny Gardens prevented this plan from being carried out. It was Mr McDougall who first told me that in his early days Balcarres Street ended at what is now No. 50, where there was a wall of railway-line sleepers. Beyond this was the nine-hole golf course where Tommy Armour learned the Royal and Ancient game. Another interesting recollection, which I was later able to confirm from written records, was that the high red-sandstone block of flats at the corner of Braid Road and Comiston Road had originally been built in 1884 as a hotel. The group of Morningside men who sponsored the enterprise, under the chairmanship of Colonel Trotter of Mortonhall, had thought first to call it the Pentland Hotel, and, later, the Belhaven. They had hoped that the opening of the suburban railway station at Morningside Road in 1884 would have attracted visitors to the district. However, the project failed through lack of finance and was abandoned.

Proceeding up Braid Road, it may be worth recording that, a few years ago, the two large stones in the road opposite No. 60, which in January 1875 formed the base for the gallows used to hang "the Braid Road robbers", were uplifted and reset. It is interesting to note, Britain having recently "gone metric", that the stones were exactly one metre square.

Further up Braid Road, as it descends to cross the Braid Burn, the Hermitage of Braid, still a sylvan dream-world, is a welcome retreat from the nearby traffic's roar. Its enchanting path, winding beside the burn under an avenue of great trees, leads one, through a profusion of wild flowers, onwards to Blackford Dell and Liberton Dams. The future of Hermitage House itself, built for Charles Gordon in 1785 to the design of Robert Burn, has in recent years been uncertain. It had long since passed from private ownership when its lands became a public park in 1938, and after being used as a Boy Scout Centre it remained for long unoccupied, so that an inevitable deterioration set in. Fortunately the mansion-house has now been restored to serve a most appropriate purpose. Under the auspices of the Recreation Department of the City of Edinburgh District Council, it has become a Countryside Information Centre, open seven days a week as an information and display centre for the use of the general public and, in particular, of schools. One recent exhibition there traced the origins of the house back to the twelfth century. Four nature trails are provided in the extensive grounds and a wide variety of wild life may be observed. The increasing interest in this new function of the Hermitage of Braid by people of all ages ensures that this house with its unique setting and ancient traditions will be preserved in a most fitting manner.

The Braid Hills Hotel, opened in 1881, commands a magnificent panorama of Edinburgh and far beyond. A pleasant rendezvous for local residents and a relaxing "19th green" for those "who have wearied at the gowf" on the nearby public golf course, it has over the years also proved a desirable residence for many world-famous artists arriving in the city to take part in the Edinburgh International Festival. Regular guests have included the late Dame Sybil Thorndyke and Rachmaninoff, whose valuable concert pianos were brought out to the hotel for his practice sessions.

A modern link in the history of this area is the Rotary Club of Braid, founded in 1972, which recently published an interesting illustrated booklet, *The Story of the Braids Area*. The author, Murray Donald, endorses my reason for writing the present book when he says that the many other published histories of the city have been largely confined to "old Edinburgh", although the origins and growth of the southern suburbs merit their own presentation.

The Chain of Office of the President of the Rotary Club of Braid bears a representation of the nearby Buckstane, and in the Braid Hills Hotel ties bearing a motif of the Buckstane may be purchased. This ancient stone may still be seen along Braid Road, a short distance to the south of the Braid Hills Hotel. Cross the road and you will see it to the left of the gateway of Buckstane farmhouse, just beyond the entrance gates to Mortonhall Golf Course. The stone had previously been built into the exterior garden wall of a villa named Allermuir slightly to the north on the other side of Braid Road, where it was scarcely noticed by the passer-by. In 1964, as a result of the interest of Mr James S. Bennet, F.R.I.A.S., who wrote an account of its history, published by the City of Edinburgh's Libraries and Museums Department in the same year, the Buckstane was transferred to the outside wall of Mr Bennet's residence, Buckstane farmhouse. At the special installation ceremony, the principal participant, Sir John Clerk, 10th Baronet of Penicuik, provided a living link with the ancient story of the Buckstane which I recounted in an earlier chapter. It may be remembered that, when the hunting party of the thirteenth-century King Robert the Bruce rode out by what is now Braid Road to the lower slopes of the Pentland Hills — where the royal standard was hoisted in the Buckstane (a march stone indicating the boundary of the Crown lands) to announce his presence — the royal buck-hounds were soon repulsed by a ferocious stag which the King then challenged his courtiers to set their dogs on. It was Sir William St Clair, Baron of Roslin and Penicuik, who pledged his life upon his dogs' succeeding where the King's had failed. This they did, whereupon large areas of land in the Pentland district, and part of what is now Buckstane, were granted to Sir William. There was one condition attached: "that the Lairds of Penicuik henceforth and in all the time coming are obliged to appear at the Buckstane when a monarch shall pass in a royal hunt, and to give three blasts of the horn."

When I talked to Sir John Clerk, the 10th Baronet of Penicuik, I asked him if he had any obligations under the ancient condition attached to the tenure of his lands, and when his family had succeeded to them. He said that the lands of Penicuik and Buckstane had passed to his family in 1634, and with them various obligations including the three blasts of the horn for a royal hunting party. This situation seemed unlikely to arise in modern times, but should it do so, he would, he said, take his place beside the Buckstane with the horn which hangs at the ready in his house in Penicuik.

The original Penicuik House, the ancestral home of the Clerks of Penicuik, was built between 1760 and 1765, the architect being John Baxter. The ceilings of the dining-room and hall, painted by Alexander Runciman around 1770, after his return from Italy, portrayed scenes from the Ossianic legends which had then just been published by James MacPherson. They were considered the finest series of romantic-style decorative paintings in Britain. Unfortunately, as the house and all its treasures were totally destroyed by fire in 1899, the only record of its paintings is in a collection of Victorian work in the National Portrait Gallery of Scotland in Edinburgh. Another of Alexander Runciman's paintings was *The Prodigal Son,* which had as its subject the poet Robert Fergusson. This was uncovered on one of the walls of St Patrick's Roman Catholic Church in the Cowgate some years ago.

Another less ancient but nevertheless interesting historical link in

Mrs Betty Millar, the Buckstane Fish-Wife

Photograph by Mr W. R. Smith

Buckstane is a familiar figure dressed in the traditional colourful dress of a Fisherrow fish-wife. Mrs Betty Millar is one of the last of this breed. For half a century she has been coming out to Buckstane by tram, bus and, in recent times, car, with her creel of "Caller herrin' and other fish, fresh frae the Forth." "It was a hard life," she told me, "but I have enjoyed every minute of it." As one newspaper writer remarked: "Her skirts are shorter, the creel is now on wheels and the fish-wife of Buckstane now lives in a bungalow — nevertheless she still brings something of Musselburgh's ancient traditions into the very different modern residential area of the Braids and Buckstane." Her open air "shop" is set up, on certain days, at the corner of Riselaw Crescent.

The life of fishing is, as the saying goes, "in Mrs Millar's blood". The wife, sister and mother of fishermen, her husband is skipper of the *Amaranth* while her brothers "all went to sea" and two of her sons have followed the family tradition. She began as a fish-wife as soon as she left school. "We used to learn everything from our mothers," she told me,

501

"who had learned from our grandmothers." It was expected that the daughters of a fishing family would continue the tradition. But times have changed. Mrs Millar's own daughters have entered the Civil Service. "The work is too hard," she commented, "The life of a fish-wife is dying out. It certainly does not appeal to young people in the present day." The traditional fish-wife's dress of navy-blue-and-white merino-wool apron and coat can no longer be bought: Mrs Millar has to make her own clothes — except the red-and-white Victorian shawl she wears around her head. This she inherited from her grandmother. Mrs Millar has achieved some renown in recent years and has been featured on radio and television. The headline of one newspaper story summed up the changing scene: "From Fish-wives to Fish-Fingers"!

In the Plewlands district of Morningside, between Balcarres Street, its continuation Craighouse Gardens, and Morningside Drive, a number of links between past and present are worth recording. When carrying out my original research on the district, I quite by chance discovered a valuable feuing plan of the area published in 1882 by the Scottish Heritages Company, which had by then obtained superiority of the Plewlands estate. I had been to Morningside Cemetery to find the burial place of Robert Louis Stevenson's famous nurse, Cummy. The graveyard was then privately owned by a family who resided in the little villa within the main gateway in Belhaven Terrace. I was taken into the office which formed part of the house and was shown the register which recorded the date of Cummy's interment and the location of her grave. I looked round the office, then, and there on the wall was a plan which, at first glance, might simply have been of the layout of the cemetery; on closer examination, however, I realised that it was the feuing plan of Plewlands of 1882, illustrating the proposed new streets and the various types of houses which it was intended to build. When, a few years ago, the cemetery was taken over by a property development company, the plan passed into their possession, and I was able to purchase it.

Earlier I gave a history of Morningside College based on printed sources held in the Edinburgh Room of the Central Public Library, which related that it was established in 1884 in the former Morningside Hydropathic, which stood at the corner of Morningside Drive and what is now Morningside Grove. Subsequently, and quite by chance, I discovered further details in a collection of press cuttings in the library which gave the actual opening date as October 1st, 1883. In the *Scotsman* of August 22nd, 1882 there was an announcement under the heading "Morningside College Company" pointing out the need for additional public school accommodation in South Edinburgh. Such schools as had been established were already overcrowded "as a result of Edinburgh University and its present public schools attracting pupils from all over the world". The article continued:"One thousand families annually come to reside in Edinburgh on account of its educational facilities. It is necessary for a first-class academy to be established in Morningside which, during the past few years, has more than doubled in its population." A large building, it continued, a former hydropathic on the estate of Plewlands, had been obtained for £20,000, a quarter of the original cost of building the Hydropathic, for the establishemnt of Morningside College. The building, on rising ground, was five storeys in height, with six large rooms and one hundred others. Each boy would have his own bedroom — unique in British public schools. The few minor alterations required to adapt the building would cost only £3,500. The notice also anticipated the effect of the new suburban railway station at Morningside Road, which was to be opened in 1884, and the projected building of many villas in the district for "the merchant class". The college was to specialise in preparing its boys for entrance to Oxford and Cambridge.

A provisional foundation committee of prominent Edinburgh men was nominated. These included W. F. Skene, Historiographer-Royal for Scotland, Sir Henry Littlejohn, the city Medical Officer of Health, and Josiah Livingston, Master of the Merchant Company. The support of some four thousand shareholders was invited, each to buy shares to the value of £5. In another *Scotsman* announcement, in June 1883, members of the General Assembly of the Church of Scotland had been invited to visit the proposed college, being advised that tramcars would take them to within a ten minutes' walk of it.

On October 1st, 1883, the opening ceremony of Morningside College duly took place. The first — and last — Principal of the College was Dr D. Fearon Ranking, M.A., S.C.L., (Oxon), LL.B., and the Vice-Principal Mr Donald Macleod, M.A.(Hons), Master Scholar of Edinburgh University. Patron of the college was Lord Reay. An invitation card for the opening is preserved in the Edinburgh Central Public Library. Despite the suggested need for a new college in Morningside, its existence in the former hydropathic was, as previously related, brief. It closed after six years, the vacated building then providing temporary accommodation for the Royal Edinburgh Hospital for Sick Children. Morningside College opened briefly at Rockville in the Merchiston district, and then at Falcon Hall in Canaan, before its final closure.

Now as we near the end of our search for living links with South Edinburgh's past we have time for just a brief visit to the Convent of the Sacred Heart, that impressive landmark under the shadow of Wester Craiglockhart Hill, and, finally, Swanston. At the convent, I talked to Sister Valerio, who lectures on English Literature at Craiglockhart College of Education. She wrote a valuable history of Craiglockhart in the May 1968 issue of the Training College magazine, *The Buckle,* which included a particularly interesting chapter on the period during the First World War when the convent premises, then Craiglockhart Hydropathic, were requisitioned to become Craiglockhart Military Hospital. Among those sent here from the front line — because they were suffering from nervous disorders — were the two great war poets, Siegfried Sassoon and Wilfred Owen, whose stay here was described in an earlier chapter of my book. They were the particular interest and subject of study of Sister Valerio. Consequently, over many years, students of the poets have visited the convent to discuss with her this important period in the lives of Sassoon and Owen. Sister Valerio has also remained in touch with members of both of their families. To mark the publication of Jon Stallworthy's book, *Wilfred Owen,* published in 1974, she was invited to attend a reception in London, at which she met various relatives of Owen's family, including the widow of his brother, Harold, who died shortly before the publication of Stallworthy's book, and Siegfried Sassoon's son, Michael. This reception also marked the opening of an exhibition in the Imperial War Museum of the work of six First World War poets. In a recent BBC schools' programme on the two poets, Sister Valerio was consulted about their stay at Craiglockhart.

Sister Valerio was anxious that early issues of *The Hydra,* the hospital magazine edited by Sassoon and Owen, should be lodged in the National Library of Scotland. However, these have, instead, been presented to the library of All Souls College, Oxford, certain issues having also been preserved elsewhere.

For a short time, while Wilfred Owen was at Craiglockhart Military Hospital, he taught English literature at what is now Tynecastle High School in McLeod Street, Gorgie. Frequently he would take groups of pupils on walks around Craiglockhart, Swanston and Colinton, and he became a very popular teacher. I talked to Mr James Taylor, Head Teacher of the school today, who told me that Owen's association with the school was still of interest to many.

As a souvenir relic of the old Craiglockhart Hydropathic, Sister Valerio kindly gave me a valuable copy of the "Hydro's" prospectus printed on silk. This provided much fascinating detail of facilities once offered.

Proceeding from Craiglockhart to Swanston by way of Colinton Mains and Oxgangs, we may note in passing that, at Oxgangs Primary School in Colinton Mains Drive, a little museum of Stevensonia includes part of a door from nearby Oxgangs Farmhouse (now the local police station), on which the youthful Stevenson carved his name and his height. There remains in the grounds of the police station the now rather fragile cyprus tree under which Stevenson drafted many an early poem which was later to appear in *A Child's Garden of Verses.* Up Oxgangs Road North, to the left of St John's Church, is the Pentland Community Centre, opened in 1965 to serve the extensive new housing area of Colinton Mains, Firrhill and Oxgangs, which, half a century ago, was fertile open farmland. Beyond this, the well-appointed Hunter's Tryst Inn may be compared with

Old milestone at Hunter's Tryst

Photograph by Mr Brian Smith

MILES From the General Post Office EDINBURGH Erected to regulate the Post Horse Duties Payable by Hackney Coach 1824

the old stage-coach inn of centuries ago which, in its later days, was a dairy farm.

We descend at last, via Oxgangs Road and Swanston Road, to Swanston itself. To the left we may observe that the building of houses has proceeded steadily, although the Swanston Conservation Study published by the City of Edinburgh Town Planning Department in 1973 promises that encroachment beyond a certain point will not be permitted, so that the character and setting of the village will be preserved. In seeking first-hand recollections of Swanston's earlier days I was fortunate to meet Mrs Joan H. Boyd, who was village schoolmistress from 1927 until the closure of the school in 1931. The schoolhouse building, now a pleasant private residence, may be seen on the right as one enters the village. In 1954 it was named The White House. The original village school had been a small cottage near the club-house of Lothianburn Golf Course, on the Biggar Road.

Mrs Boyd told me that, when her predecessor Miss Agnes Graham had retired, a circular was sent out by the Edinburgh Education Committee to all schools in the city, inviting applications for the Swanston vacancy but without receiving any response at all. Mrs Boyd, who was at the time teaching in Bonnington Road School, then received a personal appeal from Bailie Peter Allan, Chairman of the Education Committee, asking her to accept the post. This she agreed to do. It was to be a most fortunate decision for the future development of Swanston and the welfare of its villagers. Mrs Boyd and her husband were given tenancy of the residential part of the old schoolhouse. During their stay they were to transform it and its garden into one of the most attractive features of Swanston. In 1927 twenty-five pupils between the ages of five and eleven attended the school, coming from twelve families who lived in the village at that time. As in so many Scottish village schools, the education was truly "comprehensive". Pupils were helped to advance individually in accordance with their age and ability. The subjects taught were English, arithmetic, handicrafts, sewing and Bible knowledge. Such was the success of Mrs Boyd's teaching methods that, before long, many students from Moray House Teacher Training College were asking to spend a short period assisting her, and there was soon a valuable "feed-back" of new methods to the infant-teaching training course at Moray House. Indeed, as many student teachers from outside the United Kingdom visited Swanston to study Mrs Boyd's methods, her influence may have been very wide.

Prior to 1927, most of the Swanston pupils left the village school at fourteen to work in the neighbouring fields, but Mrs Boyd encouraged many to continue their education at other Edinburgh schools. When the Swanston schoolhouse was closed in 1931, pupils were transferred to South Morningside Primary School in Comiston Road, and Mrs Boyd herself served on the staff of this school for six months, before taking up the post of Infant Mistress in Preston Street School, which she held for twenty years. After the Swanston village school was closed, Mrs Boyd and her husband were allowed to retain tenancy of the residential part, and they eventually purchased the premises in 1946. This was their home until 1954.

Mrs Boyd's educational influence in Swanston did not end in 1931, when she ceased to be village schoolmistress. In September of that year she organised adult evening classes in handicrafts, which included teaching needlework to women and carpentry to men. One of the men students eventually made all the furniture in his cottage, and various pieces for neighbouring families. Mrs Boyd's enterprise in stimulating what would now be termed "community development" began to attract attention and many feature articles on the improved quality of life in Swanston appeared in the Press, notably in the former *Weekly Scotsman*. Villagers were soon enjoying a rich social life. At the instigation of Mrs Boyd, and largely organised by her, annual Burns suppers, whist-drives, Sunday school picnics, outings and Christmas parties were held, and every Christmas she presented each family in the village with a Christmas tree. On Sundays she would play the organ for the religious service held in the old schoolhouse. As if all this involvement in the life of Swanston was not enough, she also found herself acting as the village midwife, and, as her house was the only one in Swanston with a telephone, she was constantly called upon to deal with emergencies.

Then came the Second World War. Mrs Boyd took charge of Fire Watching in the village and was a member of the Civil Defence Group at Fairmilehead. She obtained a certificate in First Aid from the British Red Cross and St Andrew's Ambulance Association and assisted at the City Fever Hospital at Greenbank.

One of the events in the life of the village which she most vividly recalled was the campaign she led for the introduction of piped water to the cottages of Swanston at the time of their preliminary restoration. In 1948 there was another campaign — for the installation of electricity to replace traditional paraffin lamps. The year 1953 was recalled as a milestone in the history of Swanston. The first television set in the village was then installed in her home and she had a "full house" of friends and neighbours to watch the Coronation of Queen Elizabeth. After the inauguration of the Edinburgh International Festival in 1947, many overseas visitors came to Swanston, where the charming setting and garden of the old schoolhouse attracted their attention. Many such unexpected visitors were made welcome by the Boyds, and were frequently served a seven-course dinner!

While landscape painting is another of Mrs Boyd's many talents, her late husband, Mr James Boyd, was a musician who taught the cello and bass in many of Edinburgh's fee-paying schools. He was a member of the Reid Symphony Orchestra, when its conductor was Sir Donald Tovey, and also of the Chester Henderson Quintet.

Finally Mrs Boyd and I talked of Swanston farmhouse. She recalled its occupancy by Mr Gavin Jack and his family. At the time of writing, this essential and picturesque feature of the Swanston scene has suffered from many years of disuse and deterioration, but there are now plans for its restoration.

When I remarked to Mrs Boyd that her contribution to the life of Swanston has been most impressive, she dismissed such praise: there were just so many things that required doing, she said, and over the years it was a pleasant experience and a privilege to be involved in village life. That her services had been appreciated was evident from the comment of a friend

Group of villagers at Swanston, c. 1864, showing (second right, second row) the wife and son of John Todd, the Swanston Shepherd

By courtesy of Mrs J. Slater

who knew Swanston well: he told me that, when Mrs Boyd and her husband eventually left the village in 1954, one of the villagers was heard to remark, "When Mrs Boyd left, she took Swanston with her." Further evidence of her impact was that the late Mr John Bowman, a former Edinburgh City Water Engineer who for a considerable period lived in Swanston Cottage, had been so impressed by Mrs Boyd's contribution to the life of the village that he had begun writing an account of her achievements. However, this manuscript remains unfinished.

A link with the earlier period of Swanston's history when Robert Louis Stevenson lived here was provided by Mrs Joanna Grimmond, grand-daughter of John Todd, the Swanston shepherd who became a close friend of Stevenson and profoundly influenced his young imaginative powers. Her grandmother's maiden name was Ann Somerville. I was able to show Mrs Grimmond a photograph, kindly given to me by Mrs Janet Slater of Jordan Lane in Morningside, who is the great-grand-daughter of Ann Somerville. Taken during a school outing in 1864, it shows John Todd's wife among a group of Swanston villagers, with David Todd, her youngest son, sitting on her knee.

John Todd was born in 1809 at Friarton on the lands of Spittal between Habbie's Howe at Nine Mile Burn and the Carlops. He worked for some time in these hills before moving to Swanston. Mrs Grimmond's father, William Todd, was also born at Friarton, and lived with his family at Swanston until he was fifteen, when he returned to a herding job near Carlops. In 1891 he became the Keeper of the North Esk Reservoir above Carlops, between Spittal farm and Fairlie Hope, built in 1848 by Robert Louis Stevenson's father, Thomas Stevenson, to supply water to the paper mills in Penicuik. Here at North Esk Cottage, Mrs Grimmond spent her early life. The way up to the cottage was on foot, along a path leading from Carlops past Patie's Mill. Was it a lonely life, I asked her? Far from it! There was always plenty to do — feeding the hens, working in the garden, helping in the house . . .

Mrs Grimmond's maternal grandfather, Mr John Garnock, Keeper of the North Esk Reservoir in 1850, had, she told me, discovered, on a little island in the reservoir, a number of very old graves with human remains. I was able to check this find with records in the Edinburgh Central Public Library. The graves were examined by Mr J. W. Loney, a Morningside archaeologist, who wrote a paper on them. He considered them to be of an early Christian period.

Mrs Grimmond was christened Joanna Maria Teresa Bonar Garnock and I was curious as to why she had been given such names, which were certainly unusual for a child born of hill-farming people in the Pentlands. She explained that her maternal grandmother had from an early age served as a governess in the household of a clergyman who was a member of the famous Bonar family (which included several Free Church of Scotland ministers, most notably Dr Horatius Bonar, the famous hymn-writer and first minister of the Chalmers Memorial Free Church, later to become St Catherine's-in-the-Grange). When she left the service of the Bonar family, the wife of the minister requested that, were she to have a daughter, she should name her Maria Teresa Bonar after her, in token of her service to the household. Despite considerable research on the subject of the wives of Bonar ministers, I have been unable to find any who bore the names Maria Teresa.

Mrs Grimmond's uncle, David Todd, the son of the Swanston shepherd who appears in the photograph referred to above, became a carpenter, entering into a partnership with the Millar family who built Millar Crescent and Millar Place in Morningside and who were also, Mrs Grimmond told me, engaged in the building of the Astley Ainslie Hospital in Canaan Lane.

There is an interesting reference to Mrs Grimmond's early home at the North Esk Reservoir in *Border By-Ways and Lothian Lore,* one of many books from the prolific pen of the late Rev. T. Ratcliffe-Barnett, who for many years was minister of Greenbank Parish Church. In one chapter he describes a visit to Mrs Grimmond's early home during which her father, the Keeper William Todd, read to the gathering of the Robert Louis Stevenson Club a poem which he had written on "Swanston's Whinney Knowes". Mrs Grimmond showed me the original handwritten

17 Heriot Row.
Edinburgh, 10ᵗʰ May 1887

Sir,

    *The favor of your Company to attend
the Funeral of my Father, from his house
here, to the place of Interment in the New
Calton, Burying Ground, on Friday the 13ᵗʰ curt.
at ½ past 2 o'clock, will much oblige,*

        Sir,

        Your obedient Servant,

        Robert Louis Stevenson

Invitation, signed by R. L. Stevenson, to his father's funeral

By courtesy of the Rt. Rev. Ronald Selby Wright and Mrs K. McFie

version of the poem which she still treasures, and also gave me a hand-written copy of "A Story of Swag, the Collie Dog of John Todd, Shepherd of Swanston". This tells how the dog which appears in the well-known photograph of Todd, taken outside his cottage in Swanston, was given to a shepherd friend in Biggar but constantly found its way back to Swanston. The same thing happened with several other sheep dogs Todd gave away, such was their attachment to their original master.

    On the occasion of the golden wedding of Mrs Grimmond's father and mother, sixty people, who, when walking over the Pentland Hills by the Carlops, had been regular visitors to their home at the North Esk Reservoir, where they had always been hospitably received, clubbed together to present them with a wireless set — one of the earliest versions of that new invention. Among the contributors were Dr T. Ratcliffe Barnett, Mr. J. W. Loney and the Morningside writer Mr Joseph Laing Waugh.

While dealing with Swanston I attempted to search for other links with its famous author and found that there are many relatives of Robert Louis Stevenson, some of whom reside in Edinburgh. I contacted some of them, and also visited the former family residence at 17 Heriot Row, where I was kindly received by Mrs Kathleen McFie, a member of the City of Edinburgh District Council, who, with her husband, purchased the house in 1971. After the death of Stevenson's father, his mother had gone to live with her son and his wife in Samoa and most of the furniture from Heriot Row was eventually shipped out there. Though the house has had a succession of owners since the Stevensons — including the late Lord Clyde and Lord Kinross, both judges of the Court of Session in Edinburgh — its structure has survived without alteration.

Mrs McFie kindly allowed me to look around the house, at the rooms of Stevenson's parents and, on the top floor, that of Cummy who gave young Louis his "first feeling for literature". Along the landing from her room, which had a magnificent view across the Forth to her native Fife, was Stevenson's bedroom (where as a sick child, he was so frequently confined) and adjoining study (where, in his University days, he locked himself in so as not to be disturbed).

Although all relics of the Stevensons' residence at 17 Heriot Row have long since been removed, many to Lady Stair's House, Mrs McFie does have a number of valuable books and other items, including a signed invitation from Robert Louis Stevenson to relations or friends to attend his father's funeral.

It is evident that there is still a very great interest in Stevenson today, encouraged by the Robert Louis Stevenson Club. This does not now meet as frequently as in earlier days, but it does organise an annual lunch. It also sponsors an essay competition for Edinburgh high schools on some aspect of Stevenson's work, the two principal prizewinners of which are invited to the lunch.

The Robert Louis Stevenson Club was founded in 1920 by Lord Guthrie, a distinguished Senator of the Court of Session. He was a close friend of Stevenson and published his recollections of their association, and their correspondence. Lord Guthrie obtained the tenancy of Swanston Cottage in 1889, a few years after the Stevenson family had left the house. I talked to Mr Euan Guthrie, grandson of Lord Guthrie and a former President and long-standing member of the Robert Louis Stevenson Club. He had himself for some years lived in Swanston Cottage, leaving

511

it for service in the First World War, after which he returned to Swanston. He recalled the relative isolation of Swanston in the early 1900s, when he had to walk to the cottage from the old cable-car terminus at the Braids. There were for long no telephone communications and frequently in winter he and his family were cut off by heavy snowdrifts. Mr Guthrie's present house in Barnton has also been named Swanston Cottage.

For many years visitors to Swanston have been able to look at Swanston Cottage only from afar — either from a stance above the village or, at best, from the gateway to its grounds at the end of a cart-track. While the cottage has had a succession of tenants, visitors have been rare. Happily, in February 1978, however, during the Winter Festival organised by the Scottish Tourist Board, an "open evening" was held at Swanston Cottage. A stream of cars poured down Swanston Road, their headlamps floodlighting the old farmhouse and village. People trudged through deep snow along the cart-track to the welcoming warmth of the cottage, where they were received by Mr and Mrs T. L. Thomson, its present tenants. The well-known Scottish actor Mr John Sheddon then gave readings from Stevenson's works. It was a case of "standing room only", and Mr Sheddon had to perform again to a second house. Mrs Thomson, who has

John Sheddon gives readings from Stevenson at Swanston Cottage,
February 1978

By courtesy of the Scottish Tourist Board

512

"The purple magistrates" at Swanston Cottage

had a life-long interest in Stevenson, conducted visitors round the cottage, showing them the upstairs bedroom in which Stevenson wrote much of his early work. There was a most lively interest and many questions were put. No Stevenson relics remain in Swanston Cottage, though above the fireplace in one of the rooms there is an interesting painting of the coat of arms of the old Edinburgh Guild of Tailors, which bears the inscription, "Sine me nudus".

When the visitors had gone, I talked to Mrs Thomson about life in Swanston Cottage. The atmosphere of remoteness and closeness to the changing seasons remained, she said. She has worked hard to restore the long-neglected gardens, and the Quarry Garden is now almost completed. I showed her an illustration by T. Hamilton Crawford which appeared in early editions of *Edinburgh: Picturesque Notes,* the publication of which, a century ago, was being celebrated. This shows Swanston Cottage with two Edinburgh magistrates in traditional dress standing on the path, and, to the south-east, a nearby large building, which Mrs Thomson thought must be an inaccuracy. During Lord Guthrie's tenancy there had been a bungalow in the neighbourhood, but this had stood north-west of the cottage. Strangely enough, Mrs Thomson later telephoned me to say that she had been sent some old photographs by a Mr Reynolds of Fowey in Cornwall, who had found them in a local bookshop, and in some of these the same building appeared. Apparently it was a large garden shed.

Mrs Thomson raised another interesting point. Whereas, in *Picturesque Notes,* Stevenson wrote that, when St Giles Cathedral was being restored in 1830, "they brought crockets and gargoyles . . . and disposed them on the gables and over the door and about the garden" of Swanston Cottage, according to George Fothergill's *Stones and Curiosities of Edinburgh and Neighbourhood,* thirty-two years before Burn's restoration of St Giles in 1830, a twelfth-century Norman archway on the north side of the cathedral had been taken down and the crockets and gargoyles at Swanston Cottage had come from this source.

Numerous people claiming to be relatives of Stevenson still call at Swanston Cottage. Many are descended from the Balfour branch of the family, of which there were many children. Mrs Thomson is keen that Swanston Cottage should become increasingly open to visitors interested in Stevenson, and we talked of the possibility of recitals and dramatic presentations during the Edinburgh International Festival. It would seem, therefore, that Swanston Cottage, far from being a museum piece, may become the focus of a great revival of interest in Stevenson.

Thus we conclude our journey through the extensive area of modern South Edinburgh during which we have sought signs of a living past. "The present is but the past modified by circumstances," it has been said, and throughout this book I have recorded some of the "circumstances" which, over the centuries, led to the unpromising wasteland of the ancient Burgh Muir becoming a pleasant residential part of Edinburgh — the city's "other New Town". History is primarily about, and shaped by, people. In my account, based on historical records and the recollections of residents who have confirmed known facts or contributed others not previously recorded, I have sought to present not only the story of a place, but also of its people and institutions. Around the early mansion-houses of the once separate districts of South Edinburgh, communities developed in which, alongside residents of fame and distinction who have loomed large in this story, ordinary folk have lived out their lives. It has always been a constantly changing scene, especially in recent times with the quick rise of modern suburbia, bringing a new era. Nevertheless, in the midst of modern features, there is always some relic of the past, be it a ruined castle, a foundation stone, or just a street name. Not least, in the memories of residents, traditions live on. The "other New Town" has been "a long time a-growing". To gather together its recorded history which has long lain fragmented — and scattered in frequently elusive sources — has been my aim. Such an account can never be definitive, but I hope that this work will be taken as a useful chapter in the history of our city.

BIBLIOGRAPHY

BASIC SOURCES

Anderson, William Pitcairn, *Silences that Speak*, Edinburgh, Alexander Brunton, 1931

Arnot, Hugo, *History of Edinburgh*, Edinburgh, W. Creech, 1779

Book of the Old Edinburgh Club, Vols. I, II, IX, X, XI, XII, XV, XVI, XVIII, XIX, XXVI, XXXI, XXXII, Edinburgh, Constable, various dates

Bryce, William Moir, "The Burgh Muir of Edinburgh", *Book of the Old Edinburgh Club*, Vol. X, Edinburgh, Constable, 1918

Cadell, Henry M., "A Map of the Ancient Lakes of Edinburgh", *Edinburgh Geological Society Transactions*, Vol. 6, Edinburgh, the Society, 1893

Comrie, John D., *History of Scottish Medicine to 1860*, London, Bailliere, Tindall & Cox, 1927

Dictionary of National Biography, 63 vols. and supplements, London, Smith, Elder & Co., 1885-1900

Dixon, Norman, *The Place Names of Midlothian*, 2 vols., typescript, (1947)

Eddington, Alexander, *Edinburgh and the Lothians at the Opening of the 20th Century*, Brighton, Pike, 1904

Edinburgh Almanac, Edinburgh, Oliver & Boyd, various dates

Edinburgh and Leith Street Directories, Edinburgh, various publishers, 1773-1976

Fothergill, George Algernon, *Stones and Curiosities of Edinburgh and Neighbourhood*, Edinburgh, John Orr, 1910

Grant, James, *Old and New Edinburgh*, 3 vols., London, Cassell & Co., 1882

Gray, John G., comp., *The South Side Story*, Glasgow, Knox, (1962)

Guthrie, Douglas, *The Medical School of Edinburgh*, Edinburgh, University Press, 1964

Harrison, Wilmot, *Memorable Edinburgh Houses*, Edinburgh, Oliphant, Anderson & Ferrier, 1898

Hunter, David Lindsay George, *Edinburgh's Transport*, Huddersfield, Advertiser Press, 1964

Institute of Public Administration, *Studies in the development of Edinburgh*, London, Hodge, (1939)

Kay, John, *A Series of Original Portraits*, 2 vols., Edinburgh, Hugh Paton, 1837

Littlejohn, Sir Henry Duncan, *Report on the Sanitary Condition of the City of Edinburgh*, Edinburgh, Colston, 1865

The Lord Provosts of Edinburgh, Edinburgh, Constable, 1932

McElroy, Davis Dunbar, *Scotland's Age of Improvement*, Washington, State University Press, 1969

MacGibbon, David & Ross, Thomas, *The Castellated and Domestic Architecture of Scotland*, 5 vols., Edinburgh, David Douglas, 1887-92

Mair, William, *Historic Morningside*, Edinburgh, Macniven & Wallace, 1947

Ritchie, James Neil Graham & Anna, *Edinburgh and South East Scotland*, (Regional Archaeologies of Scotland), London, Heinemann, 1972

Scotland: Development Department, *Buildings of Special Architectural or Historic Interest: City of Edinburgh*, Edinburgh, S.D.D., (1971)

Scotland: Royal Commission on the Ancient and Historical Monuments and Constructions, *An Inventory of the Ancient and Historical Monuments of the City of Edinburgh*, Edinburgh, H.M.S.O., 1951

Scotland: Royal Commission on the Ancient and Historical Monuments and Constructions, *Tenth Report with Inventory of the Monuments and Constructions in the Counties of Midlothian and West Lothian*, Edinburgh, H.M.SO., 1929

Smith, Jane Stewart, *The Grange of St Giles*, Edinburgh, Constable, 1898

Watson, Charles Brodie Boog, *(Notes on Edinburgh)*, 15 vols., manuscript, 1922-47

Wilson, Sir Daniel, *Memorials of Edinburgh in the Olden Time*, 2 vols., Edinburgh, A. & C. Black, 1891

Youngson, Alexander John, *The Making of Classical Edinburgh, 1750-1840*, Edinburgh, University Press, 1966

VOLUME I

CHAPTER 1

Breviarium ad usum Sarum for Jean Richard, 3rd November, *1496,* manuscript

Chambers, Robert, "The Meadow Walks", *His Select Writings,* Vol. 1, Edinburgh, Chambers, 1847

Craig, William Stuart, Royal Hospital for Sick Children, 1895-1970, Edinburgh, the Hospital, 1970

Evangeliarium et Constitutiones Sororum Ordinis Predicatorum, manuscript

Goodfellow, James, *The Print of His Shoe,* Edinburgh, Oliphant, Anderson & Ferrier, 1906

Guthrie, Douglas, *Royal Edinburgh Hospital for Sick Children, 1860-1960,* Edinburgh, Livingstone, 1960

Laing, Henry, *Supplemental Descriptive Catalogue of Ancient Scottish Seals,* Edinburgh, Edmonston & Douglas, 1866

Lyndesay, Sir David, *Ane Pleasant Satyre of the Thrie Estaitis,* Edinburgh, n.p., 1802

McAra, Duncan, *Sir James Gowans,* Edinburgh, Paul Harris, 1975

Maidment, James, ed., *Liber Conventus S. Katherine Senensis Prope Edinburgum,* Edinburgh, Abbotsford Club, 1841

Maxwell, Thomas, *St Catherine's in Grange, 1866-1966,* Edinburgh, St Catherine's Church, 1966

Miller, Hugh, *Edinburgh and its Neighbourhood,* Edinburgh, A. & C. Black, 1864

National Library of Scotland, *Treasures of Scottish Libraries,* Edinburgh, N.L.S., 1961

Saxby, Jessie Margaret Edmonston, Joseph Bell: An Appreciation of an Old Friend, Edinburgh, Oliphant, Anderson & Ferrier, 1913

Scott, Sir Walter, *The Abbot,* 2 vols., London, Nimmo, 1893

Scott, Sir Walter, *Marmion,* Edinburgh, Ballantyne, 1808

Seton, George, *The Convent of Saint Catherine of Sienna near Edinburgh,* privately printed, 1871

Smith, John, *Highways and Byways of the Bristo and St Leonards Districts,* manuscript, 1931

Tait, Margaret, "William's Hut", Book of' the Old Edinburgh Club, Vol. XXX, Edinburgh, Constable, 1959

Towill, Edwin S., "Minutes of the Merchant Maiden Hospital", *Book of the Old Edinburgh Club,* Vol. XXIX, Edinburgh, Constable, 1956

Towill, Edwin S., "Minutes of the Trades Maiden Hospital", *Book of the Old Edinburgh Club,* Vol. XXVIII, Edinburgh, Constable, 1953

Watt, Hugh, *Thomas Chalmers and the Disruption,* Edinburgh, Nelson, 1943

CHAPTER 2

Bryce, William Moir, "The Burgh Muir of Edinburgh", *Book of the Old Edinburgh Club,* Vol. X, Edinburgh, Constable, 1918

Bryce, William Moir, "The Lands of Newington", *Book of the Old Edinburgh Club,* Vol. XXIV, Edinburgh, Constable, 1942

Gray, John G., comp., *The South Side Story,* Glasgow, Knox, (1962)

History of St Margaret's Convent, Edinburgh, Edinburgh, John Chisholm, (1886)

Lauder, Sir Thomas Dick, *Scottish Rivers,* Glasgow, Morrison, 1890

Smith, Jane Stewart, *The Grange of St Giles,* Edinburgh, Constable, 1898

CHAPTER 3

Aitchison, Thomas, S., & Lorimer, George, *Reminiscences of the Old Bruntsfield Links Golf Club,* Edinburgh, Privately printed, 1902

Book of the Old Edinburgh Club, vols. I, II, III, VIII, X, XI, XII, XIV, XVIII, XX, Edinburgh, Constable, various dates

Hyatt, Alfred H., *The Charm of Edinburgh,* London, Chatto & Windus, 1913

Kinghorn, Alexander Manson, & Law, Alexander, *Poems by Allan Ramsay and Robert Fergusson,* Edinburgh, Scottish Academic Press. 1974

McGregor, Alasdair Alpin, *The Turbulent Years,* London, Methuen, 1945

Pottinger, George, *Muirfield and the Honourable Company,* Edinburgh, Scottish Academic Press, 1972

Robbie, John Cameron, *The Chronicle of the Royal Burgess Golfing Society of Edinburgh, 1735-1935*, Edinburgh, Morrison & Gibb, 1936

Ross, Alice M., "James Gillespie's: History of a Popular Girls' School in Edinburgh", *The Weekly Scotsman*, March 6, 1937

Topham, Edward, *Letters from Edinburgh, Written in the Years 1774 and 1775*, London, J. Dodsley, 1776

Warrender, Margaret, *Walks near Edinburgh*, Edinburgh, David Douglas, 1895

CHAPTER 4

Bryce, William Moir, "The Burgh Muir of Edinburgh", *Book of the Old Edinburgh Club*, Vol. X, Edinburgh, Constable, 1918

Geddie, John, "Sculptured Stones of Old Edinburgh", *Book of the Old Edinburgh Club*, Vol. IV, Edinburgh, Constable, 1911

Kay, John, *A Series of Original Portraits*, 2 vols., Edinburgh, Hugh Paton, 1837

MacGibbon, David, & Ross, Thomas, *The Castellated and Domestic Architecture of Scotland*, 5 vols., Edinburgh, David Douglas, 1887-92

Smith, Jane Stewart, *Historic Stones and Stories of Bygone Edinburgh*, Edinburgh, Constable, 1924

CHAPTER 5

Davies, Roderick, & Pollock, Alexander, *Morningside Congregational Church: The Story of Fifty Years, 1887-1937*, Edinburgh, Bishop, 1937

Eddington, Alexander, *North Morningside Church, Edinburgh: History of the Congregation, 1863-1930*, Edinburgh, Oliver & Boyd, 1930

Kirk, E. W., *Book of Tried Favourites*, Selkirk, Lewis, 1900

Kirk, John, *Memoirs*, Edinburgh, John B. Fairgrieve, 1888

(Plan of the Lands of Greenhill), n.d.

Skelton, Harold, *History of Christ Church, Morningside*, typescript, 1955

Smith, John, *Greenhill Gardens, Bruntsfield Links: With Notes on Some of its Early Residenters*, manuscript, 1930

Smith, John, *Notes on the Lands of Greenhill, Bruntsfield Links and their Owners*, manuscript, n.d.

Plan of the Lands of Greenhill. n.d.

CHAPTER 6

Bryce, William Moir, "The Burgh Muir of Edinburgh", *Book of the Old Edinburgh Club*, Vol. X, Edinburgh, Constable, 1918

Guthrie, Douglas, *The Medical School of Edinburgh*. Edinburgh, The University Press, 1964

Harris, Stuart, "The Tower of Merchiston", *Book of the Old Edinburgh Club*, Vols. XXXI & XXXIII, Edinburgh, Constable, 1962 & 1969

McAra, Duncan, *Sir James Gowans*, Edinburgh, Paul Harris, 1975

Napier, Mark, *Memoirs of John Napier of Merchiston*, Edinburgh, Blackwood, 1834

Waugh, Hector L., ed, *George Watson's College, 1724-1970*, Edinburgh, R. & R. Clark, 1970

CHAPTER 7

Book of the Old Edinburgh Club, Vol. XXXII, Edinburgh, Constable, 1966

Brown, Thomas, *Annals of the Disruption*, Edinburgh, Macniven & Wallace, 1893

Bryce, William Moir, "The Burgh Muir of Edinburgh", *Book of the Old Edinburgh Club*, Vol. X, Edinburgh, Constable, 1918

Davidson, David, *Memories of a Long Life*, Edinburgh, David Douglas, 1890

Ewing, William, *Annals of the Free Church of Scotland*, 2 vols., Edinburgh, Clark, 1914

Ferrier, Susan Edmonstone, *Memoir and Correspondence of Susan Ferrier 1782-1854*, ed. John A. Doyle, London, John Murray, 1989

Hanson, Laurence, & Elisabeth Mary, *Necessary Evil, London, Constable*, 1952

Parker, William Mathie, *Susan Ferrier and John Galt*, London, Longmans Green, 1965

Morningside High Church Mazagine, November, 1944, Edinburgh, Morningside High Church, 1944

CHAPTER 8

Brown, Dr John, *Pet Marjorie*, Edinburgh, Foulis, 1911

Donaldson, Gordon, ed., *Common Errors in Scottish History*, London, George Philip, 1956

Gowans, John Stuart, *Morningside Parish Church*, Edinburgh, privately printed, 1912

Hanson, Laurence & Elisabeth, *Necessary Evil*, London, Constable, 1952

Lockhart, John Gilbert, *Cosmo Gordon Lang*, London, Hodder & Stoughton, 1949

Mair, William, "History of Morningside Parish Church", *Book of the Old Edinburgh Club*, Vol. XXIV, Edinburgh, Constable, 1942

Mair, William, *Morningside Parish Church: An Illustrated Centenary History, 1838-1938*, Edinburgh, Pillans & Wilson, 1940

Paton, Henry M., "The Bore Stone", Book of the Old Edinburgh Club, Vol. XXIV, Edinburgh Constable, 1942

CHAPTER 9

Brown, Alexander Crum, *Dr John Brown and His Sister Isabella*, Edinburgh, David Douglas, 1890

Cadell, Henry M., 'Some Ancient Land marks of Midlothian", *The Scottish Geographical Magazine*, Edinburgh, Constable, 1893

Cochrane, Robert, "Memories of Morningside", *About St Matthew's, Morningside*, Edinburgh, R. & R. Clark, 1908

Cochrane, Robert, *Pentland Walks with their Literary and Historical Associations*, Edinburgh, Elliot, 1920

Feu Charters and Other Documents Relating to Morningside Schoolhouse, manuscript, various dates

Mair, William, *Historic Morningside*, Edinburgh, Macniven & Wallace, 1947

Morgan, Alexander, *The Rise and Progress of Scottish Education*, Edinburgh, Oliver & Boyd, 1927

Potter, W. D., *Morningside: A Study of its Social and Physical Development*, unpublished archectural thesis, Duncan of Jordanstoun College, Dundee, 1970.

Ross, George, *Memorandum by Mr Ross, Woodburn, regarding Lady Maxwell's (of Pollock) Charity School in Rose Street*, manuscript, 1856

Ross, William, *Life of Darcy, Lady Maxwell of Pollock*, London, Atherton, 1839

Scotsman, "Morningside: Recollections of the Old Village by an Octogenarian", *Scotsman*, 5th March, 1955

St Cuthbert's and Dean School Board Minutes, October, 1892, manuscript

St Cuthbert's Parish Church Minutes, September, 1892-October, 1894, manuscript

CHAPTER 10

Cockburn, Harry A., "An Account of the Friday Club", *Book of the Old Edinburgh Club*, Vol. III, Edinburgh, Constable, 1910

Duncan, Andrew, *A Letter to the Rt. Hon. Neil MacVicar, Lord Provost of Edinburgh*, Edinburgh, Neill & Co., 1803

Dunlop, Alison Hay, *Anent Old Edinburgh*, Edinburgh, R. & H. Somerville, 1890

Fergusson, Robert, *Scots Poems*, ed. Alexander Law, Edinburgh, Saltire Society, 1974

Gillies, James Brown, *Edinburgh Past and Present*, Edinburgh, Oliphant, Anderson & Ferrier, 1886

Grosart, Alexander Balloch, *Robert Fergusson*, Edinburgh, Oliphant, Anderson & Ferrier, 1898

Haddow, C. S. "Tipperlinn", *The Watsonian*, Edinburgh, Oliver & Boyd, 1965

Law, Alexander, *Robert Fergusson and the Edinburgh of His Time*, Edinburgh, Edinburgh City Libraries, 1974

Mitchell, Sir Arthur, *Memorandum on the Boarding Out of Pauper Lunatic Patients by St Cuthbert's Combination*, Edinburgh, Edinburgh, James Turner & Co., 1889

Mitchell, Sir Arthur, *Memorandum on the Position of the Royal Edinburgh Asylum for the Insane, 28th December, 1882*, Morningside, Royal Edinburgh Asylum, 1882

Reid, Robert, *Observations on the Structure of Hospitals for the Treatment of Lunatics*, Edinburgh, James Ballantyne & Co., 1809

Ritchie, William K., *Edinburgh in its Golden Age*, London, Longmans, 1967

Robertson, George M., "The History

518

of the Teaching of Psychiatry in Edinburgh, and Sir Alexander Morison", *Edinburgh Medical Journal*, Edinburgh, Oliver & Boyd, 1928

Royal Edinburgh Asylum for the Insane, *Regulations*, Edinburgh, William Grant, 1847

Royal Edinburgh Asylum for the Insane, *Regulations*, Edinburgh, William Grant, 1847

Royal Edinburgh Hospital, *Focus on Change, 1955-1965*, Edinburgh, Pillans & Wilson, 1965

Royal Edinburgh Hospital, *Psychiatry in Edinburgh*, Edinburgh, Robert Mitchell, n.d.

Scott, Violet Redpath, *The Royal Edinburgh Hospital*, typescript, 1968

"Unveiling of a Bust of Pinel at the Royal Hospital, Morningside, Edinburgh, by the French Ambassador", *Journal of Medical Science*, London, Adlard & Son, 1930

Smith, Sydney Goodsir, ed., *Robert Fergusson, 1750-1774*, Edinburgh, Nelson, 1952

CHAPTER 11

Anderson, John, "Falcon Hall College", *Illustrations*, 1889

Bonnar, Thomas, *Biographical Sketch of George Meikle Kemp*, Edinburgh, Blackwood, 1892

Brown, Dr John, *Rab and His Friends*, Edinburgh, Nimmo, Hay & Mitchell, n.d.

Bryce, William Moir, "The Burgh Muir of Edinburgh", *Book of the Old Edinburgh Club*, Vol. X, Edinburgh, Constable, 1918

Cochrane, Robert, "Memories of Morningside", *About St Matthews, Morningside*, Edinburgh, R. & R. Clark, 1908

Cochrane, Robert, *Pentland Walks with their Literary and Historical Associations*, Edinburgh, Elliot, 1920

Comrie, John D., *History of Scottish Medicine to 1860*, London, Bailliere, Tindall & Cox, 1927

Crockett, Samuel Rutherford, *The Raiders*, London, Unwin, 1894

Dilworth, Mark, *(Letter to Charles J. Smith about St Andrew's Priory and School, Canaan Lane, August,)* manuscript

(Feu) Plan of Canaan, 1802

Grant, Will, *The Call of the Pentlands*, Edinburgh, Robert Grant, 1927

Guthrie, Douglas, *Janus in the Doorway*, London, Pitman Medical Publ. Co., 1963

Hamilton, James, *Memoirs of the Life of James Wilson of Woodville*, London, Nisbet, 1859

Macrae, F. J. L., *A Short History of the Astley Ainslie Hospital*, typescript, 1966

Scott, Sir Walter, *Marmion*, Edinburgh, Ballantyne, 1808

Scott, Sir Walter, *Provincial Antiquities of Scotland*, 2 vols., London, Cornhill, 1826

Sewell, Brocard, *Footnote to the Nineties*, London, Woolf, 1968

Sewell, Brocard, *My Dear Time's Waste*, Aylesford, St Albert's Press, 1966

Sewell, Brocard, *Two Friends*, Aylesford, St Albert's Press, 1963

Shepherd, John Alfred, *Simpson and Syme of Edinburgh*, Edinburgh, E. & S. Livingstone, 1969

Stewart, Agnes Grainger, *The Academic Gregories*, Edinburgh, Oliphant, Anderson & Ferrier, 1901

Taylor, Wilfred, *Scot Easy*, London, Max Reinhardt, 1955

Taylor, Wilfred, *Scot Free*, London, Max Reinhardt, 1953

Waddell, Helen, *(Letters to Charles J. Smith on the Subject of the Falconars of Falconhall, September, 1967)*, typescript

VOLUME 2

CHAPTER 1

Abercrombie, Patrick, & Plumstead, Derek, *A Civic Survey and Plan for the City and Burgh of Edinburgh*, Edinburgh, Oliver & Boyd, 1949

Lauder, Sir Thomas Dick, *Scottish Rivers*, Glasgow, Morison, 1890

Taylor, Wilfred, *Scot Easy*, London, Max Reinhardt, 1955

Taylor, Wilfred, *Scot Free*, London, Max Reinhardt, 1953

Young, James, *The Protocol Book of James Young, 1485-1515*, Edinburgh, Scottish Record Society, 1941

CHAPTER 2

Cochrane, Robert, "Memories of Morningside", *About St Matthew's,*

Morningside, Edinburgh, R. & R. Clark, 1906

Cochrane, Robert, *Pentland Walks with their Literary and Historical Associations*, Edinburgh, Elliot, 1920

Feu Plan of the Lands of Plewlands Belonging to the Scottish Heritage Co. Ltd., 1882

Hunter, David Lindsay George, *Edinburgh's Transport*, Huddersfield, Advertiser Press, 1964

Institute of Public Administration, *Studies in the Development of Edinburgh*, London, Hodge, (1939)

MacGibbon, David, & Ross, Thomas, *The Castellated and Domestic Architecture of Scotland*, Vol. 4, Edinburgh, David Douglas, 1887

Mair, William, *Historic Morningside*, Edinburgh, Macniven & Wallace, 1947

Mitchell, Alexander, *The Story of Braid Church, 1883-1933*, Edinburgh, Oliver & Boyd, 1933

Robarts, F. H., "The Origins of Paediatric Surgery in Edinburgh", *Journal of the Royal College of Surgeons of Edinburgh*, Vol. 14, November, 1969, Edinburgh, Morrison & Gibb, 1969

Smith, Jane Stewart, *The Grange of St Giles*, Edinburgh, Constable, 1898

Stevenson, Robert Louis, *Edinburgh: Picturesque Notes*, London, Rupert Hart-Davis, 1954

Thomas, John, *The Tay Bridge Disaster: New Light on the 1879 Tragedy*, Newton Abbott, David & Charles, 1972

Weekly Scotsman, (The Plewlands Panic, or the Eyes of Siva), *Weekly Scotsman*, 10th March, 1906

CHAPTER 3

B., J., *Craiglockhart Hills: Why Should Not the Public Have Access to Them?*, n.p., 1886

Beattie, George, *New City Poorhouse at Craiglockhart*, Edinburgh, n.p., 1865

Bell, John Munro, *The Castles of the Lothians*, Edinburgh, R. & R. Clark, 1893

Blunden, Edmund, *War Poets, 1914-1918*, London, Longmans Green & Co., 1958

The Buckle, May, 1968, Edinburgh, Lindsay & Co., 1968

Cadell, Henry M., "Some Ancient Landmarks of Midlothian", *Scottish Geographical Magazine*, Edinburgh, Constable, 1893

Comrie, John D., *History of Scottish Medicine to 1860*, London, Bailliere, Tindall & Cox, 1927

Dalrymple, Sir James, *Collections Concerning the Scottish History*, Edinburgh, Andrew Anderson, 1705

Duncan, Andrew, *An Account of the Life, Writings and Character of the Late Dr Alexander Monro, Secundus*, Edinburgh, Constable, 1818

The Edinburgh Fever Hospital, Edinburgh, George Stewart & Co., 1903

Edinburgh Parochial Board Minutes, 5th July, 1860 - 19th December, 1867, manuscript

Greenbank United Free Church, *An Illustrated Description of Greenbank United Free Church*, Edinburgh, McLagan & Cumming, 1927

McAra, Charles, "Wilfred Owen's Sojourn in the City", *Edinburgh Evening News*, December 30th, 1950

Murray, Thomas, *Biographical Annals of the Parish of Colinton*, Edinburgh, Edmonston & Douglas, 1863

"Opening of South Morningside School", *Scotsman*, 4th October, 1892

Owen, Wilfred, *Collected Letters*, ed. Harold Owen & John Bell, London, Oxford University Press, 1967

Paterson, Audrey, *A Study of Poor Relief Administration in Edinburgh City Parish between 1845 and 1894*, unpublished thesis, Edinburgh University, 1973

Pollard, James, *Care of Public Health and the New Fever Hospital in Edinburgh*, 2nd edn., Edinburgh, Constable, 1898

Portrait of a Parish, Edinburgh, Macrae & Patterson, 1968

Ritchie, James Neil Graham, & Anna, *Edinburgh and South East Scotland*, (Regional Archaeologies of Scotland), London, Heinemann, 1972

Sassoon, Siegfried, *Sherston's Progress*, London, Faber, 1936

Sassoon, Siegfried, *Siegfried's Journey, 1916-1920*, London, Faber, 1945

Scheme for the Administration of the Endowments Known as Dr Bell's Schools &c. and Standing Orders, 1889

Shankie, David, *The Parish of Colinton*, Edinburgh, John Wilson 1962

South Morningside School, *Log Books, 1892-1975*, manuscript

Stewart, James, *Notes for a History of Colinton Parish*, Edinburgh, Oliver & Boyd, 1938

Wright - St Clair, R. E., *Doctors Monro: a Medical Saga*, London, Wellcome Historical Medical Library, 1964

Young, James, *Protocol Book of James Young, 1485-1515*, Edinburgh, Scottish Record Society, 1941

CHAPTER 4

Bennet, James S., *The Buckstane: Its History and Romance*, Edinburgh, Edinburgh Corporation Libraries & Museums Committee, 1964

"Braid Road Robbery, High Court Trial", *Edinburgh Evening Courant*, 22nd December, 1814

Bruck, Hermann Alexander, *The Royal Observatory of Edinburgh, 1822-1972*, Edinburgh, University Press, 1972

Bryce, William Moir, *Book of the Old Edinburgh Club*, Vol. X, Edinburgh, Constable, 1918

Bulloch, John Malcolm, *The Gordons of Cluny*, (Buckie), privately printed, 1911

Cockburn, Lord Henry Thomas, *Memorials of His Time*, Edinburgh, Foulis, 1909

Edinburgh Corporation: Libraries and Museums Committee, *Thomas Keith, 1827-1895: Surgeon and Photographer*, Edinburgh City Libraries, 1972

Findlay, H. J., *South Morningside Church of Scotland: A Jubilee Retrospect, 1889-1939*, Edinburgh, Bishop, 1939

L., R. H., "A Flight of Fifty Years Ago", *The Evening Dispatch*, May 26, 1939

Lauder, Sir Thomas Dick, *Scottish Rivers*, Glasgow, Morison, 1890

Malcolm, Charles, "The Hermitage of Braid", *Book of the Old Edinburgh Club*, Vol. XXVII, Edinburgh, Constable, 1949

Reid Memorial Church: Descriptive Brochure, Edinburgh, Pillans & Wilson, 1934

Ritchie, James Neil Graham, & Anna, *Edinburgh and South East Scotland*, (Regional Archaeologies of Scotland)

London, Heinemann, 1972

St Matthew's Parish Church of Scotland, *About St Matthew's Morningside*, Edinburgh, R. & R. Clark, 1908

Scott, Sir Walter, *Marmion*, Edinburgh, Ballantyne, 1808

Scott-Dodd, A., *Braid Recreation Club*, typescript, 1944

Skelton, Sir John, *The Table Talk of Shirley*, Edinburgh, Blackwood, 1896

Stevenson, Robert Louis, *St Ives*, London, Dent, 1897

St Matthew's Parish Church of Scotland, *About St Matthew's, Morningside*, Edinburgh, R. & R. Clark, 1908

Waterston, Robert, "Early Paper Making near Edinburgh", *Book of the Old Edinburgh Club*, Vol. XXV, Edinburgh, Constable, 1945

Waugh, Joseph Laing, *Robbie Doo*, Dumfries, Thomas Hunter, Watson Co., 1912

CHAPTER 5

Fairmilehead Parish Church, 1938-1959, *Fairmilehead, the Parish Church and a Mile Around*, Edinburgh, Waddie & Co., 1959

Good, George, *Liberton in Ancient and Modern Times*, Edinburgh, Andrew Elliot, 1893

(Kerr, Archibald), *The Genealogie of the Trotters of Mortoun-Hall and Charter-Hall*, typescript and manuscript, 1704

Lyford-Pike, James D., "Roman Roads at Fairmilehead", *Scotsman*, 17th April, 1957

Margary, Ivan Donald, *Roman Roads in Britain*, 3rd. edn., London, John Baker, 1973

Scotland: Royal Commission on the Ancient and Historical Monuments and Constructions, *Tenth Report with Inventory of the Monuments and Constructions in the Counties of Midlothian and West Lothian* Edinburgh, H.M.S.O., 1929

Stevenson, Robert Louis, *Edinburgh: Picturesque Notes*, London, Rupert Hart-Davis, 1954

Whyte, Thomas, "An Account of the Parish of Liberton", *Transactions of the Society of Antiquaries of Scotland*, Vol. I, Edinburgh, (1792)

CHAPTER 6

Caw, James L., *Scottish Painting Past and Present, 1620-1908*, Edinburgh, Jack, 1908

Colston, James, *The Edinburgh and District Water Supply*, Edinburgh, privately printed, 1890

Dobson, William, S., *Six Walks Round Colinton Parish*, typescript, c. 1968

Fothergill, George Algernon, *Stories and Curiosities of Edinburgh and Neighbourhood*, Edinburgh, John Orr, 1910

"The Hunter's Tryst Ghost", *The Echo & Dreghorn College Review*, Edinburgh, n.p., 1865

Hunter's Tryst Primary School & Moray House College of Education, *The Environment of Hunter's Tryst*, Vol. I: A Collection of Descriptions, Extracts and References for Part of S. W. Edinburgh, typescript, 1969

Kirkwood, Robert, *Draught of Braid's Burn &c.*, n.d.

Laurenson, A., *The Ecology of Edinburgh's Water Supply: A Paper Delivered to the Edinburgh Geological Society, May 8th, 1963*

Lewis, David, *Edinburgh Water Supply*, Edinburgh, Andrew Elliot, 1908

The Lord Provosts of Edinburgh, Edinburgh, Constable, 1932

Queen Victoria in Scotland, 1842, Edinburgh, A. & C. Black, n.d.

Ritchie, James Neil Graham, & Anna, *Edinburgh and South East Scotland*, (Regional Archaeologies of Scotland), London, Heinemann, 1972

Robertson, W. B., *Pictures of Colinton in the Early 20th Century*, (1964)

Scotland: Royal Commission on the Ancient and Historical Monuments and Constructions, *Tenth Report with Inventory of the Monuments and Constructions in the Counties of Midlothian and West Lothian*, Edinburgh, H.M.S.O., 1929

Shankie, David, *The Parish of Colinton*, Edinburgh, John Wilson, 1902

Stuart, James, *Notes for a History of Colinton Parish*, Edinburgh, Oliver & Boyd, 1938

Stevenson, Robert Louis, *Edinburgh: Picturesque Notes*, London, Rupert Hart-Davies, 1954

Stevenson, Robert Louis, *Memories and Portraits*, London, Chatto & Windus, 1887

CHAPTER 7

Balfour, Sir Graham, *The Life of Robert Louis Stevenson*, 2 vols., London, Methuen, 1901

Black, Margaret Moyes, *Robert Louis Stevenson*, Edinburgh, Oliphant, Anderson & Ferrier, 1898

Cochrane, Robert, *Pentland Walks with their Literary and Historical Associations*, Edinburgh, Elliot, 1920

Cunningham, Alison, *Cummy's Diary*, preface and notes by R. T. Skinner, London, Chatto & Windus, 1926

Edinburgh Corporation Town Planning Department, *Swanston Village Conservation*, Edinburgh, The Corporation, 1973

Findlay, Jessie Patrick, *In the Footsteps of R.L.S.*, Edinburgh, Nimmo, Hay & Mitchell, 1911

Geddie, John, *Romantic Edinburgh*, Edinburgh, Sands, 1900

Grant, Will, *The Call of the Pentlands*, Edinburgh, Grant, 1927

Grant, Will, *Pentland Days and Country Ways*, Edinburgh, Nelson, (1934)

Guthrie, Lord Charles John Guthrie, "Alison Cunningham", *Scotia*, Vol. 3, 1909

Guthrie, Lord Charles John Guthrie, *"Cummy", the Nurse of Robert Louis Stevenson*, Edinburgh, Otto Schulze, 1913

Guthrie, Lord Charles John Guthrie, *Robert Louis Stevenson: Some Personal Reflections*, Edinburgh, Green, 1924

Masson, Rosaline Orme, ed., *I Can Remember Robert Louis Stevenson*, Edinburgh, Chambers, 1922

Orr, Robert Low, *Lord Guthrie: A Memoir*, London, Hodder & Stoughton, 1923

Simpson, Evelyn Blantyre, *Robert Louis Stevenson's Edinburgh Days*, London, Hodder & Stoughton, 1913

Stuart, James, *Notes for a History of Colinton Parish*, Edinburgh, Oliver & Boyd, 1938

Stevenson, R. H., *Chronicles of Edinburgh*, Edinburgh, Whyte, (1851)

Stevenson, Robert Louis, *Edinburgh: Picturesque Notes*, London, Rupert Hart-Davis, 1954

Stevenson, Robert Louis, *Memories and Portraits*, London, Chatto & Windus, 1887

Stevenson, Robert Louis, *St Ives*, London, Dent, 1897

London, Dent, 1897

Warrender, Margaret, *Walks Near Edinburgh*, Edinburgh, David Douglas. 1895

Watt, Lauchlan Maclean, *The Hills of Home*, Edinburgh, Foulis, 1913

CHAPTER 8

Beilby, William, *Address Delivered at the Opening of the New Hall of the Royal College of Physicians, November 27, 1846*, Edinburgh, Constable, 1847

Bruntsfield Hospital Magazine, September 1972, Edinburgh, Bruntsfield Hospital, 1972

Burgon, Rev. John W., *The Portrait of a Christian Gentleman: A Memoir of Patrick Fraser Tytler*, 2nd edn., London, John Murray, 1859

Burnett, Isobel and William, *Give us . . . the Quiet Mind*, 2nd edn., London, Mitre Press, 1974

Burnett, W. B., *Scotland Laughing: The Humour of the Scot*, Edinburgh, Albyn Press, 1955

Duncan, Flockhart & Co., publ., *The History of Duncan, Flockhart & Co., Commemorating the Centenaries of Ether and Chloroform*, Edinburgh, Duncan, Flockhart & Co., 1947

Evans, Andrew J., *Across the Cevennes in the Footsteps of R. L. Stevenson and His Donkey*, Edinburgh, Libraries & Museums Committee, 1965

Hennessy, James Pope, *Robert Louis Stevenson*, London, Jonathan Cape, 1974

James Gillespie's High School Magazine, une 1977, Edinburgh, James Gillespie's High School, 1977

McRoberts, David & Oman, Charles, "Plate Made by King James II and VII for the Chapel Royal of Holyroodhouse in 1686", *Antiquaries Journal*, Vo. XIVIII, Pt. II, 1968

Moffatt, J. A. R., ed., *Mayfield 100, 1875-1975: A Selection of Historical Notes, Recollections and Illustrations to Record the Centenary of Mayfield Church*, Edinburgh, Mayfield Church, 1975

Newman, Noel N., comp., *Genealogy of the Children of William Beilby, M.D., and Maria Catherine Moller*, Birmingham, J. C. Hammond & Co., 1886

Payton, Mary & Geoffrey, *The Observer's Book of Glass*, London, Frederick Warne, 1976

Ritchie, James T. R., *Golden City*, Edinburgh, Oliver & Boyd, 1965

Ritchie, James T. R., *The Singing Street*, Edinburgh, Oliver & Boyd, 1964

Rush, James, *The Ingenious Beilbys*, London, Barrie & Jenkins, 1973

Stallworthy, Jon, *Wilfred Owen*, London, Oxford University Press, 1974

Tait, Haldane Philip, *A Doctor and Two Policemen*, Edinburgh, Edinburgh Corporation, 1974

The Rotary Club of Braids, *The Story of the Braids Area*, Edinburgh, (1972)

Todd, Margaret, *The Life of Sophia Jex-Blake*, London, Macmillan & Co., 1918

Wilson, Charles, *The History of Unilever: A Study in Economic Growth and Social Change*, 2 vols., London, Cassell & Co., 1954

Index

525

527

528

491, 492, 493, 495, 509
Canaan Lodge 205, 218, 220, 373, 408
Canaan Park 151, 222, 233, 238, 494
Canaan Park College 238
Canaan Villa 239
"Canaanites" 238
Candlemaker Row 10
Cannonball House 298
"Canny Man's, The" *See* "The Volunteer Arms"
Canongate 150, 373, 411, 432, 452, 465, 469
Canongate Burgh School 155
Canongate Church 2
Canongate Churchyard 191
Canonmills 111, 405
Cant, Andrew, *of Comiston* 160
Cant, Henry 50
Cant, John, *of the Grange of St Giles and Comiston* 37
Cant, John, *of the Grange of St Giles, Morton and Comiston* 95, 160, 364, 403
Cant, Ludovic, *of Morningside* 160
Cant, Walter, *of the Grange of St Giles* 39, 95
Cant family 143
Cant's Loan 3, 39, 132, 134, 143, 160, 170, 205, 460
Cap and Feather Close 185
Cape Club 184, 186, 187, 188, 190, 490
Capelaw 397
Captain of the Orange Colours 133
Captain's Road 391
Cargill, *Mr* 351
Carlops 209, 508, 509, 510
Carlyle, Alexander 143, 278
Carlyle, Edward 143
Carlyle, Jane Welsh 124, *129*-30, 131
Carlyle, Jean 143
Carlyle, Oliver 143
Carlyle, Thomas 124, 130-2, 143, 236, 303, 370
Carlyle, Thomas. *Reminiscences* 370
Carmichael, Marie 287, 291
Carnegie, Andrew 303
Carrick, Alexander 343
Carrubber's Close 459
Carrubber's Close Mission 481
Carters' parade 173
Castle Terrace 101
Castle Wynd North 298
Castlehill 298; reservoir 220, 393, 394, 404, 408, 432
Cathcart, *Sir* Reginald 369
Causewayside 12, 13, 24, 29, 44, 182, 447-56,
Causewayside School 454
Cauvin, Jean 15
Challenger Lodge 356
Chalmers, Charles 96, 140, 182
Chalmers, David *of Redhall* 181, 182
Chalmers, George 115
Chalmers, *Dr* Thomas 12, 29, 43-4, 96, 109, *110*, 111-15, 124, 140, 141, 148, 150, 153, 181, 182 412, 478, 480
Chalmers Crescent 43, 454
Chalmers Hospital 115
Chalmers Memorial Church 115
Chalmers Memorial Free Church *See* St Catherine's-in-Grange Church
Chalmers Territorial Church 115, 480
Chamber of Commerce 345
Chamberlain Road 76, 77, 81, 85, 86, 87, 142, 232
Chambers, Robert 22
Chambers Street 16, 24, 82, 234, 450, 455, 466
Champanye *See* Blackford

Champunzie *See* Blackford
Chantrelle, Eugene Marie 31
Charity Workhouse 188, 189, 308, 309
Charles I, *King of Great Britain* 58-9, 95, 287, 365, 417
Charles II, *King of Great Britain* 33, 58, 287, 465,
Charles Edward Stuart, *Prince* 39, 123, 134, 192, 262, 417, 436
Charles Edward Stuart, *Prince, thistle* *38*
Charlotte, *Queen of Great Britain* 179, 182
Charterhall 387
Charterhall Grove 342
Charterhall Road 342
Charteris, *Professor* Archibald Hamilton 82-3
Charteris, *Lady* Caroline 15
Chepman, Walter 14, 33
Chester Henderson Quintet 507
Chiesly, John 321
Chinese House *See* Rockville
Chinnery-Haldane, Rev. James 82
Chloroform 462-3
Christ Church 84, 89, 247, 354, 360, 371, 497
Christison, *Professor* Robert 194, 219
Church Lane *See* Newbattle Terrace
Church of Scotland, Disruption 109-14, 130, 141, 153, 301, 303, 412, 438
Churchhill 3, 84, 104, 105, 107-33, 134, 136, 138, 144, 147, 148, 170, 176, 195, 205, 224, 265, 268, 272, 280, 301, 354, 382, 423, 455, 478, 480, 481, 484
Churchhill Place 109, 115, 135
Churchill Theatre 90, *108*-9, 114, 135, 142, 301
City Boundary 155, 253, 265, 266, 338
City Hospital 182, 259, 268, 270, 298, 304, 306, 307, 310, *313*-17, 412, 417, 472, 479, 484, 493, 507; opening ceremony *316*
City Observatory, Calton Hill 345, 347
City Poorhouse *See* Craiglockhart Poorhouse
City Quarry 50
Clapperton, Margaret 46
Clare Academy 44, 454
Clark, Campbell 195
Clark, *Lord Provost Sir* Thomas 376
Clavering, Charlotte 117, 118
Cleghorn, Alexander 417
Clerk, *Sir* George *of Penicuik* 114
Clerk, *Sir* John, 2nd *Baronet of Penicuik* 390
Clerk, *Sir* John, 10th *Baronet of Penicuik* 383, 500
Clerk family *of Penicuik* 383
Cliftonhall, *Lady* 44-5
Clinton House 126
Clinton Road 84, 115, 122, 123, 125, 126, 127, 128, 129, 220, 241, 480, 481
Clouston, *Dr* Thomas 87-8, 201-3, 289-90, 489
Cluny 148, 177, 210, 265, 370, 484, 498
Cluny Avenue 141, 142, 209, 215, 354
Cluny Drive 209, 357, 358, 371
Cluny Gardens 272, 353, 354, 356, 407, 498
Cluny Parish Church (formerly St Matthew's Parish Church) 84, 142, 268, 353-8, 497
Cluny Parish Church *See also* St Matthew's Parish Church *and* South Morningside Parish Church
Cluny Rugby Club 485
Clyde, *Lord* 511
Clyde Street 280.
Cobden, Richard 288
Cochrane, Robert 211
Cockburn, Andrew Myrtle *152*-3, 304, 483
Cockburn, *Lord* Henry 11, 25, 31, 40, 67, 184, 214

529

Grant, John 481
Granthill 180
Granton 413, 457, 476
Granton Harbour 478
Granton Hotel 478
Grantown-on-Spey 278
Grassmarket 115, 180, 406, 408, 480
Graves, Robert 334
Gray, *Cardinal* Gordon Joseph 43, 85-6, 418
Gray, *Canon* John 249-51, 495, 496
Gray, Roddy 470
Gray, William Forbes 53
Gray's Annual Directory 147, 156, 157
"Great Michael" 225
Green, Charles Edward 125
Green, W. *and* Son 125
Greenbank 105, 148, 259, 298-317, 318, 338, 339, 363, 399, 507
Greenbank Crescent 265, 298, 395, 397, 482
Greenbank Drive 182, 259, 260, 268, 298, 304, 307, 317, 472
Greenbank Farm 298, *299,* 492
Greenbank Parish Church 269, 298-300, 301, 493, 509
Greenbank United Free Church 299
Greenbank United Presbyterian Church 299
Greenend 264, 397
Greenhill 5, 76-90, 104, 105, 124, 143, 151, 473
Greenhill Cottage *See* Bruntsfield Lodge
Greenhill Gardens 11, 76, 77, 82, 83, 84, 86, 211, 460, 473, 478, 479
Greenhill House 3, *77,* 78-82, 105, 122, 140; demolition 82; owners 78, 79-82
Greenhill Lodge 76
Greenhill Park 83, 87, 478
Greenlea 259, 298, *307,* 312, 317
Gregory, *Professor* James 35, 192, *218*-20, 345-6, 373
Gregory, John 220
"Gregory's mixture" 35, *219*
Greyfriars Church 11, 82, 308; destruction by fire 41
Greyfriars Churchyard 245, 247, 360, 385, 414
Greyfriars Monastery, destruction 10
Gribbell, Florence Truscott 250
Grierson, *Sir* Herbert 251
Grimmond, Joanna 508
Groome, F.H. *Ordnance Gazetteer of Scotland* 325
Grose, Francis. *Antiquities of Scotland* 222, 495
Grove Street 308
Grove Street Dispensary 55, 489
Gunn, William 470, 471
Guthrie, Euan 511-12
Guthrie, *Lord* 334, 434, 435, 438, 444, 511, 513
Guthrie, *Dr* Thomas 342
Gypsies 205, 206-7, 209, 493, 494

Habbie's Howe 153, 420, 508
Hackney coaches 209
Hadden, Thomas 344
Haddington 124, 131, 132
Haig, James 22
Hailes Street 69
Halkerstone's Wynd 185
Hamilton, Alexander 126
Hamilton, *Rev.* James 240
Hamilton, Thomas 478
Hamilton Place Academy 98
Hampany *See* Blackford
Hanging stones, Braid Road 358-*359,* 360, 391

Hankya, Kharul 296
Happy Valley 256, 337
Hardie, Charles Martin 13
Harding, Gilbert 218
Hare, Henry, *of Newgrange* 151
Hare Burn 427, 428, 430-1, 432, 434
Hare Spring 406
Harlaw House 141, 483
Harlaw Lodge 168
Harmony House 241, 243
Harris, Stuart 97
Harrison, Agnes 476-7
Harrison, *Lord Provost Sir* George 102, 158, 344-5, 477
Harrison, *Sir* John 102, 158, 345, 476
Harrison Arch *344,* 477
Harrison family 345
Harrison Park 345, 477
Harveian Society 196
Hawkhill 225, 475
Haxton, Robert 241
Hay, David Ramsay 216
Hay, William 479
Haymarket 270
Heart of Midlothian Football Club 459
Hebron 205, 217
Helen's Place *See* Braid Hill Cottage
Hellfire Club 184
Hen Burn 430-1
Henderson, Alexander 479
Henderson, *Rev.* D. 87
Henderson, *Dr* David Kennedy 203
Henderson, George 479
Henderson, *Sir* John 389
Henderson, John 140, 478
Henderson, *Professor* Thomas 347
Henley, William Ernest 281, 444
Henrison, Josina 8
Henry VIII, *King of England* 224
Henry, Alexander 422
Henrysoun, *Dr* James 230-2
Henshaw, *Mr* 182
Hepburn, James, 4th *Earl of Bothwell* 44
Hepburn, *Lady* Jane 7-8
Herdman, Patrick 321
Heriot Croft 21
Heriot Row 278, 435, 437, 438, 442, 511
Heriot Trust 268
Hermitage 177, 484, 498
Hermitage Drive 173, 272, 350, 360, 485, 493
Hermitage Gardens 479
Hermitage of Braid 107, 159, 170, 215, 265, 268, 351-3, 362, 366-76, 373-6, 378, 397, 407, 445, 493, 499; acquired by Town Council 371; corn-mill 367-8; Countryside Information Centre 499; paper mill 368; watermark *368*
Hermitage of Braid (mansion) 107, 170, 265, 362, 366-8, *369,* 370, 371, 373, 499; architecture 367; dovecot 367; owners 367-71
Hermitage Terrace 498
Hertford, *Earl of, See* Seymour, Edward, 1st *Earl of Hertford*
Herzfelt, *Dr* Gertrude 15
High Street 24, 25, 73, 150, 163, 179, 184, 185, 245, 309, 313, 360, 365, 459, 466, 481; piped water *406,* 410; timber-fronted houses *4*; wells 405-6
Highland and Agricultural Society 453
Hill, David Octavius 28-9, 112, 340
Hill, Robert Gardiner 195
Hill Street 215
Hillend 391, 393, 400

535

545

547

548

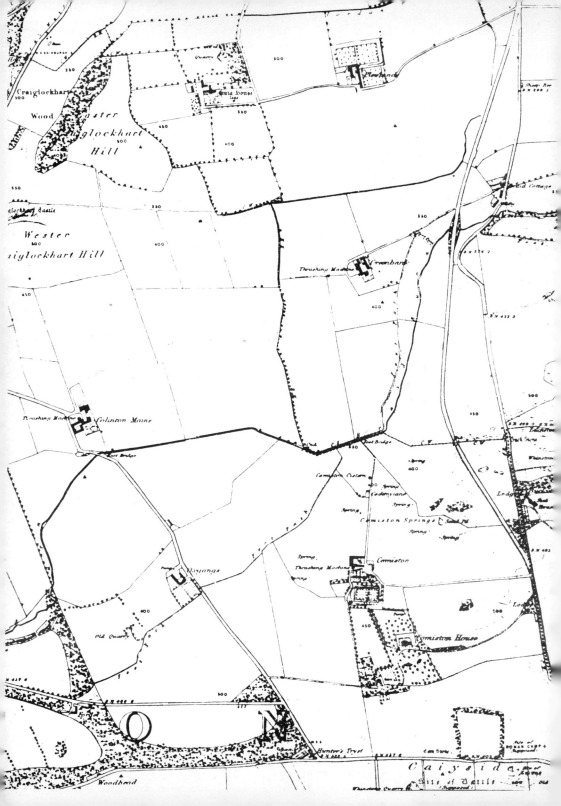